The Road to Comedy

THE FILMS OF BOB HOPE

Donald W. McCaffrey

 **PRAEGER**

Westport, Connecticut
London

Library of Congress Cataloging-in-Publication Data

McCaffrey, Donald W.
  The road to comedy : the films of Bob Hope / Donald W. McCaffrey.
     p. cm.
  Includes bibliographical references and index.
  ISBN 0–275–98257–2 (alk. paper)
  1. Hope, Bob, 1903– I. Title.
PN2287.H63M39 2005
791.4302'8'092–dc22   2004017655

British Library Cataloguing in Publication Data is available.

Library of Congress Catalog Card Number: 2004017655
ISBN: 0–275–98257–2

First published in 2005

Praeger Publishers, 88 Post Road West, Westport, CT 06881
An imprint of Greenwood Publishing Group, Inc.
www.praeger.com

Printed in the United States of America

The paper used in this book complies with the
Permanant Paper Standard issued by the National
Information Standards Organization (Z39.48–1984).

10 9 8 7 6 5 4 3 2 1

To Edmund L. Hartmann, screenwriter and producer, author of seven screenplays for Bob Hope. This raconteur's interviews inspired the creation of *The Road to Comedy*.

Contents

Acknowledgments

Two personal assistants, Christopher Jacobs and Tanya Everhart, contributed their expertise in the completion of a complicated study for my seventh book on film comedy and satire. The inspiration for *The Road to Comedy: The Films of Bob Hope* evolved from many interviews with Edmund L. Hartmann, screenwriter and producer, who wrote seven screenplays for Bob Hope. A memorial gathering of over a hundred people a month after his death in November 2003 proved to be a celebration of his accomplishments and a tribute to his fame as a raconteur with anecdotes of Hollywood in the '40s and '50s plus his work in television as writer and producer in the '60s.

It certainly is necessary to acknowledge theatre and film critic Robert Nott, at *The Santa Fe New Mexican*, who wrote about Hartmann before I developed a book on Ed. Also, film critic John Bowman, working for the same newspaper, has evaluated this screenwriter's contributions to the art of the cinema. These two film critics made me realize how important the relationship between Hartmann and Hope was. In this evaluation, there is one portion of the book that shows Ed's contribution to the career of Bob Hope—Chapter 4, "There Was Hope and Hartmann."

The research facilities at the Fogelson Library of the College of Santa Fe, Santa Fe, New Mexico, assisted in the creation of this work. My wife, Joann, possessed great tolerance for a husband too often closeted away and chained to a computer.

Francesca Zozi, the research assistant and photocomposition specialist as an artist from Switzerland, provided the added touches to this book. For the final composition of text, Kike'lomo Adedeji edited the index.

I also wish to thank Eric Levy for his support and direct assistance as editor for Praeger Publishers. He was an important guide for an author as he traveled a road in the process of creating a book on the films of Bob Hope.

Introduction

The Road to Comedy: The Films of Bob Hope explores the nature and quality of Hope's films in a historical context. A strong relationship exists between the movies and the performance media of vaudeville, radio, and television. Focusing on the screenwriting, directing, and acting will show the significance of the films in the comic milieu of American motion pictures. The range of acting skills exhibited by Bob Hope needs in-depth examination. Following the progression of the quality of his movies from the Thirties through the Sixties and Hope's development as an actor is important to the historical perspective. Starting as a song and dance man plus a monologist or emcee, his vaudeville background shaped the characteristics of his personal style as a film comedian. There is a concerted effort here to examine the variety of humor employed by Hope. Classifications of these comic types are analyzed in each chapter according to the specific periods of Hope's career. Since he relied on the material created by screenwriters, he served as an editor for their jokes and the plot. He was skilled at moving from a standup comedian to the dramatic medium—which became a prototype for many comedians who followed him, such as Woody Allen, Steve Martin, and Bill Murray, plus television host comedians such as Steve Allen, Jack Paar, Johnny Carson, Jay Leno, and Conan O'Brien. While there are differences in the material used by these standup performers, Bob Hope's influence is obvious and a very important factor in his legacy.

1 Song, Dance, and Gags: From Vaudeville to Radio

"By the time I did say something funny, half the audience would laugh and wake up the other half."[1] This self-deprecating statement was the type of gag Bob Hope used to obtain his job as master of ceremonies on the vaudeville stage in the late '20s. As a teenager, however, Hope held odd jobs and, influenced by visits to see vaudeville skits and movies, performed as a pantomime artist. His model, Charles Chaplin, came from the cinema:

> Hope performed at Luna Park in Cleveland, entering a contest emulating the comic genius, winning enough prize money to buy a cooking stove that he and his friends carried home to the delight of his mother. Les Hope was distinctly proud of his effort and was now totally struck with the idea of a career in show business.[2]

Biographies of Bob Hope give rather lengthy accounts of the comedian as starting out as a dancer with Mildred Rosequist and, later, with George Byrne. Vaudeville, it should be realized, had many variety acts, of which dancing teams provided one type of entertainment. A hodgepodge of monologists, blackface singers, contortionists, ventriloquists, dog performers, and jugglers provided the fare in a vaudeville theater. This variety seemed to appeal to an easily satisfied, low-class audience, and anyone who is old enough to remember early television may recall how simple and lowbrow the fare was. With the exception of the blackface acts that made Al Jolson and Eddie Cantor headliners, early television contained this same conglomeration of entertainment. Viewers saw similarly incongruous features on the variety shows developed by Milton Berle and Ed Sullivan.

The transition from the simple dance act to the song, dance, and gag man seems obscure to most biographers, who cannot pinpoint the exact year or event that led to the important movement to the three talents of Bob Hope. The comedian moved toward a successful career when he formed a dance duo with Lefty Durbin. They appeared in small towns, called "tank towns," in Ohio, Pennsylvania, Indiana, North and South Carolina, Virginia, and West Virginia. While it meant an inauspicious beginning, some of the greats, such as Will Rogers, Eddie Cantor, and Al Jolson, played these states. It was called the Gus Sun Circuit.[3]

A tough life in small towns on the circuit could take its toll. Lefty Durbin became sick from what first was thought to be a minor case of food poisoning, but after Bob had him sent home to Cleveland he died in the hospital. Hope had a new partner, George Byrne, assigned to aid him in the dance act. Many years later, Bob indicated the nature of at least one of their turns on the vaudeville stage. He told of their dance to the song, "If You Knew Susie," with a rapid soft-shoe routine. Bob and George wore Eton jackets, high hats, and spats and carried black canes. According to Hope, "All solid class." For a finish they put on fireman hats and squirted water into the orchestra pit.[4]

With this kind of tomfoolery, there might have been a lack of taste or a juvenile taste of the times. Comedians put into their one-liners simple puns, topical references, and visual gags with handy props. In the '40s, I remember ludicrous puns thought to be funny and repeated by teenagers, sometimes to a chorus of laughter. Here is a groaner example: "Mother, get off the rafters. That is no way to get on the beam." Naturally, to understand the joke, it was necessary to know the idiom of the day. "Get on the beam" meant "get with it" or understand the situation. Consequently, this example illustrates how contemporary language jokes, in this case puns, sometimes do not translate from one age to another. Biographer Richard Grudens provides an anecdote that Hope used in his travels with Byrne. Partner George came on the stage with the handy prop, a suitcase, set it down, and stepped over it. Bob would ask how he was doing. George would answer, "Fine. Just getting over the grippe." Obviously, the idiom of the past does not allow most people a clue to help them with the meaning of the joke. A pun, the gag referred to a suitcase called a grip. Most puzzling of all is the term

Hope and Mildred Rosequist on the Vaudeville
circuit with a dance routine in the late '20s.

From the collection of Donald McCaffrey

spelled "grippe." It is a word that loosely means a cold, flu, or influenza. This language problem from vaudeville, to radio, to television explains why the bulk of the humor in the popular media has a limited existence.

While Bob and George could team up with dancing spiced with jokes, the producer of the circuit, Fred Hurley, became furious when the two entertainers added the seasoning of song. On their own they had practiced singing together with the dancing act. Lawrence Quirk, in his book, *Bob Hope: The Road Well-Traveled*, mentions that this addition altered the sketch somewhat:

> Nonetheless, Hurley recognized the boys were tired of the old routine and realized they both needed—and were ready for—a change. Singing, though, was out. But maybe comedy was the answer. Hope hadn't done badly in some of the sketches, and he was sure Byrne could carry his end.[5]

The duo, Hope and Byrne, looked for their fortune in New York. They realized after another assignment with a circuit that their lot was not much better than with the Gus Sun Circuit. After that tour, for more money with the RKO-Keith Circuit, they went on tour with a grotesque freak show act, the Hilton Siamese Sister Twins. Bob and George actually danced, however awkwardly, with the joined-from-birth twins. Strange as it may seem, the Hilton Sisters were headliners, so Hope and Byrne ended up eclipsed. The Ohio boys struggled with the act for a year—from 1926 to 1927.

Finally, fortune smiled on the boys from Ohio.

Bob and George auditioned for a Broadway show and became part of the cast of *The Sidewalks of New York*. It opened at the Garrick Theatre in Philadelphia on September 5, 1927. Hope and Byrne remained together with small parts as chorus boys—"brief specialty dance bits in the show's opening scene."[6] They also had a few lines of dialogue. But the role of a chorus boy would not make Hope an instant success. He had to go where some people say you can't go: "You can't go home again." Hope went back to Cleveland and got bookings in the city he knew best and in surrounding cities in the region. However, he thought he could achieve success in Chicago, even though he had no contacts there. Hope kept on as a vaudevillian. He was an emcee, a dance man, a monologist, and a singer, but his career remained a slow boat to fame. The most significant steps would take place in the '30s. Broadway, radio, and movies eventually would embrace him.

From 1928 to 1932 Hope traveled as a solo standup comic for the vaudeville stage and also the nightclub stage. Both the movies and radio became competitor media as vaudeville began to decline; nevertheless, it did not die. This medium and its poor, sleazy cousin, burlesque, helped carry on the traditional variety show. As if surrogates taking over a similar type of presentation, radio and television actually resuscitated the medium, which evolved into the most popular entertainment of the late Nineteenth and early Twentieth centuries.

An unusual discovery revealed that Lawrence Foy, who is no relation to Eddie Foy, was an uncle of one of my personal assistants for this book on Hope. She is Tanya Everhart, whose uncle played a role in raising her as a child. Foy had a trio dance group that used to open for headliners Bob Hope and Bing Crosby in the '30s. Because Bing had a drinking problem, Larry Foy, a sober athlete and dancer, received extra pay for keeping the crooner out of bars.[7]

Larry Foy with his two dance partners in a vaudeville dance
routine in the '30s. Hope had a bazaar dance
act with two women, Siamese twins.

From Tanya Everhart's Foy album

Larry performed as head of the dance trio that was completed by Vera Turner and Maureen Johnson—two attractive women dancing with a handsome man. This act, which prospered during the '30s executed a variety of styles, from ballroom, ballet, athletic, and exotic dance. A diversity of costumes, from formal wear to bodily exposure, indicated the exotic appeal to the act. Larry exhibited bare-chested beefcake, and the women, with perfect legs, were appealing. Larry and company played the exclusive Palace in New York at the top of their career. Earlier, it was similar to Bob Hop's career—you had to go on tour. In a vaudeville and nightclub circuit, they performed in major cities in the eastern United States. A prize in Larry Foy's book of photos and newspaper clippings is a signed eight-by-ten photo of Bob Hope with the inscription: "To Larry Foy. My Sincere Wish for Success. Bob Hope '35."[8]

What makes this find by Tanya and her family important is the personal reminiscence of an age long past and an age that illustrates the movement on the stage from the variety show to the story-scripted song and dance musical. By 1935, the date of the signed photo to Larry Foy, Hope had been a Broadway comedian in the 1933 musical *Roberta* and another musical in 1934, *Say When*. Yet, despite these legitimate stage successes, the comedian still did vaudeville stints. Also, Rapid Robert, as he was sometimes called, began his movie career in two-reel comedies for Warner Brothers.

Uncle Larry Foy did not find the life of a vaudeville and nightclub entertainer to his liking. It may have been the traveling on a circuit from town to town and city to city. Naturally, the hotels and restaurants sometimes left much to be desired, for the hardships he and his two dancers, Vera and Maureen, experienced. The trio traveled by car from place to place. Shortly after the Japanese attacked Pearl Harbor, Foy left the life of the stage to join the Navy. He never returned to vaudeville. And to his nieces and nephews he asserted, "Vaudeville is not a life to live." Larry would shake his head.

Bob Hope traveled by train in the '20s, but the places to sleep and eat were inferior to those in larger cities in the '30s. Bob seemed to see all this not as a struggle but as an adventure. Screenwriter Edmund L. Hartmann, who wrote seven pictures for the comedian in the '40s and '50s, reported to me that Bob was resilient and weathered the hard times in vaudeville. Even with a loaded schedule when Hartmann knew the comedian, Hope found success. He kept a grueling agenda with extra shows and benefits. And his persistence

An example of Foy's departure from ballroom dancing
to an athletic routine.

From Tanya Everhart's Foy album

finally paid off when he landed a good comic role in the 1933 stage musical, *Roberta.* Bob got the role of Huckleberry Haines, a rapid-talking sidekick of a college football player who inherits a Paris dress salon. Hope, unlike some vaudevillians and standup comics, made the transition to an acting role in a musical. This is a credit to his ability to conquer all media: vaudeville, musical comedy, radio, cinema, and television. From the experienced critic, British actors have made the leap to other media more easily than American actors with Hope as one of the exceptions. For example, Peter Sellers, Dudley Moore, Peter Cook, and Alec Guinness were able, like Hope, to perform effectively in most media.

When *Roberta* opened on November 18, 1933, at the Amsterdam Theater in New York, it received mixed critical reviews. William Robert Faith gave three examples of the mixed reactions:

> Brooks Atkinson of *The New York Times* wrote, "The humors of *Roberta* are no great shakes and are smugly declaimed by Bob Hope, who insists on being the life of the party and who would be more amusing if he were Fred Allen." But Percy Hammond of the *Herald-Tribune*, describing Hope as an "airy sort of a chap" and "a quizzical cut-up," approved his comedy style. The influential Robert Benchley, writing in *The New Yorker*, didn't help box-office receipts when he quipped, "Its bad points are so distracting that it turns out to be one of those praiseworthy musicals during which one is constantly looking at one's program to see how much more of it there is going to be."[9]

Atkinson must have wanted a comedian from vaudeville and radio who had a dry, slow-talking witty persona when he preferred Fred Allen. Hardly the Huckleberry Haines that Hammond describes. Benchley obviously became bored with it all. He did not like the book created for the musical. Despite the critical opinions, *Roberta* went on and on. With an excellent Jerome Kern song, "Smoke Gets in Your Eyes," the audiences determined, not the critics, that *Roberta* became a solid hit that year. Kern's musical would have revivals on the stage and screen, even in the year 2003.

While Hope received the label of Rapid Robert because of his machine-gun delivery and the demeanor of a person always on the move, he was reluctant to take on radio programs in the early '30s as he did when entering television in the '50s. It should be remembered that Hope played a radio master of ceremonies in his role in *The Big Broadcast of 1938*. However, he had played the emcee for many of his vaudeville shows since the late '20s. A radio show with comedy and variety would have similar ingredients. So, starting with a Bromo-Seltzer radio program, Bob launched his talent for the airwaves on January 4, 1935. Female partners were the rage, and every major male comic had a woman sidekick for laughs. Fortunately, wives became show business smart. George Burns had not planned it that way. He hoped to be the one who got the laughs, but Gracie was a comedy natural and got chuckles and guffaws from straight lines. George then became the feeder and straight man. Much of the comedy came from the woman baffling the man with strange but sometimes intuitive logic. Jack Benny used his wife

Bing Crosby and Bob Hope acted as a duo in the '30s vaudeville and here on radio before they were paired for the seven Road Pictures.

From J. C. Archives, Inc., photos

Mary Livingstone. Sometimes laconic Fred Allen used an excitable Portland. Interestingly different was the small town husband and wife team of Fibber Magee and Molly.[10]

Bob Hope took a different tack. His wife, who did not have an interest in a comic role, remained a singer. Bob recruited a woman named Patricia Wilder, who received laughs for her naïve statements using a southern accent. She had the radio name of Honey Chile. An off-the-wall eccentric, Jerry Colonna, became one of the regulars Hope used in his radio shows, his USO presentations, and, occasionally, his films.

Since I was a child of the Depression and a teenager at the start of World War II, my main entertainment consisted of sprawling on the floor listing to the radio. Secondarily, Saturday matinees provided swashbuckler Errol Flynn and Tyrone Power movies plus comedies featuring the favorite stars of radio. At first, the kids' radio programs I enjoyed were *The Lone Ranger*, *Sky King*, *Jack Armstrong*, and *Orphan Annie.* My introduction to humor came from Jack Armstrong's sidekick, Billy Fairfield. The neighborhood boys and I thought Billy made stupid remarks. Jack, naturally, proved to be our idol. Reading Jim Harmon's *The Great Radio Comedians*[11] stimulated my memory that Billy was supposed to be Jack's comic sidekick when he urged "Jack Armstrong, The All-American Boy," on with inane, humorous comments as our hero became the conqueror of any foe. However, this boys' adventure series was only part of the milieu. Ventriloquist Edgar Bergen manipulated his dummy Charlie McCarthy on the radio show that entertained the whole family. Here, on radio, existed the type of humor vaudeville had spawned. Even Fred Allen had a ventriloquist act on the stage until he moved to radio.

At the time I listened to Charlie McCarthy and Edgar Bergen (my order of importance as a child listener), I probably did not catch the cleverness of that McCarthy vs. W. C. Fields battle of words. Here is an example:

FIELDS: To be perfectly frank with you, Edgar, I've never trusted you.

CHARLIE: What do you mean by that crack? I want you to know that Bergen is just as honest as you, you crook, you.

FIELDS: That tips off the whole thing. You'd better come out of the sun, Charles, before you get unglued.

CHARLIE: Do you mind if I stand in the shade of your nose?

FIELDS: Quiet, you termite flophouse.[12]

This banter became the essential ingredient of radio comedy shows—a type of humor derived from vaudeville battles between the straight man and the comic. In the case of the Bergen-McCarthy show it was two comedians, the dummy and W. C. Fields. There developed the two-comedian rivalry: Hope vs. Benny, Benny vs. Allen, and Hope vs. Crosby. The word battle between Hope and Bing Crosby continued longer than most duo playful confrontations—from vaudeville and radio in the early '30s, through seven Road Pictures, from the first, *Road to Singapore*, in 1940, to *Road to Hong Kong*, in 1962.

When one of Bob's less successful Broadway shows, *Ballyhoo of 1932*, neared its closing, the actor got a variety show booking at the Capitol Theater in New York for December 2, 1932. His name appeared on the marquee with Bing Crosby's. This early pairing with Bing has not been much remarked by many people who remember the long collaboration of these two pals. Biographer William Robert Faith indicates the nature of the encounter. He gives Hope's reflection on the possible reference to his nose and Bing's prominent stomach, a type of insult comedy focused on one's anatomy that blossomed in the encounter quoted above between Charlie McCarthy and W. C. Fields: "Hope cannot recall whether 'ski-nose' and 'butter-belly' were born during the engagement or not, but the camaraderie that later spawned such sobriquets formed at the Capitol."[13]

Jim Harmon uses an example of radio put-downs tied to Bing's poor bets on racehorses and Bob's lowly position in his theater and radio pursuits:

CROSBY: Sorry I'm late, Bob. I had trouble finding a place to park.

HOPE: What do you mean? The stable's right outside.

CROSBY: Is that what that was? I thought it was your dressing room. It was—last time I was on your show.[14]

Hope, in the media of vaudeville, radio, and film, employed a comedienne named Patricia Wilder. Her thick Georgia accent and natural talent for comedy helped sell her persona with the stage and radio name of Honey Chile. Her fame was short-lived and came more from her radio programs with Hope than from her vaudeville and film career. She had a curious, naïve logic similar to that possessed by Gracie Allen. A sample of her role as a comedienne with Hope as the straight man went this way:

HOPE: You know, Honey Chile, there are a lot of comedians on the air. Why did you pick me as your partner?

HONEY CHILE: 'Cause ah had a fight with mah folks and ah wanted to do something to disgrace 'em.

HOPE: Uh-huh. Well, you picked the right partner.[15]

Such a put-down by a naïve person does have a special risible quality. We laugh because this person is almost unaware of how severe the invective is. Also, Hope, as the recipient of the insult, comments wearily as he does not know what to do with Honey.

Patricia Wilder had a very short career in films. Her Honey Chile on the radio gave her a role in one of Hope's pictures, the 1938 *Thanks for the Memories*, as an odd femme fatale. An early attempt to examine almost the total amount of effective films of 1938, Frank Vreeland notes that Patricia Wilder lures Hope away from his wife, played by Shirley Ross—the woman who sang "Thanks for the Memories" in *The Big Broadcast of 1938*. Vreeland writes that Wilder as the "Virginia creeper" is found in the bedroom by the wife. This results in a split between husband and wife, but since the wife is going to have a baby, they reunite.[16]

One of the earliest radio programs now available on tape, *The Bob Hope Show* was broadcast in 1938 with the designation of "Blondie and Dagwood," from the popular cartoon strip that still runs in newspapers today. The first Blondie movie, simply called *Blondie*, came out the same year as Hope's December radio show. The series had great audience appeal, and twenty-seven pictures followed—ending with *Beware of Blondie* in 1950. Penny Singleton bleached her hair and played the title role. Arthur Lake, already a movie actor, looked like a dead ringer for Dagwood and only needed the makeup department to give him a cowlick hairdo. Odd as it may seem, Bob interviewed the two actors on his program and used political jokes to poke fun at both Democrats and Republicans:

HOPE: I bet you two had a lot of fun making the picture.

LAKE: We always get along swell. Don't we Penny?

SINGLETON: The only thing we don't agree on is politics.

HOPE: I see. You're both Democrats. (*A big laugh from the audience*) Tell me why you didn't bring Baby Dumpling along with you?

LAKE: He had to stay home. He's filing his income tax.

HOPE: Oh, he's a Republican.[17]

Political jokes were more common in vaudeville and radio skits, but some of this type of humor slipped into a few movie scenes. In the 1940 *Ghost Breakers*, Hope and Paulette Goddard meet a zombie wandering and stumbling around the haunted house. Hope's character wisecracks about the creature being like the Democratic Party, not knowing where it is going.

A radio program ten years later, in 1948, exploited the character flaws of Hope's good friend, Jack Benny, who visits Bob after he had an accident:

HOPE: It was awfully nice of you to drop by and see me, Jack.

BENNY: Well, I was sorry to know about your accident, Bob.

HOPE: It's a little less comfortable. But the worst of it is whenever I hobble down the street people throw money in my hat.

BENNY: (*Long pause*) They do? (*Laughter*) That's embarrassing. Must be awful. What's your take per block? (*Much louder laughter*)

The radio audience anticipated the character flaw of Benny's with "They do?" because of Jack's almost lustful passion for money that he must grab even when it might be beneath him as a millionaire. Hope's character in many of his movies, especially the Road Pictures with Bing Crosby, has the character flaw of groveling for the affection of a woman and not getting any response or being rejected.

Later in the 1948 program, Jack objects to the weak lines he has been given for this radio show. The classic duel of comedians develops when Hope insults Benny. Hope says, "We wanted to give you something you could get your teeth in, but didn't know if you'd have them with you." It seemed like the age insult that Hope used to attack both Benny and Crosby. The influence of vaudeville and radio would transfer to the movies. Physical abnormalities became fair game in the fight. Bing's extended ears became an object of comic derision; Hope's ski-slide nose received the most invective remarks from Crosby. And people think Don Rickles invented insult comedy.

The contemporaries of Hope reveal something about his style. Eddie Cantor, Edgar Bergen, and Fred Allen have comic modes different from Hope's. While Hope possesses enthusiasm, he does not match the manic energy of Cantor, who gained fame by singing and dancing patter songs. In looks and manner, Cantor proved to be an eccentric comic. Bergen plays straight man to Charlie McCarthy, but since Charlie has a life of his own—as if the wooden dummy is a real person—the humor is unique. Hope could play straight man in any medium.

Fred Allen a third person who is different in his comic style, comes closer to satire than Hope. In his jostling with Hope and Benny, Fred comes close to dipping his words in acid. Allen's comments on certain people had the twist of a rapier into the chest. For example, he stated that only an orange existed well in California. Also, he wondered about the intelligence of a radio audience that came to see a program that is only heard.

Three other comedians could be said to be closer to Hope in style or to complement his mode. Jack Benny, George Burns, and

Bing Crosby, like the three comedians discussed above who have different styles, all came from vaudeville. All six were emcees in radio and television. But three with a manner and comedy techniques come closer to Hope. Especially in radio, Benny, Burns, and Crosby had an easygoing delivery. Bob also used slowly delivered understatement, but he could switch into rapid fire and a more energetic utterance. While this greater use of variety did not occur all the time, available radio tapes show that Hope attempted diversity. Benny, Burns, and Crosby all had techniques that they perfected in vaudeville and radio. Benny developed the long pause before the punch line. Burns had a wry drawl on the punch line. And Crosby perfected the nonchalant delivery that sometimes was very low-key. This subdued technique worked best when Hope played the excitable man and switched his delivery to low-key mode. He occasionally made this switch when he believed he was being neglected or misused. This comic exchange of complementary characters evolved in the Hope and Crosby Road Pictures. All of these devices carried over to the films of all six comedians. But here Hope reigned. In film, Bob Hope clearly outshone his contemporaries, not only in quantity but in quality as well.

Hope was more then a verbal comedian; he could handle more varied physical humor than the six comedians who were his popular contemporaries. And Hope's visual skills blossomed in cinema and television.

2 Hollywood Embraces a Song and Dance Man

With the deluge of musical and variety shows adapted to early sound film, Bob Hope became a natural for the medium. However, the two genres were not well executed in the early, primitive stages of the so-called "All Talking, All Singing, All Dancing" films at the end of the '20s. Most of the titles used words such as "Broadway," "Revue," "Melody," and "Follies"—indicating clearly some adaptations from the theater. Magazine and newspaper evaluators were critical of these fledging efforts in 1929. In this transition year of 1929, for example, an unnamed evaluator in the *Time* magazine found the film musicals unsatisfactory: Under the heading of "Song-&-Dancies," he complained about the *Fox Movietone Follies of 1929*. He stated that the movie had "the conventional cinema story about an understudy who got her chance." His comments about "The faint, yellowish color which tints this film most of the time," is a fault the evaluator found with another musical, *On with the Show*. And he questions if the clowning of the Marx Brothers in *The Coconuts* will seem funny in rural regions of the United States.[1]

Fortunately Bob Hope entered the musical *Paree, Paree* in 1934 when technical and acting skills had improved. A critical comment should say it was "somewhat improved." This Warner Brothers two-reel work appears to be a cut-down version of the 1931 *Fifty Million Frenchmen* that featured the stage musical comedians Ole Olsen and Chic Johnson. In *Paree, Paree*, Hope enacts the role as a light-comedy, romantic young man—unlike the usual Chic Johnson manic demeanor. This two-reel derivative of the stage presentation employs the hackneyed concept of a poor, young man named Peter Forbes (Hope) yearning to wed the beautiful woman Lulu (Dorothy Stone). This, of course, is love-at-first-sight and Peter's male companions bet that the woman will "look at his bank book." Fortunately Cole Porter's hit songs come to the rescue of this meandering story and help the picture. Peter sings "You Do Something to Me" to Lulu. Thus the song and dance man, Bob Hope, doesn't get to show his deft hoofing and instead, Dorothy Stone goes into an odd dance as she kicks high in a long dress to the Cole Porter song.

Unusual musical numbers are packed into this short work. One song features a female chorus line and later, a production number entitled "A Primitive Man," doesn't have a logical continuity with the main plot of *Paree, Paree*.[2] By pluck and luck Peter finally wins the hand of the woman and collects the bet from the men who thought he couldn't do it.

The print available on DVD can be found in the third part of *The Ultimate Collection: Bob Hope*,[3] includes *Paree, Paree* and also includes the two-reel short, *Calling All Tars* (1936), a Warner Brothers Vitaphone comedy. With this movie the comedian received top billing—the 1934 *Paree, Paree* had Hope second to Dorothy Stone. *Calling All Tars* is a typical short of the period with a series of loosely-related scenes. The opening portion shows Hope developing his con man and would-be womanizing humor. He has a pal, enacted by Jimmy Berkes, whom he instructs in the art of getting a date with a woman. Hope, of course, is the pretender who is repeatedly rejected until he and his pal go to a costume shop and rent sailor suits. Bob and Jimmy get dates with this deception. However, just as they start dancing with them, the ruse gets them ordered back to a ship, even though they are not Navy inductees. Both men show their incompetence as sailors in a series of contrived and artless skits using on-ship scenes. While *Calling All Tars* is a weak two-reeler, it employs the manipulator or con man aspect of Hope's evolving character—a persona that fluctuates from film to film.

Bob Hope's career in movies actually received its initial step from the popularity of these two-reel works as he obtained fame with his stage performance in *Roberta*. The short comedies brought his talent to the average person who went to the movie houses throughout the United States. Hope was offered a handsome $2,500 for the shorts, and he continued his stage appearances. Educational had a studio in Queens so the shooting of the shorts could be during the day.[4] Most of these mini films were only important as the perfecting of Hope's

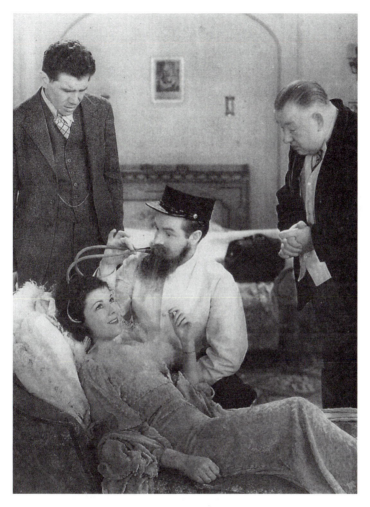

The third two-reel comedy, *The Old Grey Mayor* (1936).
Hope is shown here with Lionel Stander,
Ruth Blasco, and Sam Wren.

From the collection of Donald McCaffrey

savvy as a film comedian. *Going Spanish* (1934) and *The Old Grey Mayor* (1935) are examples of hastily-created works without the skilled writing and directing needed to make them even as acceptable as the 1936 *Calling All Tars*. Nevertherless, the exposure these little movies and the stage hit *Roberta* gave him provided the boost that would lead to Hollywood and a contract with Paramount.[5]

It is not always clear what the comedian thought of his two-reel shorts. Anyone who has seen his Educational film, *Going Spanish*, reports that it is inferior to most of his early works and has ethnic humor that insults Latinos with few redeeming gags. Hope, who often created jokes about his efforts, referred to the fugitive bank robber of the '30s: "After the premiere, Hope was asked by Walter Winchell what he thought of it. Hope's answer, printed by Winchell, was 'When they catch Johnny Dillinger, they're going to make him sit through it twice.'"[6]

Less important than *Paree, Paree* in 1934, Hope had a contract for one short with Educational Pictures. *Going Spanish* sets up a basic situation with Bob driving in South America with his fiancée to encounter a strange festival. In a town named to evoke crude humor, Los Ham and Eggos, a person may insult someone and then sing. The recipient of the put-down must not be offended, but must smile graciously regardless of the nature of the insult. Practically no one who has seen this short has anything complimentary to say on the quality of the comedy and acting portrayed.

Fortunately, Hope moved on to Warner Brothers' comedy short department, with better screenwriting and not as much tasteless humor. *Paree, Paree* is one of six of the mini movies Hope appeared in while he still continued his Broadway career. In 1935 he improved his screen presence with *The Old Grey Mayor*, *Watch the Birdie*, and *Double Exposure*. Playing a role close to the ones he enacted on the stage, *Calling All Tars* in 1936 probably ranks the best of the lot.

Bob Hope and his contemporaries from vaudeville entered films with short movies in the early '30s. Comedians George Burns and Gracie Allen, Jack Benny, and Bing Crosby followed a tradition firmly established in the 1920s by the genteel comedians. Much of the material used in the tales of breezy, young, humorous characters came from the popular magazine short stories of the decades of the '20s and '30s. Burns wrote nine short films for Gracie Allen as a clerk (or other service employee) confronting a customer played by George Burns. The comedy of frustration develops from the employee who uses weird logic that has a strange thread of truth even as she rambles off the subject of a possible sale. Five of these mini movies are directly tied to a sale in a store. Four of the encounters have a medical nurse, an infant-care nurse, a dance hostess, and a manicurist—all service-oriented positions. Both Burns and Allen produced humorous works related to everyday characters in everyday situations. Women comedians going back to the 1910s embraced such light comedy. Such famous women as

One of the comedian's Broadway musicals—the 1936 *Red, Hot and Blue*—with music by Cole Porter, starring for the first time with the leads Jimmy Durante and Ethel Merman.

From the collection of Donald McCaffrey

Mary Pickford, Dorothy Gish, Zasu Pitts, and Mabel Normand found light comedy features their province. So, Gracie Allen, with the help of the stories from her partner George Burns, became popular before Bob Hope. Their shorts became creations more related to light comedy with very little physical comedy. Thereby movie audiences saw the fading of the slapstick comedy so popular in the early days of silent cinema. The tramp figure with the tattered coat and baggy pants of Charlie Chaplin begins to disappear as the more popular light comedian dons a new coat—often that of an ambitious young man with all the faults of an eager, naïve fellow. This was similar to the material and character used by silent screen star, Harold Lloyd.

It is seldom realized that Jack Benny and Bing Crosby appeared in such 1930s shorts where they enacted similar young men often bent on romantic attachment. Such was true in the motivation of Jack Benny in *Broadway Romeo* (1931) and Bing Crosby in *Billboard Girl* (1932). A bit of a masher, Benny finds a mate in the big city with some rather odd humor that reflects the economic stress of the depression. Bing falls in love with a college girl who has become an advertising model for billboards. Falling in love with her image, Bing meets her on campus and woos her with his famous, mellow, golden baritone. Only in the final scene does the Mack Sennett–produced short revert to an angry father trying to stop Bing and his daughter from eloping. The mini movie ends with an automobile chase. The plot has the same material of the genteel silent screen comedians such as Johnny Hines, Douglas MacLean, and Charles Ray.

One of the best examples of Bob Hope inheriting the light comedy traditional material from the past is in the 1936 *Shop Talk*. A contributing evaluator from overseas, Minffordd, Wales, offers his description to the Internet Movie Database:

> "Shop Talk" has a clever premise. Bob Hope stars as a young playboy who considers settling down and becoming the manager of his father's department store. He visits the store to find out what all the employees do. The current manager doesn't want to lose his job; he bribes all the store's employees to act strangely so that Hope will be scared off and go back to his playboy life. There are several funny bits in which a shop girl or a clerk does something bizarre, prompting Hope to react with one of his famous double takes. (By F. Gwynplaine MacIntyre, Borroloola@aol.com)

This type of humorous complication became standard fare for the polite comedians Johnny Hines, Douglas MacLean, and Charles Ray, who were important comedians in the silent age of American cinema. However, they did not make the transition to sound in the '30s. Harold Lloyd, using similar material in both silent and sound films, did make the transition and created popular comic films in the '30s. Bob Hope's *Shop Talk* has all the makings of a Lloyd movie. The 1923 *Safety Last* feature showcases one of the leading comedians of the '30s as a clerk in a big city department store in many of the scenes and total sequences. There are more comic situations of frustration (as in Hope's *Shop Talk*) than most people remember because their minds fixate on the classic image of Harold trying to climb a building and winding up hanging on the minute hand of a huge clock. In a sound picture reprise of climbing a building in *Feet First* (1930), Lloyd starts out as a clerk once more, this time a shoe sales clerk.

Bob Hope, however, kept his feet on the ground and never handled the thrill-type comedy. His occupations were a step above the sales clerk including a master of ceremonies, a small-time traveling song and dance entertainer, a fledging dentist in the Old West, a children's photographer, a radio commentator, a soldier, a sailor, a French barber, a racetrack tout, a British actor who becomes a butler, and a bank teller. There are even more occupations, but throughout his movie career Hope holds many humble jobs. More often he portrays a low-class entertainer. Only occasionally does he enact a wealthy person. One of the exceptions is his role as a multimillionaire hypochondriac in *Never Say Die* (1938). Nevertheless, the situation of extreme wealth has been used for the comic characters in light humorous films.

Leading actors in *The Big Broadcast of 1938*. Left to right: Ben Blue, Dorothy Lamour, W. C. Fields, Shirley Ross, Bob Hope, and Martha Raye.

From J. C. Archives, Inc., photos

From the relatively insignificant two-reelers, Bob moved to features for Paramount. He has a role that combines the radio commentator and master of ceremonies. The most significant scene in Hope's first feature, *The Big Broadcast of 1938*, appears when Hope sings "Thanks for the Memory" to Shirley Ross. Throughout his career this piece became the actor's signature tune, his theme song in many radio and television broadcasts and for the live stage shows—for the troops and for his master of ceremonies appearances.

An example of the lyrics in "Thanks for the Memory":

> Thanks for the memory, / Of rainy afternoons
> Swinging Harlem tunes, / And motor trips and burning lips,
> And burning toast and prunes, / How lovely it was.
> Thanks for the memory / Of candlelight and wine,
> Castles on the Rhine, / The Parthenon and moments on
> The Hudson River Line. / How lovely it was.
> Many's the time that we feasted, /
> And many's the time that we fasted,
> Oh, well, it was swell while it lasted,
> We did have fun, / And no harm done

Another important feature of this *Broadcast Film* potpourri is Hope's introduction to a wider audience, since variety movies were very popular. Additionally, "Thanks for the Memory" received an Academy Award for the best musical number. Maybe less important but worth noting is that the most risible scenes are delivered by W. C. Fields in his golf and pool skits from vaudeville. Besides these variety items, Fields became a plot mover with his huffing and puffing portrait of S. B. Bellows, a millionaire entrepreneur who invents a huge cabin cruiser that can achieve fantastic speeds of 100 miles per hour. On a bet he enters the ship into a race with another cruiser. With this thin plot a number of talents from Paramount take turns creating the type of entertainment that pleased audiences who wanted to see those who provided entertainment on radio programs.

Where, of course, does this mixture—besides his turn singing, "Thanks for the Memory"—leave Bob Hope with anything to do? His function in this 1938 Big Broadcast film became that of a radio master of ceremonies. He set forth lame jokes with each introduction of a routine, sketch or musical number. Unfortunately, the weak jokes were supposed to be funny, actually a poke at the stand-up comedian. Such a bit did not work for this picture. Probably one of the most literate, perceptive film evaluators, Frank S. Nugent, suggested how Hope handled a token scene to please opera goers' admiration for diva Kristen Flagstad. She sang Brünhilde's war cry from "Die Walküre":

> We admired Miss Flagstad's voice, but even more did we admire her complete detachment. Of the many extraneous interludes lugged in by a laconic Hope introduction, hers was the most offhand and the most bluntly executed. Miss Flagstad had a short aria to sing. She sang it. And we could almost see her stepping down from her crag, taking her check and going happily home.[7]

Among the four movies released in 1938 was *College Swing*, with comedienne Martha Raye.

From the collection of Donald McCaffrey

With a battery of gagmen from radio Hope would try to avoid such lampoons in the future. His skill as a master of ceremonies became his function throughout his career. In radio, television, musicals, and stage shows he could hold the audience with his energy and charm.

Like new automobiles, the movie musicals of the '30s that bore a year designation were sometimes produced a year earlier. Created in 1937, *The Big Broadcast of 1938* is reported to have been released February 18, 1938, by the American Film Institute researchers.[8]

In late April Paramount released *College Swing*, another musical that had the trappings of an all-star cast—so much so, in fact, that Hope became buried in talent. Paramount obtained a deluge of comedians such as Martha Raye, Ben Blue, Edward Everett Horton, Jerry Colonna, plus romantic singing roles for Betty Grable and John Payne. Most prominent of all were the husband and wife team George Burns and Gracie Allen, who stole the show...especially Gracie.

Gracie Allen evolved as the comedian and George Burns as the straight man. The duo, according to billing, probably fit the pattern of all other comic twosomes. A very popular radio program propelled them into pictures. The credit titles for *College Swing* gave George and Gracie top billing along with Martha Raye, and Bob Hope was listed below in smaller print. Gracie Allen became the lead for a variety of reasons: (1) She becomes the plot focus as the heiress to Alden College who must earn a college degree so that she can take possession of the 200-year-old institution for her ancestors. (2) Gracie Alden, her character's name, exhibits her tangled logic when confronted by a word or event that possesses a humorous connotation that seems to make perfect sense. (3) When she marries stuffy, fussy Everett Edward Horton as Professor Hubert Dash, she sings the love song "You're a Natural," and demonstrates a sprightly Irish jig—a skill she developed as a single act in early vaudeville. Consequently, she becomes the most important comic character in *College Swing*.

Bob Hope's character acted as an agent to tutor Gracie for her college examinations. However, the writers gave him few laughable lines. Several limp scenes with Martha Raye gave her more moments to display her brash man-hungry demeanor. Her "How'dja You Like to Love Me" provided a chance for Hope to sing with her, but the comedian was probably not happy with the role. The song by Burton Lane and Frank Loesser proved to be the hit of the movie, but

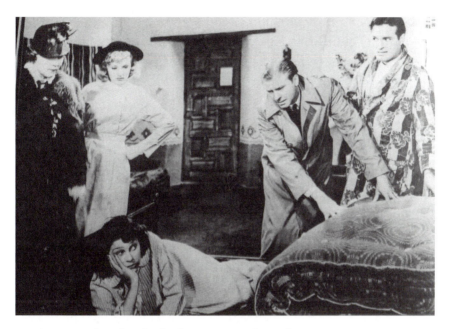

Discovered in their bathrobes, Hope and Martha Raye can't convince people they were caught in the rain in a 1938 feature, *Give Me a Sailor*.

From the collection of Donald McCaffrey

according to biographer Lawrence J. Quirk, who sometimes appears to be a Hope detractor, that was not enough for Hope. Quirk, an evaluator with a propensity to gossip, wrote: "Here, to his extreme annoyance, he was just one of a crowd."[9]

Once more teamed with Martha Raye in the 1938 film *Give Me a Sailor*, Hope surely could not complain of being "just one of a crowd." He became the leading comedian in a light, thin plot characteristic of those popular novels and magazine short stories of the '20s and '30s. Bob plays Jim Brewster, the con man, devil-may-care Navy ensign who tries to manipulate the romantic activities of his brother, Walter Brewster, a lieutenant on the same ship. The object of their affections becomes the good-looking Nancy, played by Betty Grable, who is the sister of Letty, the less attractive of the two. While this is contrived, well-worn material for a comedic drama, Hope does get a plot of sorts to help develop his character. In this work he becomes a likeable rogue with a few good scenes.

Martha Raye, in the role of unattractive Letty, tries to impress Jim Brewster with her cooking skills at a picnic. Unfortunately, the cooking fire spreads to Jim's car and it explodes. The pair walks to a remote hotel in the rain where they rent a room and try to get dry. They are caught by relatives in this compromising situation and are forced to explain. Hope, as Jim, gets the task of explaining their predicament and stammers in a humorous manner. He gives up the attempt to clarify why they are both in bathrobes.

Letty wins a contest for the woman with the best legs.[10] (Raye does have a very attractive figure, but it is her "Plain Jane" face, especially the large mouth, which serves as her negative feature.) She wins enough money to have a make over and emerges as the lovely swan—no longer the ugly duckling. Brother Walter turns his affection from Nancy to the new charms of Letty. However, Jim gets Letty because he has a kiss that thrills her.

It is evident that much of this plot is contrived and has many trivial scenes. Nevertheless, Hope makes good use of the more specific design to develop his comic con man character. Additionally, *Give Me a Sailor* provides pleasant fluff with the popular appeal of "All's well that ends well."

What could be considered Hope's best picture of the '30s, *Never Say Die* (1939), must be attributed to those talented writers, Don Hartman, Frank Butler, and Preston Sturges. Hartman and Butler had credits scripting many works for Bob Hope. In the late '30s, Sturges wrote delightful comedies such as *Easy Living* (1937). Sturges would also produce screenplays and directed *The Lady Eve* and *Sullivan's Travels* in 1941. Then, he created *Hail the Conquering Hero* and *The Miracle of Morgan's Creek* in 1944.

While it is difficult to tell the contributions of the three authors of *Never Say Die*, adapted from a 1912 Broadway play, the subject has the meat that Sturges liked to handle. He wrote humorous pictures that contained social significance but were often laced with sarcasm—and the combination of talents made this work a hit that can still be enjoyed by critics and audiences alike.

The opening shots in *Never Say Die* present the caustic commentary on how easy it is to swindle tourists visiting Switzerland:

TITLE SHOT #1 (Appearing over a photo of mountains and a foreign city.)

Nestling peacefully beneath the snow-clad Alps lies the quaintly picturesque health spa of Bad Gaswasser. It is world-famous for the curative values of its natural mineral springs.

SHOT #2 Two men are shoveling coal to heat water. DISSOLVE INTO

SHOT #3 A man in a beret with a medical coat mixes chemicals into a flow of water. PAN TO CANISTERS SHOWING THE WORDS 1. Epson Salt, 2. Bi-Carb, 3. Plum Extract, 4. Sulfur Dioxide.[11]

There is a shot of the chemical mixer sampling the water. He grimaces, obviously finding the taste offensive. However, he says, "Good." Later in the scene we see a bronze plaque reading:

BAD GASWASSER
"NATURAL HOT MINERAL SPRINGS"
"HEALTH FROM MOTHER EARTH"
KURHOTEL EDELWEISS

From the opening shots of the movie it becomes obvious that tourists coming to Bad Gaswasser are being fleeced by mineral water that is not from mother earth but a product of added chemicals and heated tap water. And hypochondriac John Kidley, worth 20 million, is one of the tourists to be swindled. Naturally, it develops as a role for Bob Hope—a part that demonstrates his comic versatility.

As the exposition develops, John is in the room about to receive a pitcher of the bogus healing spring water from his valet, Jeepers. He moans, "I am a very sick man." The valet takes his temperature and declares, "It's normal." To which John says, "It can't be." And he throws the thermometer to the floor—"It's broken." Thereby the fussy, hypochondriacal character of John Kidley is established.

Evaluator Bob Thomas wrote about this character as weak and ineffective for Hope:

Amusing though it is, *Never Say Die* fails to exploit Hope's own comic nature, fitting him instead into a script-tailored character. It is an essentially weak character, since most of the time he thinks he is sick or dying.[12]

This criticism could be questioned. A weak, complaining hypochondriac can be as funny as an aggressive con man—and Hope played many a fussy and whiny character. Surely Moliere, the French playwright of the seventeenth century, was not wrong with his satirical portrait of the quintessence of a hypochondriac in *The Imaginary Invalid*. Also, this enactment by Hope demonstrates his ability to make an atypical portrait for his acting interesting, comic, and effective.

Hope's character as John Kidley encounters the complication of a black widow spider woman, Juno Marko, pursuing him for his fortune. Hope has a scene where he tries to hide from her. When she finds him, Juno confronts him with the demand that he marry her. He objects: "You are already married." Her reply: "Not for long." She is known to get rid of her husbands by nefarious means.

An oddball physician, Dr. Schmidt, tells John he has only 30 days to live because the acidity in his system is dissolving his bones. "You are the first human dog." Thinking he will die anyway, John marries Texas heiress Mickey Hawkins, enacted by Martha Raye, to make sure she is not forced into marrying fortune-hunting Prince Smirnow. The prince believes that he is being cheated out of the fortune and challenges John to a duel.

The climactic duel scene provides Hope with some of his best humorous moments. He trembles with fear, which he tries to hide. Mickey bribes the handler who loads the pistols and learns that one of them has a blank. "There's a cross on the muzzle of the pistol with the bullet. There's a nick on the handle of the pistol with the blank." The stress of the moment, where each duelist faces death, confuses both John and Smirnow. As they attempt to recall the correct pistol markings, even the word order gets garbled. Watching this develop, expert markswoman Juno takes out her own pistol and shoots the gun from the prince's hand. She is an expert at dispatching husbands, after all. Since she decides to marry another man, the finish of this wild farce has John and Mickey embracing. Hope would not fare so well with rival Bing Crosby in the seven Road Pictures. Bing would more often than not get the woman, Dorothy Lamour.

One other '30s film, *The Cat and the Canary* (1939), needs to be briefly examined because it would spawn another "Dark Old House" mystery-comedy, one of Hope's pictures in 1940, *Ghost Breakers*. From a hit play on Broadway, *The Cat and the Canary* received its first screen version as a silent film for Universal. This earlier adaptation was tied to the stage medium. Director Elliott Nugent moved the 1939 movie rendering of the drama from a restricted number of interior scenes to numerous dark, exterior sets surrounding the mansion. The boat ferries the heirs up to the mansion (and possibly to their fortune) against a swampy background. The alligators in the water are menacing and serve as a harbinger of the horror and mystery that will greet the guests who arrive for the reading of the will. Furthermore, a new touch develops into an asset for the 1939 production. One of the heirs, Wally Campbell (Hope's role) possesses a breezy, smooth-talking sense of humor. In fact, the comedian adds an amusing counterpoint to the lurking, shadowy figure, the secret passageways, and the mystery of who is the murderer. Two men, a lawyer in charge of the execution of the will and a policeman from a nearby asylum for the mentally ill inmates, are the victims. The identity of the killer becomes clouded by an escape of "The Cat," a criminally insane man who thinks he is a cat and is bent on killing someone. In a contrived plot, the mysterious figure in the shadows stalks Joyce Norman (Paulette Goddard's role). So Joyce becomes the canary, the symbolic intention of the original play's title.

When the guests arrive at the mansion, the lights flicker and go out. Wally wisecracks, "They do that if you don't pay the bill." With a pose of nobility and male bravado he attempts to be the hero. Joyce has been promised the fortune if she stays the night in the mansion and of course the other heirs, except Wally, make her an object of their scorn. The conflict becomes a multiple one: a possible haunted house, a murderous madman is on the loose, and the relatives would like to see Joyce fail the test. Wally tells Joyce, "I'll protect you." Suddenly there comes on the scene a shadowy, menacing figure right after Crosby, the lawyer, falls dead on the floor and is eventually discovered in a secret passageway. When Wally becomes scared and tries to hide his fear he says, "I'll run and get help." His heroic attempt evaporates and he wants to escape.

One of the best parts of critic Frank S. Nugent's astute evaluation of Hope's delivery of the comic line:

> Some of his lines are good ("I'm so scared even my goose-pimples have goose-pimples.") . . . but the good and bad profit alike from the drollery of Mr. Hope's comic style. It is a style so perfidious we think it should be exposed for the fraud it is. Mr. Hope's little trick is to deliver his jests timidly, forlornly. . . When they click, he can cut a little caper and pretend he is surprised and delighted too. It's not cricket, but it is fun.[13]

By the time Hope had logged many radio programs and six features in the '30s, he had developed this technique. In *The Big Broadcast of 1938* all of his master of ceremonies jokes seemed lame. In this first feature, Hope didn't have the level of comic style that Nugent observed in *The Cat and the Canary*. Don Kaye, an Internet evaluator for All Movie Guide comments on how this movie follows the standard Dark Old House genre when other potential heirs try to drive her insane so she will not inherit millions. Kaye writes: "The frights are nonstop as hands reach out from nowhere, people disappear between trap doors, the halls echo with terrifying sounds and secret doorways that lead to hidden passageways." Wally helps Joyce through the ordeal and, according to Kaye, "Hope integrates his wiseacre comedic style into an essentially straight role, with the humor well-placed in the otherwise moody material."[14]

It would appear that Paramount thought Hope and Martha Raye would make a good comedy team. *The American Film Institute Catalog: Feature Films, 1931–1940* cites the *Hollywood Reporter* as indicating that Raye was considered for *The Cat and the Canary*. Comedian Hope obtained a starring role when he was paired with Paulette Goddard in this film and he would be considered for a sequel because the plot of *Ghost Breakers* was almost a parallel story of the Dark Old House film. Goddard played close to a straight role—again, and as in *The Cat and the Canary*, an heiress. Hope portrays the role of a protector in the haunted house. The Martha Raye and Bob Hope combination probably produced more sparks of rivalry than the complementary pairing of Goddard and Hope. Not only did *The Cat and the Canary* further the comedian's career, Paulette Goddard received a ten-year contract from the prestigious Paramount Studio.

The tradition continued from the silent days of film by the use of attractive women opposite comedians. While Charles Chaplin first played his famous Tramp role with Mabel Normand, a comedienne and director, he would switch to playing opposite women who essentially enacted a straight role. A similar casting preference existed with three other silent comedians: Harold Lloyd, Buster Keaton, and Harry Langdon. Occasionally Keaton would obtain humor from a naïve young woman who couldn't handle the simplest task. Bob Hope's exceptions of using comediennes evolved in three films with Martha Raye and four movies co-starring Lucille Ball. Raye employed an aggressive, man-chasing weirdo. Usually Ball played a sophisticated role when she co-starred with Hope. However, Ball became a brassy, rural, assertive woman in the 1950 *Fancy Pants*. Her role in this movie seems to be the harbinger of the character in the long-running television series, *I Love Lucy*.

Bob Hope's success in his movies of the '30s would give him even more character variety as he moved into the next decade, the war years, and the post war years.

3 Starring Hope During the War Years

According to most retrospective evaluators, the '40s and '50s were the period when Bob Hope created his most effective movies. During the preparation for war in the late '30s, the draft years, and the actual war from 1941 to 1945, Hope produced impressive, humorous pictures. The comedian established his star status during this time and became a valuable asset for his base, the Paramount Studio.

One of his best films was the 1942 *Louisiana Purchase,* Bob's first Technicolor feature.[1] Hope generally dominated every picture he starred in; however, Victor Moore turns in an amazing performance as the bumbling, pudgy, Senator Loganberry. Moore underplays the meek, whiney politician who has grand ideas of being president of the United States—an obvious impossible future for one who lacks charisma. Hope, as leading man Jim Taylor, has the role of a state representative who becomes the fall guy for four influential cronies who place the blame on Jim's shoulders as they bilk the state of Louisiana out of questionable projects. Bob, consequently, attempts to wiggle out of the blame. These chiselers represent various factions of old southern society: a colonel of the old school, a state police official, a son of the colonel, and the dean of the state university. Bob Hope has the persona often exhibited in the Road Pictures: a comical incrimination by con man Bing Crosby. And, with struggling, humorous protestations, he is known to utter such lines as: "Now wait a minute. I didn't do that."

The four cronies want to head off an investigation by Senator Loganberry and suggest that Jim Taylor get the senator in a sexually compromising situation. So the basic plot is for Taylor to have Oliver Loganberry accused of an indiscretion so that he can be bribed with disclosure. The malfeasance of the quartet, and fall guy Taylor, would thereby be overlooked.

Because the senator is the epitome of restraint—he doesn't smoke, drink, gamble, or fool around with women—he becomes a difficult target to corrupt. Herein develops the most laughable sequence of the film. Actress Vera Zorina, as Marina Von Duren, poses as Jim Taylor's secretary. Hope, with a handlebar moustache, disguises himself as a French headwaiter and slips the teetotaling senator liquor instead of water. When the senator becomes drunk and doesn't realize what is happening he allows Marina to sit on his lap as pictures are taken. "Couldn't I sit on your lap? I always wanted to sit on a lap of a woman," Oliver says hesitatingly. The performance delivered reveals a character with a number of nuances. Moore plays the drunk with considerable, humorous restraint—a master comedian who originated the role on Broadway. And while Hope might have appeared secondary to Moore's risible comedy, he truly isn't. Hope plays comic frustration very effectively and evokes the desperation of a man who might go to prison for the crimes of his political cronies very deftly.

Since this film explores comic political corruption, is it a pure form of satire? It is certainly as close to satire as any of Bob Hope's pictures get. However, much of the credit for the witty, satirical situations comes from the pen of Morrie Ryskind. With George Kaufman, Ryskind wrote the political lampoon *Of Thee I Sing*, a 1932 Broadway musical. On his own, Ryskind scripted the book for the Broadway musical, *Louisiana Purchase*, which was adapted for Hope and Moore into a successful movie.

Arriving on the screen five years later, *The Senator Was Indiscreet* (1947) has some similarities to *Louisiana Purchase*. Much like the portrait of Oliver Loganberry as the senator, William Powell's Melvin Ashton has no self-awareness regarding his dreams of becoming president. Powell's enactment of the foolish, self-deluded senator is, in the character's development, an equal to Victor Moore's Loganberry.

Film critic Bosley Crowther rarely found comic movies impressive, but he praised the adaptation of *Louisiana Purchase* from the Broadway musical as one of the New Year's best. In the *New York Times* on January 1, 1942, he wrote, "Surprisingly the film has not been cluttered with song and dance." And Crowther observed that Hope's performance was one of his best. Crowther particularly enjoyed the comedian's parody of Jimmy Stewart's filibuster in *Mr. Smith Goes to Washington* (1939). Hope delivered a type of Road Picture wisecrack with an in-joke by saying that he got permission from Jimmy Stewart to do the routine.

An earlier released film, the 1940 *The Ghost Breakers*, also shows Hope's skilled handling of the Dark Old House with ghosts, a ripe subject for almost all comedians. In 1953, Dean Martin and Jerry Lewis starred in *Scared Stiff,* a remake of Hope's *The Ghost Breakers.* Two other comic duos include Abbott and Costello, who appeared in *Hold That Ghost* (1941), and Olsen and Johnson, who encountered the other world in *Ghost Catchers* (1944). In 1927 the silent screen adapted a spooky mystery from the stage called *The Cat and the Canary*, which, in 1939, Bob Hope developed with a comic twist as a sound movie remake.[2]

The success of the sound version of *The Cat and the Canary* starring Hope and Paulette Goddard probably spawned the pair being cast again in *The Ghost Breakers* the following year. Although the 1940s picture was not strictly timed with the actual U.S. participation in World War II, the conflict was underway in Europe and recruitment had begun in the States. As a diversion to help escape reality, this Dark Old House comedy was wonderful entertainment.

The development of the plot leads to what is believed to be a haunted castle on a Caribbean island called Black Island. Fate puts Hope, as Larry Lawrence, a scandal-dispensing radio host, on the run to escape retribution for a supposed murder he didn't commit. This role has Hope enact a comical, cowardly person afraid to face the truth. During his escape Larry meets the heiress, Paulette Goddard's Mary Carter, and hides in her steamer trunk bound for Cuba to avoid reporters wanting to get the story on his alleged crime.

With the bravado of a would-be protector, of Mary, who is going to the mysterious island, Larry dances with the heiress before venturing into the castle. Hope delivers one of his classic, self-deprecating statements: "When I dance with women I am a pilgrim. I make little progress."[3] Such literary allusions were not often employed in a typical, popular comedy. More traditional is Hope's wisecrack as he encounters a menacing, sleepwalking zombie in the castle. The comedian says the odd creature, a stereotyped casting of Noble Johnson, is like the Democratic Party because he doesn't know where he is going.

Much of the humor of *The Ghost Breakers* emerges from the politically incorrect stereotype of black persons who are afraid of ghosts—a comedy staple from the past. Willie Best plays manservant to Hope's Larry Lawrence. Best assists Hope with a search of the castle and, in the muted style of others of his race who played in films of the period, has fear of the unknown, but stands by Hope even though he is frightened. Best played something closer to the standard role of a leading black comic as Stepin' Fetchit in Harold Lloyd's 1930 talkie, *Feet First*. Best took on the name of Sleep an' Eat. I had the privilege of asking Lloyd about the questionable use of this type of humor when I interviewed him in July of 1965. He indicated that it was derived from vaudeville and was characteristic of the racial and ethnic humor that no one thought demeaning at that time. Even Bob Hope supported Best and praised his acting ability.

To a degree the black comedian Best gets more laughs in *The Ghost Breakers*. Nevertheless, Hope has one very effective bit using physical comedy—something not always attributed to his skills that often depended on verbal gags. There is one innovative example. Reaching Cuba hiding in a steamer trunk of the heiress, Mary Taylor, Hope's Larry Lawrence emerges in a cramped, bent-over position and finds it impossible to stand straight. The comedian wobbles about the room in a squatty, legs-bent posture.

In another war years work, *You Got Me Covered* (1942), Hope plays reporter Robert Kittredge and executes an even more elaborate physical bit. Confronting Nazi spies he gets cornered by a *femme fatale* who gives him a cigarette loaded with mind-bending chemicals. He sips a drink and begins to suspect that he has been slipped a loaded cocktail. As he remarks to the lady spy that the drink has had no effect, his vision begins to whirl into multiple images of the woman. He wisecracks that he is seeing the Andrew Sisters, the popular singing trio of the World War II era. His neck and head begin to twist oddly, and he executes a tottering, sliding, staggering dance until he collapses. Obviously, Hope's deft handling of this physical, comical, yet graceful routine harks back to his vaudeville dancing days.

The German spies in *You Got Me Covered* are the stereotypical villains often used during the war years for both serious melodramas and full-fledged lampoons. Hope plays Kittredge, a bumbling foreign correspondent to Moscow who mistakenly reports that Germany will not invade Russia. Fired from his job, he tries to make up for his mistake by investigating a Nazi spy ring operating in the United States. In this rather routine intrigue comedy, Hope shines as a struggling ne'er-do-well who needs the help of Christina Hill, a

My Favorite Blonde, a take-off from Hitchcock's *The 69 Steps*,
has Hope entangled in international intrigue
with Madeline Carroll.

From J. C. Archives, Inc., photos

secretary played by Dorothy Lamour. A collection of mentally
defective characters or obsessed villains creates the film's most
laughable comedy. Donald Meek plays a crazy old man who attempts
to execute Kittredge for treason because he thinks he lives in the
Civil War of the 1860s.

A Nazi leader of the spy ring portrayed by Otto Preminger, becomes
suitably menacing in a hilarious way. After a climactic chase and
fight, Kittredge gets credit for the capture of the spies (with the help
of U.S. Marines) and, of course, gets the woman, Christina.

By far a much better intrigue comedy than *You Got Me Covered* is
another work from 1942, *My Favorite Blonde*. Starring Hope and
Madeline Carroll, this film is populated with the standard wartime
favorite collection of sinister Nazis. The casting of Gale Sondergaard,
George Zucco, and Lionel Royce as Nazi spies provides the film with
suitably fiendish villains. Also, writers Frank Butler, Melvin Frank,

and Don Hartman furnish the actors with a delightful spoof on Alfred Hitchcock's *The 39 Steps* (1935). Situations of pursuit and escape give Madeline Carroll (the heroine of the parody) a comic thriller reprise.

Essentially, Miss Carroll plays straight woman to Bob Hope's vaudevillian character, a performing-penguin trainer. His Larry Haines gets caught up in the intrigue and is chased by the spies. Actress Carroll, as Karen Bentley, uses Larry to help in her escape as she assumes various relationships with the hapless trainer. Hope gets in a one-liner as Karen tells of her plight:

> KAREN: Do you know what it feels like, followed and hounded and watched every second?
>
> LARRY: I use to, but now I pay cash for everything.

Another effective line from the comedian is uttered when the *femme fatale* spy, Gale Sondergaard, produces a gun to get a scorpion pendant that is presumed to contain microfilm:

> LARRY: (protesting) That might shoot somebody and I'm the only one here.

Hope, long admired by many other deliverers of gags, executes such lines with aplomb—even in a state of panic. Sometimes this type of delivery works as understated humor that avoids the excesses of some comedians who have a tendency to "knock themselves out" trying to be funny. Examples of such humor are the overstatements, both verbal and physical, of Milton Berle, Jerry Lewis, and Jim Carrey.

Some parallels to the plot in Hitchcock's *The 39 Steps* led the researchers for *The American Film Institute Catalog: Feature Films, 1941–1950*, to classify the humorous work as "Road, Espionage, Comedy."[4] "Road" does not refer to Hope's Road Pictures, featuring Hope and Bing Crosby. It means that this film, *My Favorite Blonde*, was a light, simple parody of the 1935 intrigue drama, *The 39 Steps*, and has many "on the road" spy escapes. *My Favorite Blonde* depicts Carroll and Hope fleeing in a taxi, a passenger train, a police patrol car, a bus, a train freight car, and even an airplane. With the melodramatic plot enhanced by the superior acting of Madeline and Bob, the film became one of the best of the genre.

My Favorite Brunette (1947), five years later, doesn't fare as well as the Hope and Carroll vehicle. In this intrigue the plot is based on

Mistaken for a detective in *My Favorite Brunette*, Bob meets Alan Ladd
who is in the cameo role of a real-life detective.

From J. C. Archives, Inc., photos

Hope's desire as Ronnie Jackson to be a hard-boiled private detective in the style of the popular crime novels and short stories of
Raymond Chandler. Next to Hope's wisecracks, probably the most
effective comedy comes from the bizarre characters of Peter Lorre
as Kismet and Lon Chaney, Jr. as Willie. Lorre is a knife-throwing
fiend who almost obscures the plot by doing mock imitations of
some of his earlier sinister roles. Chaney executes a repeat of the
character Lennie, a character he played in the 1939 movie based on
John Steinbeck's novelette and stage play, *Of Mice and Men*. Chaney
plays a man with the IQ of a boy in the body of a giant. Hope
mollifies the innocent but threatening creature with: "I'll buy you a
rabbit later." The wisecrack probably goes past the average viewer
today, but it is a literary allusion to the original story that depicts

Lennie's obsessive dream of raising rabbits. As with a number of films from the '40s, referential jokes regarding film and stage characters are common. Alan Ladd has a cameo as the tough private eye, and Bing Crosby plays an executioner who is disgusted because Hope is reprieved from a death sentence.

Before the declaration of war after the December 7, 1941, Japanese attack on Pearl Harbor, the United States instituted conscription into the military services, indicating that this country might soon go to war. This mandatory requirement produced several film comedies. Comedians Abbott and Costello had *Buck Privates* released January 31, 1941, and it became a $4 million hit on an $180,000 budget—nearly unheard of for this decade. Paramount followed with a July 4, 1941, release of the Hope vehicle *Caught in the Draft*. The plot has the comedian as the important, sensitive film star Don Bolton, who wilts at the sound of gunfire. This is discovered as the opening of the film shows the actor trying to handle a leading role in a war movie. One scene in the movie shows the desperation of Don to get out of the draft. He climbs on the top of an upright piano and jumps off with bare feet onto the floor in order to produce, he thinks, flat feet. He hopes to marry Dorothy Lamour (as Tony Fairbanks) because at the age of thirty-one he thinks he is too old for the draft. However, legislation is passed that pushes the age bracket up to thirty-five years.

When he is finally in the army he proves to be one of the worst recruits in the service. He has trouble with the standard arms drill and shows great fear on the firing range. The comedy of inefficiency prevails as he tries to drive an army tank. By good luck and pluck he attains the rank of corporal and gets the woman, Tony. One of the best lines of the movie gives Hope the wisecrack when he first sees Tony and is smitten with her. The inside-joke, with shades of the Road Pictures, states: "She looks like Dorothy Lamour with clothes on." An audience in our present-day society might not know that Lamour would often appear in films wearing a revealing sarong.

The musical genre that launched Hope's career in the late '30s with *The Big Broadcast of 1938* did not die, but waned in the '40s. Paramount would promote its many stars and other contract players in such creations as *Star Spangled Rhythm* (1942). Such movies proved to be potpourris much like earlier works—a mixture of skits, songs, production numbers, and cameo appearances of well-known actors. They might be considered variety shows derived from the tradition of Broadway in the early '30s and originating from vaudeville.

Star Spangled Rhythm had no contemporary Broadway roots. It became a studio public relations concoction. The leads—Victor Moore, Betty Hutton, and Eddie Bracken—carry the main plot. The "Miss Fixit" Hutton, as Polly Judson, becomes the plot mover by supporting Moore's pretense that he is a studio CEO instead of a lowly guard at the main gate of Paramount. Polly helps perpetuate the mildly humorous deception by allowing her U.S. Navy boyfriend, Eddie Bracken (as Moore's son) to think his father has become the head of the studio. To complete the manipulations to bring in the Paramount cream of the crop, Polly gets the studio's stars to appear in a show. Important luminaries such as Bing Crosby and Bob Hope are only two examples of stars included in the lineup. Using a one-act play, Fred MacMurray, Franchot Tone, and Ray Milland appear in George S. Kaufman's skit, "If Men Played Cards Like Women Do." Then, a trio of women—Paulette Goddard, Dorothy Lamour, and Veronica Lake—render the song "A Sweater, Sarong and Peekaboo Bang," which is an allusion to the trademarks of each woman. These are examples of some of the scenes from *Star Spangled Rhythm*. In the basic plot incorporating a variety show, Betty Hutton shines as the most comic figure with a bit more controlled version of the comical, sex-starved, aggressive female for which she was so noted. Hope, executing the role of master of ceremonies, may have helped promote himself into that position for the future Oscar presentations.[5] Bing Crosby takes the lead in the final production number, "Old Glory," with a waving flag in a background projection and a huge representation of the four presidents on Mount Rushmore.

In the 1943 musical *Let's Face It*, Hope has a much better role. Hope, as Jerry Walker, and his two army buddies, all three of whom are married, run into problems as they try to have fun with other women. In comic retribution their wives try to make the men jealous by having their own escorts. Ironically, the husbands also have dates. Despite the comic tangle of motives and humorous embroilments, the couples eventually iron out their differences. *Let's Face It* lampooned the looser moral standards during the Second World War. The *American Film Institute Catalog Feature Films, 1941–1950*, describes the history of this movie as follows:

> Source: Based on the musical *Let's Face It*, music by Cole Porter, libretto by Herbert and Dorothy Fields. (New York, 29 Oct. 1941), which was suggested by the play *Cradle Snatchers* by Russell Medcraft and Norma Mitchell (New York, 7 Sep. 1925).[6]

Cole Porter's contribution to this film was the following songs: "The Milk Song," "Let's Face It," "Let's Not Talk About Love," and "Farming," of which he was composer and lyricist.

A revival of this work appeared on television February 21, 1954, for the NBC *Colgate Comedy Hour*. The producers of the television show played it loose by adding songs from other Cole Porter stage musicals. More popular than the songs in the original 1941 stage play *Let's Face It*, "It's Delovely" from the 1936 stage musical *Red, Hot and Blue* was added, along with the ever-popular "I've Got You Under My Skin" from the 1936 MGM movie, *Born to Dance*. In an interview with screen and television writer Edmund L. Hartmann, the author explained how comedian Bert Lahr objected to the part he was assigned for the television show: "I rewrote and extended his role," Hartmann recalled. Lahr was given an even greater chance to show the range of his skills by playing two roles: the male role of Frankie Burns as written in the original musical and the comical drag role of Aunt Pamela Burns.

In the decade of the television revival of *Let's Face It*, Bob Hope starred in a period costume film comedy, *Casanova's Big Night* (1954), another work created by screenwriter Edmund Hartmann. This picture has some of the characteristics of an earlier period comedy Hope played toward the end of the war years, *Monsieur Beaucaire*.

From the novel and play by Booth Tarkington, *Beaucaire* was a comedy developed for Hope with songs by Jay Livingston and Ray Evans. In the title role, Hope plays a barber to the King and is forced to assume the role of expert swordsman, Duke de Chandre. This is a plot similar to *Casanova's Big Night*, which has a tailor impersonating his master, the lover Casanova.

A climactic duel between Beaucaire and the villainous Don Francisco becomes one of the most hilarious scenes of the 1946 film. As Hope is unmasked, Francisco says, "This is not the Duke de Chandre, he is but a common barber." Beaucaire replies with Hope's famous understated delivery: "I am not common." Of course, Beaucaire cannot duel and complains that he doesn't have a sword. A member of the court offers his weapon and Beaucaire objects to the accommodating man, "You keep out of this."

Forced to fight, Beaucaire slashes up and down as if he had a stick to ward off the blows. A series of musical instruments provide the barber an escape from the thrusts of an opponent who proves to be a master of the dueling art. The well-choreographed comedy

Hope in *Monsieur Beaucaire* (1946) hacks away instead of fencing a
champion swordsman.

From the collection of Donald McCaffrey

shows the following: (1) the comedian Beaucaire hides behind a
harp and gets his nose (often a butt of jokes on the comedian's "ski-
slide nose") caught in the strings, and for a moment the strings
sound out; (2) he tries to hide under the piano and uses his sword to
hit the courtier's shins, but a sword to Beaucaire's rear end gets the
comedian moving; (3) Beaucaire grabs a music stand and tries to use
it to fend off Francisco's sword thrusts; (4) The barber catches the
sword of his foe in the top of the piano and slams the lid of the
piano on Francisco's hand; and (5) backing into a bass violin, he
gets stuck so he tries to use the top of the bass to hit his challenger
Francisco on the head by bending forward—but he misses. The
moment evolves into one of the best moments illustrating Hope's
ability to execute physical comedy. Hope, as an actor, more often
has been cited for his delivery of one-liners.

Beaucaire is saved from certain death by the arrival of the real
Duke de Chandre. So, the not-so-common man escapes in a stolen
carriage with his girlfriend. Beaucaire says to her, "There must be
some country where you can die of old age." In the final scene of the

film he has a flourishing barber business in Colonial America with Francisco, an escapee from the guillotine for his nefarious ways, who is now reduced to serving as a shoeshine boy in Beaucaire's four-chair barber shop. Filmmaker and actor Woody Allen found this work so verbally satisfying that he paid homage to the Hope period piece by creating a parody of the Russian novel and play called *Love and Death* (1975)—an important part of Hal Erickson's All Movie Guide's internet evaluation. The performance of Hope in *Monsieur Beaucaire*, according to Allen, shows Bob at his best:

> He is very, very funny. There are a number of films where he's allowed to show his brilliant gift of delivery, his brilliant gift of comic speech. He had a very breezy attitude; he was a great man with the quip. Those one-liners and witticism, they're just like air. He does them so lightly. (*Woody Allen on Woody Allen: In Conversation with Stig Bjorkman*, p. 26)

American Film Institute Catalog: Feature Films, 1941–1950 indicated that such magazines as *Cue* evaluated Hope's movie as having one of the funniest duel scenes Hollywood ever filmed "because it used musical instruments for comic effect" (p. 1597).

Two years earlier Hope appeared in a Technicolor production for Samuel Goldwyn Productions, *The Princess and the Pirate*. This 1944 picture was as handsomely mounted as *Monsieur Beaucaire*. Also, two screenwriters, Don Hartman and Melville Shavelson, contributed to many of Hope's movies and helped to make *The Princess and the Pirate* a superior work. Other Hartman and Shavelson pictures for Hope include: Don Hartman's *Road to Singapore* (1940), *Road to Zanzibar* (1941), *My Favorite Blonde* (1942), and *Road to Morocco* (1942); and Melville Shavelson's *Where There's Life* (1947), *Sorrowful Jones* (1949), and *The Great Lover* (1949).

The Princess and the Pirate is set in the eighteenth century with Hope playing the role of an ineffective traveling actor who tries to be a one-man act. A quick-change impersonator who plays all parts, Hope's character's promotional name is "Sylvester the Great," an oxymoron for his skills as an itinerant performer. Hope is rehearsing his version of an old gypsy hag when Captain Hook takes over the ship in order to hold the incognito Princess Margaret for ransom. To escape being forced to walk the plank by the pirate gang as they get rid of all the males on the ship, the actor puts on the skirt of the

The bearded pirate Victor McLaglen in one of Bob's excellent
comedies, *The Princess and the Pirate* (1944).

From the collection of Donald McCaffrey

gypsy hag to avoid death—but due to his lack of acting skill, is not
convincing. Forced to fight with a saber he is admonished: "Die like
a man." Sylvester counters with one beat, "I'd rather live like a
woman." Featherhead, a crazy pirate played by Walter Brennan,
pleads to have the old hag for a lover. Once alone together, Sylvester
tries to convince Featherhead that he is NOT a woman. His reply,
with gay overtones, is: "I know that." Similar double meanings were
seldom used in 1944. Featherhead, as idiotic as he appears, wants to
manipulate people because he has a map that shows where Captain
Hook's treasure is hidden. And such complications become humorous when Sylvester disguises himself as Captain Hook.

When comedian Hope dons the disguise of the pirate leader, confusion reigns among the crew on board the ship because the real Hook
and the pretender Hook give contrary orders. At this point, the plot

takes a farcical turn. The story line depends on the age-old mistaken identity comedy and the humor of confusion by the crew. At one point, the real Captain Hook, played by Victor McLaglen, thinks he is looking in a mirror; however, it is Sylvester mocking his every move. It is a comic routine that goes back to the Music Hall of England and France. In fact, it is a bit used by French silent screen comedian Max Linder in a turn of the century short and by two of the Marx Brothers in *Duck Soup* (1933). Following the tradition of this sketch the person being imitated sees some variation of his movements and discovers the ruse. This is, of course, another example of Hope's skill at mime and mimicry. Noted for his verbal humor, it shows that the actor could handle physical comedy almost as well as many silent comedians.

As in quite a few of his films, Bob doesn't get the woman. He thinks he will become the princess's lover but alas, she is in love with another commoner. At the ending, Bing Crosby gives a cameo appearance and strolls across the deck of the ship to claim Princess Margaret, played by Virginia Mayo. Hope faces the camera and says indignantly that he will never again act in a Samuel Goldwyn picture. It is the kind of presentation gag from vaudeville and radio that was embraced so often in the Hope and Crosby Road Pictures. According to the *American Film Institute Catalog: Feature Films, 1941–1950* "Studio promotional materials asked reviewers not to reveal the film's ending, and not to review the picture until its release in Nov 1944." (p. 1895). Bosley Crowther obliged when he wrote in the *New York Times*, February 10, 1945:

> This film has a cutely novel finish, in which "a bit player from Paramount" steps in and snags the girl from Mr. Hope's arms. But they asked us not to tell you who it is.

Of the Hope pictures released between 1940 and 1947, four are superior to the others analyzed in this chapter. The highest quality in scripting, acting, and directing in this period are *Monsieur Beaucaire*, *My Favorite Blonde*, *Louisiana Purchase*, and *The Princess and the Pirate*. To some degree, the overall excellence in production values influences the placement of these works.

Monsieur Beaucaire shows the leading comedian in top form as he combines his rapier wisecracks with astute physical ingenuity. The climactic dueling scene illustrates Hope's ability to master the blend of verbal and physical humor. He also excels in his character's inadequate attempts to improve his status and become a formidable lover. *My Favorite Blonde* shows the comedian enmeshed in an escape from the spies, who want to capture those who have valuable information. His comic fear while attempting to be manly. This is the staple of this humorous melodrama, with Madeleine Carroll having the courage that often makes Hope seem a mouse.

Louisiana Purchase may not have given Hope as much of a vehicle as the other works in this period. This is partly a result of the strong comic role played by the Caspar Milquetoast-esque congressman, Victor Moore. Hope sometimes plays straight man to Moore, but his attempts to con the senator produce a wealth of comedy. Also, the overall situation of corrupt state politics plays footsie with satirical humor.

While the design of *The Princess and the Pirate* may seem a bit disjointed, the writers developed a plot and situations to please just about any audience. Hope is given many opportunities to show his ability to imitate characters from a gypsy hag to Captain Hook. He also has a chance to display comic cowardice in a number of scenes.

This period in Hope's development as a comedian would evolve into even more outstanding hits in a number of his post-war features.

4 There Was Hope and Hartmann

From 1948 to 1954 Bob Hope had the good fortune of having Edmund L. Hartmann as one of his screenwriters. Starting as a writer in Hollywood in 1932, Hartmann created scripts for Basil Rathbone, Lucille Ball, Joan Fontaine, Jon Hall, Abbott and Costello, Martin and Lewis, Andy Devine, and many others. One of Hartmann's most financially successful Bob Hope pictures was his first Paramount assignment for the comedian, *The Paleface*, released in 1948. Naturally, he would be slated for six more movies with the star, who came close to the zenith of his career in the '40s.

When Hope died two months after his one hundredth birthday in May 2003, a magazine designed to honor the comedian listed nine selected films of his fifty-one features. Four of Hartmann's movies were chosen: *The Paleface* (1950), *Fancy Pants* (1950), *The Lemon Drop Kid* (1951), and Casanova's *Big Night* (1954).[1] Hartmann's three other films for Hope remain important pictures in the comedian's repertoire of comic characters: *Sorrowful Jones* (1949), *My Favorite Spy* (1951), and *Here Come the Girls* (1953)—a racetrack tout, a vaudeville comedian pretending to be a spy, and an over-the-hill chorus boy. In short, the films sported Bob Hope playing the pretender—a staple of the comedian's best characterizations.

Another publication from reviews of comedy pictures in the trade weekly *Variety* selected ten Hope movies for special recognition, with *The Paleface* as one of the films from the '40s. All seven of the Road Pictures are among the Hope pictures to make the 1992 book, *Variety: Comedy Movies*, mostly containing works from the sound age. Exceptions are Buster Keaton's three silent films, along with *The Great Dictator* (1940), Charles Chaplin's first sound film.

Two other Hope films received recognition, *Call Me Bwana* (1963) and *Boy, Did I Get a Wrong Number* (1966). These movies were not considered among Hope's best. *The Paleface* did receive critical and popular acclaim, however. The *Variety* book gives it a high ranking for story development:

> *The Paleface* is a smart-aleck travesty on the west, told with considerable humor and bright gags. Bob Hope has been turned loose on a good script.... Script poses an amusing story idea—Hope as a correspondence school dentist touring the west in a covered wagon. He's having his troubles, but they're nothing compared with the grief that catches up with him when Calamity Jane seduces him into marriage so she can break up a gang smuggling rifles to the Indians.[2]

Given Ed Hartmann's story finesse, Jane Russell would become Calamity Jane. When I interviewed the screenwriter he told me how the ego of a studio head produced a strange twist:

> "The interesting thing about *Paleface*," Edmund reminisced, "[was that] we [Ed, Jack Rose, and Frank Tashlin] were under contract with Paramount to do a show. They called us in and said they wanted a Western with Hope and Jane Russell. That was the only assignment. We went up to our office and talked about the possibilities and all. And I came up with a story of Calamity Jane. We told it to the head of the studio, Frank Butler. He said, "No, it will never work. No way." He burst into the office about ten minutes later and said, "I got it, boys!" and told us the same story exactly. Exactly, no change at all. I said, "That's great!" So we did it.

Ed was the lead writer of the three, having created many stories dating back to the '30s; he took charge of what was really his idea. Coming from the world of animated cartoons, Frank Tashlin provided the gags. Jack Rose had one of the less effective Road Pictures to his credit, *Road to Rio* (1947), and would go on to associate his writing and production assignments with as many films as Hartmann. As with any multi-scripted picture, it has always been difficult to assign the contributions to duo and trio authorship. After experiencing the integrity of Hartmann's reflections, it would appear he became the central story maker with some gags as effective additions.

A posed still with Jane Russell for the picture
The Paleface (1948).

From the collection of Donald McCaffrey

The Paleface proved to be one of the best box office comedies of the year. The Hope and Russell combination worked better than the sequel, *The Son of Paleface* (1952). This film was more a product of the gag writer Tashlin, who took over as both writer and director. Part of the superiority of the original *Paleface* came from the freshness of the concept. Hope plays the character that fit him best: the novice book-trained dentist, a pretender to bravery who tries to escape from his perilous predicaments. Also, Calamity Jane outclasses him in any dangerous encounter with their enemies.

Hartmann's opening for the Hope and Russell Western pictures Calamity Jane being released from jail and awarded a pardon in exchange for the promise to capture a gang that is selling guns to the Indians. The first comedy sequence develops with Hope as the amateur dentist who advertises his trade as "Painless Peter Potter."

The first comic scene opens with Hope as Peter, who is looking at a guidebook he has received from the mail-order school. He not only reads the manual once for an overall treatment, he consults it repeatedly for each step of a procedure. And he reads the instructions out loud. A mild-mannered patient tries to tell him the problem. Potter smiles and pleasantly says, "Please, no clues. It spoils all the fun."

As he works with this man to find out his problem by an investigation of his mouth, a burly, tough miner interrupts. Growling in pain he demands to have a tooth pulled. "You're second," says Potter pleasantly. The miner pulls the patient out of the chair and takes his place. Meekly, Peter continues by drilling what he calls a "toe hold" for pulling the infected tooth. He produces a laughing gas canister, used by Nineteenth-century dentists:

POTTER: That's why they call me painless.

TOUGH: Is it safe?

POTTER: Safest thing in the world. (Off-handedly) Would you mind paying me now?

Peter takes a sniff of the gas to see if it is working. Evidently a repeated sniff gets to him, and he utters "heh, heh, heh." Soon both are laughing and Painless Potter discovers he pulled the wrong tooth. They laugh as if it were a joke. Even while laughing the tough miner roars, "I'll give you just fifteen minutes to get out of town!" Hope, using his one-beat timing, suggests casually, "Last town they gave me twenty minutes." The miner socks Peter in the jaw, and the dentist falls backward and topples over a desk.

This scene, given in specific detail, remains one of Hope's great moments of both verbal and physical comedy. It almost becomes the shining scene of the comedy. But more would follow, and the comedian did not disappoint the audience viewing *The Paleface*. To this day, *Paleface* remains one of the best, if not the best, of Hope's film comedies.

With more realistic embellishments, the humorous touches have some of the characteristics of the silent screen and early sound comedy shorts treatment of the visit to the dentist. It certainly seems odd that a visit to what some people might call an "office of pain" could be the subject of amusement. Nevertheless, it is. W. C. Fields, in his 1932 two-reel *The Dentist,* explored the laughter "comic pain" delivers. Fields enacted, as most know, a type of "off the wall" burlesque of oddball incidents in many of his films. And, he often wrote his own screenplays. In *The Dentist*, this comedian from the '20s through the '40s plays a character who struggles to be a dentist with a patient who has a beard so full that W. C. has troubles finding the man's mouth. An addition, a woman client becomes a contortionist and wraps her legs around the dentist in an intense, suggestive, sexual joke. As indicated, the first scene with Painless Peter Potter employs a more realistic type of burlesque.

In one of the best Western comedies of his career, Hope gets the chance to employ his skills at humorous mimicry. When the Indians attack, Calamity Jane shoots down the invaders as they try to overtake a log-constructed hotel. Potter jumps into a wooden barrel and tries to shoot the Indians through a hole from his hiding place. He misses repeatedly but thinks he is downing them one after the other. It is, of course, sure-shot Jane. The wagon train pioneers see the pile of dead Indians and think Potter shot them. They declare him a hero.

Overcome with the adoration shown by the settlers, Painless, as Calamity calls him, purchases attire that makes him look like a drugstore cowboy. This becomes an unconscious, inadequate, and humorous attempt to be the hero. Potter struts, swaggers, and addresses people in a pseudo-aggressive, Southwestern twang.

When Calamity Jane becomes victim to the Indians and is tied to a stake, Peter gets into the garb of a medicine man and attempts her rescue. He produces strange whoops and yips in a pathetic impersonation of an important man of the tribe. By pluck and luck, he finally frees her, and they get into Painless Potter's covered wagon to move on to another town.

Throughout the plot of *The Paleface*, two running gags persist: First, Calamity uses many excuses not to go to bed with Potter. Second, Potter takes the reins of the team of two horses and the animals bolt, pulling him behind them in the dirt. This happens to him as a running gag. Then, in the final scene, Calamity takes the reins and gets pulled off the wagon and dragged away. Out of character for the first time, Hope looks at the camera and exclaims, "What do you want, a happy ending?" It seems to be a device borrowed from the Road Pictures.

The picture became one of the highest grossing films of the year. Hope had a perfect vehicle to show comic meekness, cowardly withdrawal under stress, and pretension to manliness in an attempt to con his adversaries. Jane Russell provided a comic counterpoint since her character had no fear and usually was in control of any situation. This scene plus many to follow are sprinkled with a wealth of the comedian's well-delivered one-liners. This was his trademark for *The Paleface* and six other films scripted by Hartmann.

Furthermore, Hope proves that he has deft abilities to employ physical humor as well as wisecracks. He has two important sequences where he pretends to be another person. When crack-shot Calamity dispatches Indians on the attack, Painless mistakenly becomes hero of the moment. So he tries to be a manly cowboy, which produces a comic effect since his strutting postures and affected deep voice with a Western twang become a lampoon of the champion. Painless is also a caricature when he dons Native garb and imitates a medicine man. He dances around Calamity, who has been tied to the stake by Indians. This ineffective disguise, of course, becomes part of a feeble attempt to rescue her. By pluck and good luck, however, such an effort eventually brings success. Underneath his attempt at bravado there always lurks his true, chicken-livered demeanor.

Broad comedy using fights and the chase promote a fast pace in the film. Even the song, "Buttons and Bows," is inserted and delivered by Hope in a way that almost seems to be tossed off. With tongue in cheek, critic Bosley Crowther wrote, "The great things in human progress—and in art—usually happen this way. 'The Paleface' deserves primarily a marker as the birthplace of 'Buttons and Bows.'"[3] Crowther becomes more clever than correct. Time has been kind to *The Paleface*, and most evaluators now rank this Western comedy starring Bob Hope as one of the actor's best.

While *Son of Paleface*, the sequel to Hope's box office success, came only two years later in 1950, the remake of the original by Universal released twenty years later. It is perhaps more accurate to say that a supposed new version came to theater screens in 1968. Instead of characters called Painless Peter Potter and Calamity Jane, the new authors scripted Dr. Jesse W. Heywood and Penelope "Bad Penny" Cushings. The two screenwriters, James Fritzell and Everett Greenbaum, plus the director, Alan Ratkin, seemed intent on improving the original by eliminating and changing many of the aspects that were effective in the original comic drama. The director and screenwriters, of course, did not want to create a mere copy of the 1968 version. Some plot situations from the original remained, however, in the work called *The Shakiest Gun in the West*.

Don Knott, the dentist protagonist of this Western, moves from the East, as he puts it, "to fight oral ignorance." When he gets drunk, he states he is "going to spread dental health like a plague." As in the original *Paleface*, a lady robber receives a pardon from the governor provided she cooperates in bringing gunrunners to jail who are trading with the Indians. To carry out the task, she must marry so that her husband will serve as a cover for her secret investigation. This is a direct take of the pledge Calamity Jane must make in *The Paleface*. In the remake, Jesse wants to go to bed with Penelope, just as Peter longs to consummate his marriage with Calamity Jane in the original; so, the sexual frustration of the male becomes a risible subject for both movies. Also in both movies, the wife is captured by Indians, while the bungling husband tries to rescue her. The rescue in the original concept is attempted by Peter Potter (Hope) dressing up as a medicine man to free Jane from her bonds. Jesse Heywood (Knott) dons the garb of an Indian maiden to provide access into a wigwam to help in Penelope's escape. This revision gives the added comedy of a man in drag, complicated by one of the braves falling in love with the disguised Jesse. While it is not explained, Don is suddenly wearing a wig replete with two well-braided, black pigtails. The climactic gag comes when the lustful brave carries off Jesse for his own prize. Penny, as she is sometimes called, lands a solid right to the jaw of the Indian trying to abduct her man and pulls Jesse back with her as her lover.

Besides some plot variations, the strongest contrast between the films involves the portraits of Knott and Hope. Don Knott gives a performance of a man excitably frustrated, afraid, and embarrassed in any confrontation. Bob Hope executes the role of a person trying to wiggle out of any situation that he cannot handle by bluster and deception. He develops the comic character of Painless Peter Potter as an inadequate pretender. Hope, in *The Paleface*, plugs along as best he can, not using Knott's humor of embarrassment. In conclusion, the original version has special merits of plot, laughable lines, and a character that surpasses the remake.

Hartmann's next work for the comedian has a long history of various versions with different actors. Adapted from the short story *Little Miss Marker* by Damon Runyon, the 1934 version uses the original title, with Adolph Menjou and Shirley Temple in the lead roles. The 1949 remake employs the title *Sorrowful Jones*, the name of the slippery con man as a Broadway bookie enacted by Hope. In 1962, a third version has the questionable casting of Tony Curtis not as the racetrack bookmaker but as a manager of a nightspot. Additionally, the picture has the odd title of *40 Pounds of Trouble*. This title refers to the lost little girl named Penny Piper. Not only are the names and characters changed but there are drastic plot alterations in this version. The next version of the basic Damon Runyon story comes closer to the original and thereby offers a closer comparison with Hope's portrait of Sorrowful Jones. In 1980 more effective casting gave Walter Matthau the lead, and the film returned to the original 1934 title and the short story. The little girl in the story is left behind by her father at a booking agency to serve as a "marker" (IOU), the father thusly borrowing money to bet on a horse race (hence the story title *Little Miss Marker*). With these repeated productions, a highly popular movie story evolved through many modifications to fit the actors' talents.

A picture that could more properly be called a drama with comic moments, *Sorrowful Jones* shows a sharp departure from the 1947 *Road to Rio* and the 1948 *The Paleface*. The comedian proves he can depart from the style and pace of his standard wisecracking character. A basic plot of a racetrack tout being forced to care for a little girl whose father is killed by the mob provides this change of humor tied to Hope's character.

Some remnant of the clever remark emerges when Sorrowful meets his girlfriend, Gladys, a role well developed by Lucille Ball. She is not the airhead and perky domestic troublemaker she plays in *I Love Lucy*. She starts the banter between Sorrowful and herself in this way:

GLADYS: (Seeing Sorrowful observing a woman mannequin in a store window.) You better take the dummy, Sorrowful. She doesn't have to eat. It doesn't cost a penny to say "Hello."

SORROWFUL: Hello, Gladys.

GLADYS: You know, it's been almost four years since I saw you, Sorrowful, but I recognize the suit.

SORROWFUL: It's been lucky for me—up to now. Some people seem to forget what some people spend on some people.

GLADYS: Spend? Where did you ever learn that word? I always figured you invented the Dutch treat.

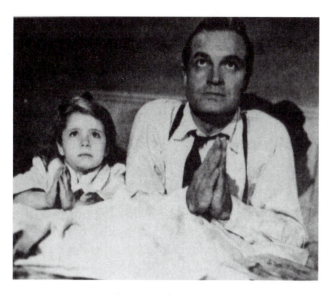

Mary Jane Saunders says her prayers for the horse
and the bookie in *Sorrowful Jones* (1949),
a remake of the 1934 Shirley Temple
picture *Little Miss Marker.*

From the collection of Donald McCaffrey

Oozing sarcasm, Ball sets her would-be boyfriend back almost every time they meet. When he comes to the nightclub to see the owner and boss, Big Steve, he catches Gladys rehearsing a song for her routine at the club. He tries to get back at her with, "You're off key—as usual." When she sings another song, he attempts a second dig: "You have been taking lessons, but not enough."

Gladys takes the lead in their banter with her sharp cut-downs. Her verbal fencing with Sorrowful provides much of the best humor. Part of this is tied to his weak defensive reactions. Although there is a type of innocence in the tightfisted nature of this bookie, he carries this trait to the extreme. He would even take money from a little girl who has been given a racehorse called Dreamy Joe. The stallion has been used for a cover by the mob, and the little girl gets the ownership of the horse. It is put in her name to protect the gangsters from being identified by the law.

Hartmann told me of his contribution to one of the scenes of this movie. The foster child pushes Sorrowful to help with her evening prayer, "Now I lay me down...." She asks for the care of everyone she knows, including her horse Dreamy Joe. Then she asks God to give Sorrowful a new suit. The bookie adds, "With two pairs of pants, please." Ed indicated that he gave Hope this line. It was, of course, fashioned for one of the types of lines Hope does best—an added, humorous request. This also helped to avoid what might have become a sentimental scene—something Runyon himself avoided given his brand of comic, shady characters.

"All's well that ends well" is the end of *Sorrowful Jones*. Big Steve, the head of the gang who orders the killing of little Martha Jane's father, is arrested. Sorrowful and Gladys are married and adopt Mary Jane. Gladys asks her husband what his real first name is. He tells her it is Humphrey. She tells him to stick with Sorrowful.

During his many stints as master of ceremonies for the annual Academy Award presentations, Hope honed many gags about his failure to win an Oscar for any of his movies. One of his best one-liners came at the introduction of this television program: "Welcome to the Academy Awards or as it's known at my house, Passover."[4] When a member of the audience in a taped television interview asked him why he never received an award, Hope indicated that only certain types of films win. Hope thought either *Beau James*, *Sorrowful Jones,* or *The Facts of Life* might have won an Oscar if someone had submitted them. These, of course, are movies with serious as well as comic elements.[5]

Most critics would rate *Sorrowful Jones* as one of the comedian's top-notch pictures. Even in a contemporary review, Bosley Crowther, who usually saw Hope's films as slight fare, stated:

> Mr. Hope has occasion to go through the streets collecting bets (and passing out wise-cracks for gratis), to give the little orphan girl a bath, help her to say her prayers, fight gangsters, and eventually to woo a night-club girl. All of them he does in his most airy and hilarious comedy style. It may not be Runyon humor, but it is laughable just the same.[6]

An important comparison can be made with *Sorrowful Jones'* third rendering titled *Little Miss Marker*. This 1980s version returns to the original Runyon story with some variation. First of all, the casting changes the focus by using Walter Matthau as Sorrowful Jones and Julie Andrews as Amanda, his romantic interest. Matthau, skilled at playing disgruntled comic characters, brought a change from the portrait created by Hope in 1949. The orphaned moppet, who is often referred to as "The Kid," does not as easily charm

Matthau's curmudgeon. Andrews plays it very straight as a sympathetic Miss Fixit. She takes care of this racetrack tout and the orphan. In effect, Andrew's portrayal gives a strong sentimental twist to the remake. Matthau's crusty Sorrowful Jones counteracts the tendency to move close to bathos, something the screenwriters avoided in the Hope version by Edmund Hartmann and Jack Rose. Walter Bernstein is both writer and director for the Walter Matthau and Julie Andrews remake. Bernstein had received recognition for the screenwriting of *Fail Safe* (1964) and *The Molly Maguires* (1977). The scripting of a comedy with a touch of the serious appeared in the 1976 *The Front*, starring Woody Allen. Its theme pertained to the blacklisting period in Hollywood. *Little Miss Marker* became Bernstein's first full-fledged humorous screenplay.

Walter Matthau and The Kid (played by Viola Kates Stimpson) have their best comic moments when they engage in the type of portions that mirror the previous film with Hope and Mary Jane Saunders, who plays the cute kid in *Sorrowful Jones*. These scenarios involve the awkward attempts of the surrogate fathers to feed, clothe, and get the little girl to bed. In the 1980 *Little Miss Marker*, Walter feeds The Kid a donut and corn flakes without milk. Irritated by the crunching sound, he finally pours milk in her bowl. Sorrowful puts the child in a Murphy bed that springs back into the wall, enclosing the child so that she is out of sight. A little head pokes out and says, "Do it again."

Bernstein's script must have had some shadow from the past—possibly Charles Chaplin's *The Kid*. As director he even gets humor from the little girl's determined attempt to keep up with Sorrowful as they walk down the streets of New York. Even with the grumpy disposition, affection for the child creeps slowly into his crusty heart. Not so with Amanda's advances. She asks, "Have you ever been married?" Sorrowful replies gruffly: "What a stupid question." When it comes to an appearance before the judge who might send The Kid to an orphanage, Amanda is forced to propose marriage to the flinty bachelor. It appears that he only marries her to keep the child, but in the fade-out we see the unlikely couple embracing and kissing. And the final shot shows them holding hands before the judge. At the hearing, The Kid looks up at them wondering why they are arguing about the disposition of Sir Galahad, the horse. This is director and scriptwriter Bernstein's attempt to avoid sentimentality. But this vehicle for Matthau has some scenes that come very close to mawkishness. The fault lies with the female leads. Julie seems to sometimes be in another movie playing Mary Poppins, lost in another movie, playing her lead in *Mary Poppins*, the successful 1964 film with the protagonist as an excellent Miss Fixit.[7] Only in the final scene does she assert herself by proposing marriage and matching Sorrowful in argument. While The Kid has many humorous moments, in some scenes she becomes almost too precious. Hope's vehicle has a more restrained moppet, and Lucille Ball has the brass to put Sorrowful in his place throughout the 1949 version.

The strongest contrast exists between the two portraits of Sorrowful. Matthau forcefully and stubbornly tries to control every situation, even bribing all the jockeys in a race so that a horse called Sir Galahad can win. Hope, however, struggles to hold his own. As a bookie he loses even when he thinks he has sure-fire information. Only occasionally does he match the banter with the assertive nightclub singer played by Miss Ball. This character contrast produces two versions of the Runyon story that have different overall tone and humor.

Another loosely based Runyon adaptation starring Hope appeared on the screen in 1951. While *The Lemon Drop Kid* proved to be a solid picture, it is most known for its Christmas opus entitled "Silver Bells," with music and lyrics by songsmiths Jay Livingston and Ray Evans. Naturally some seasonal tunes live on forever and bring in royalties for the creators and performers; however, although Hope and Marilyn Maxwell sing "Silver Bells" in the movie, they didn't get to cut the record at the time. Ironically, the "White Christmas" crooner, Bing Crosby, received that privilege, and the money. Not so with Hope. Hartmann told an interesting anecdote about the title of the song "Silver Bells." The composers came up with the title "Tinkle Bells," but Jay's wife pointedly asked: "You know what tinkle is?"

Anyone wishing to see *The Lemon Drop Kid* may find it on television during the Christmas season; some programmers realize that it has a holiday theme. This theme revolves around a plot to raise money for what the New York racetrack tout Kid calls "An Old Dolls' Home"—a boardinghouse for down-on-their luck elderly women. The Lemon Drop Kid, whose name is Sidney Melbourne, devises a scam to collect money for himself during the Christmas season. He gives a battery of unsavory companions Santa Claus bells and attire to collect money so he can pay a mob leader (Steve). The Kid needs a ten thousand dollar restitution for a bad racing tip to the boss's girlfriend. Steve demands that Sidney raise and return the money. Eventually, the girlfriend convinces the Kid to give the money, which was falsely collected, to the "old dolls." And, when he reforms his ways, she switches her affections from Steve to the Kid.

It becomes necessary for the Kid to get back the money that his boss, Steve, had loaned him to pay off his personal debt. Comedian Hope has a chance to employ a disguise as he does in a number of his pictures. In this film he plays something akin to a "Charlie's Aunt"— a man in drag for comic effect. Hope makes the most of the struggle to retrieve the money, and a comic chase ensues that harkens back to the silent age of motion pictures. The movie ends with a reformation of the Kid. He has a party with the elderly ladies and "Brainy," who is now his girlfriend.

The portrait of the Lemon Drop Kid employs the humor of the con man. This facet is muted, however, in *Sorrowful Jones*. It ultimately proves to be a serious film with a three-dimensional character. The two movies show the two poles of Hope's humor. Often in *Sorrowful Jones* Hope is the butt of the gag. In *Lemon Drop Kid* he reigns as the wisecracking con man.

Another Western comedy by Hartmann, *Fancy Pants* (1950), has some similarities to the 1948 *The Paleface* but probably could have used the previous film's director, Norman Z. McLeod. Director George Marshall was Ed's least favorite associate in the creative process. He told me about a monologue he had written for the actor:

> Hope is in a picture called *Fancy Pants*—which I wrote. Bob Welch produced it. There was a scene of a cricket match. George Marshall, an old mean son-of-a-bitch, was director. Producer Welch did *The Paleface* and this was only his second picture. After we did that, we were doing *Fancy Pants*. There were maybe fifty tables around the cricket field. I had an idea for a monologue for Hope. The day before I told it to Welch and he loved it, but he said we had to shoot it the next day. We stayed up late working on the monologue. The director comes on the field the next day and Welch comes up to him and told him it was the monologue to be shot this day. So, Marshall, being a real prick, takes it and doesn't look at it. He says, "I've written some things on the back of the envelope and that's what we're going to do today." He takes my script and throws it on one of the tables and walks away. Some of the cricket scene was shot. There was a break to set the lights and cameras for more shooting. Hope sat down at the table and saw the script. Picks it up and reads it. "Hey, this is great. This is very funny." He calls Marshall and says "Let's do this. It's great!" Marshall says, "What's this?" pretending to have never seen it. Marshall read it and said, "That's very funny. Yeah." They did it. By sheer accident of Hope sitting down at one of fifty tables.

I couldn't resist interrupting with the key word we mentally shared: "Fate."

Fancy Pants became a perfect work for comedian Bob Hope to exercise his skill at humorous deception. As a bumbling actor playing the role of a butler named Humphrey in a British theatrical piece, he is able to convince a naïve family that he is from England and has had dangerous adventures. Mrs. Effie Floud, the aggressive head of her *nouveaux riche* family, hires the actor Humphrey. Effie wants him to teach her daughter Agatha and her husband Mike some high-class manners. To some degree this part of the plot follows director Leo McCarey's 1935 *The Ruggles of Red Gap*, of which the 1950 *Fancy Pants* was a remake. The '30s movie features Charles Laughton as the butler, who is believed to be English nobility. The '50s version depicts an American actor who is mistaken for a manservant from England. As such, Bob Hope plays a more complicated deception in this film and humorously uses his imaginary interpretation of British manners as superior social behavior. There is also an overall tonal change from the 1935 film. Whereas the McCarey movie seems whimsical, director Marshall handles much broader humor. Much of this may have been fashioned to display Hope's skills, as well as the comedic talents of his co-star, Lucille Ball.

A nearly ditched, innovative monologue occurs when Humphrey appears at a tea party and entertains the guests with his manufactured feats of daring. The impossible details of the confrontation show Hope dealing in the comedy of the tall tale.

Aggie, as her mother and father call her, tries to give Humphrey a flower for his lapel buttonhole.

"I can't wear them, you know. Disturbs my medals," he explains. Then he is asked about his exploits to earn the decorations.

"Which medal shall I explain first? I think it was my first year of service out East.... Things were becoming very nasty,... trying to wipe us out, you know. But they were only waiting for the end of the monsoons."

"Monsoons. That's French for mister," Aggie naïvely interrupts.

Humphrey agrees, "Exactly. Those infernal drums cease. Imagine it, three against a thousand."

Humphrey goes on in his overly serious tone to cite the dangers of the river and jungle—vicious crocodiles and hissing pythons. Aggie interjects again, "And you hissed right back at them." He gives out a hiss to agree once more, which indicates he is improvising the tall tale and is prone to any suggestion. He keeps repeating the odds "three against a thousand."

At one point he declares, "I had a spear right through my body," and he utters a weak cough as if in pain. "Didn't it hurt?" Aggie interjects. "Only when I laughed," he says jauntily. With elaborate detail and with a cutting motion of his arms he tells how he used a cutlass to hack away at the enemy. Suddenly, he drops his narration off. He must take a nap, he declares, "before I go to sleep."

Asked what happened, he off-handedly concludes, "We finally put them to rout. But we all agreed they were the three toughest rascals we had ever fought. Goodnight, goodnight."

Hope executes this extended Hartmann monologue with vigorous animation, displaying his deft combination of verbal and physical comedy. It remains one of the comedian's best examples of his command of his art. In her third Hartmann script, Lucille Ball, as Agatha, becomes one of the best comediennes to co-star with Hope. In *Fancy Pants*, she develops a brassy, naïve young woman who contrasts with Gladys, the sharp, witty attacker in *Sorrowful Jones*.

The precursor to *Fancy Pants* vividly depicts how screenwriters sometimes change the content of the basic story to suit the leading character. There is a sharp contrast in the comedic styles of Charles Laughton and Bob Hope. Laughton produces a character suited to the devoted manservant who finds repulsive any movement to amend or blur the class structure. The 1935 version is memorable for the handling of the division between two ways of life—the formal existence of a British butler and the rugged, freewheeling life of a U.S. cattleman. Ruggles must go along with the master even though, as a servant, he cringes when Egbert, the American, wants to drink with him. Not accustomed to drink, Ruggles becomes inebriated. Charles Laughton adroitly enacts a hilarious scene as he tries to maintain his dignity while reeling drunk, periodically expressing joy by shouting, "Whoopee!" Eventually, the worm turns. Sentiment evolves as he courts and marries an American woman. The master, Egbert, must also change due to the influence of Ruggles, who has discovered from a speech by Abraham Lincoln that all men are equal. The head of the household has been the wife, who has been trying to develop fine manners with the help of their manservant. Egbert utters a clever line as he takes control: "Men are created equal to women. That is why you have no right to order me around." And the trait of the sentimental drama develops with this so-called "return to normal" social code. Ruggles has become Americanized and also becomes an independent person. *Fancy Pants* exhibited a much different style and form.

With the talents of Hope and Ball, the screenwriters and director did not favor sentimental content. Screenwriter Edmund Hartmann, with director George Marshall, painted with a much broader comic brush. Marshall had his co-stars engage in the physical comedy of trying to ride a horse, and the tenderfoot Hope has his difficulties. Hartmann contributes the pretender's tall tale, which shows a much different tone than that of director Leo McCarey's highly successful sentimental version of the basic story. This elaborate monologue (already described above) shows the contrast between the comedic styles of Charles Laughton and Bob Hope. Also a superior serious actor, Laughton blends some the comic with the serious. Hope would, in the fifties, show this ability with *The Seven Little Foys* and *Beau James*, in which he portrays two real-life characters, Eddie Foy and Jimmy Walker.

Another character by Hope shows him engaged in droll depiction. This becomes evident in the opening sequence of *My Favorite Spy* (1951). Burlesque comic Peanuts White, played by Bob is retained by the police because he resembles the infamous spy Eric Augustine. U.S. government officials, seeking persons engaged in espionage, convince Peanuts to impersonate the spy by giving him an elaborate briefing on the spy's sophisticated manners. Since Peanuts imagines he is a superior actor, even though he isn't, he is flattered by the challenge. Peanuts gets a complete makeover—changing from a cheesy clown into a suave, gentleman operative. However, some of the negative aspects of his inferior persona crop up to generate problems. And, naturally, comic plot twists evolve. As Augustine, Peanuts travels to Tangier where he becomes involved in international intrigue. When he realizes that he has become the target for assassination, he immediately wants to fly back to the United States. Instead of portraying the daring spy, he becomes the cowardly person Peanuts always has been.

To provide even more complication and intrigue, the impersonator must convince the spy's girlfriend, Lily Dalbray (played by Hedy Lamarr), that he is the true Eric Augustine. Although Peanuts has received elaborate coaching on Eric's woman-conquering kissing talents, Lily outdoes his embrace. He had developed such romantic skills that an embrace could produce such powerful emotion that the woman's stocking would run. Instead, when Lily kisses him, the impostor's expensive silk socks rip up in several branches, but hers do not.

Hope and Hedy Lamarr, a girlfriend of the spy
Augustine, provide romance and comedy
in *My Favorite Spy* (1951).

From the collection of Edmund L. Hartmann

At a critical juncture in the tight plot, Eric returns to threaten Lily
and Peanuts. Killed by a spy versus spy encounter, Eric's death becomes an important moment in the film. One of the best and wacki-
est lines comes from Peanuts when he discovers Eric's body: "Ach
du lieber, Augustine." (A play on words of an old German song.)

Hope employs one of those monologues he often used that show
comic overstatement. He exhibits a kooky stream-of-consciousness
when his enemies give him the so-called truth serum. The drug

affects Peanuts strangely as he portrays many parts: Cyrano de Bergerac, Hyde—the ghoulish creature from *Doctor Jekyll and Mr. Hyde*—and Hamlet from the Shakespearian play. While this turn isn't as humorous as Hope's monologue in *Fancy Pants,* it fits well with the intrigue of the spy versus spy of *My Favorite Spy.*

In an April 19, 2001, interview, Hartmann referred to Jay Livingston and Ray Evans, two of the most prolific and talented tunesmiths who not only created hit songs for movies but were also able to score the entire picture. These music men would make a significant contribution to the next to last of the seven films Ed penned for Bob Hope, *Here Come the Girls*, a movie released in 1953.

After I viewed this sixth movie in Ed's long-term link with the comedian, I asked him if this work wasn't more of a musical than any other that he wrote for the actor. "I was told this was the best Hope picture I did," he explained. As lead screenwriter he created the original story and co-wrote the motion picture with Hal Kanter. "You mean *Here Come the Girls* wasn't designed as a musical?" With an uncharacteristic use of an expletive, he said, "They [screwed] up." The very proper gentleman from St. Louis obviously disliked the final results. Ed thought the use of a male actor who was a noted crooner brought more songs into the picture than was needed. His excellent memory failed him because he had to be told the lead's name—Tony Martin. Obviously this name was one he wished to forget. And his view proved to be correct since some of Martin's songs were cut from the final release.

Hartmann's basic story for the lead comedian can be revealed by Hope's character, Stanley Snodgrass, who bemoans his fate when he is fired from a stage show: "I'm the oldest living chorus boy. Failing is the only thing I've been a success at." The premise seems very fruitful for a comedic character extension of Hope's best work. Snodgrass's self-analysis shows a new sympathetic dimension not often realized in the comedian's portraits. To complicate the situation, a madman threatens the leading man (Tony Martin's role) because the killer wishes the leading lady (Arlene Dahl's role) to turn her affections toward him. Snodgrass becomes a substitute target as bait to catch the potential murderer. The fall guy thereby gets unbridled flattery from the producer and lead actors to keep him in the show—even though his performance results in many mistakes and even clumsy falls. Unaware of his inept portrayal of a leading man, Sidney becomes inflated with the compliments he receives. In the climactic scene, he realizes that he is the target of the killer, who throws knives at him as he is on stage struggling to escape death. The situation of the comedian as a coward who hides behind people and stage sets gives Hope a chance to show how he can execute risible physical actions.

Since there are eleven musical portions in *Here Come the Girls*, songwriters Jay Livingston and Ray Evans provide significant contributions to this comic genre—to the point where the film can be classified as a musical. One of the best numbers is a duet by Bob Hope and Rosemary Clooney, "You Got Class." The comedian reaches back to his earlier profession as a dancer and handles this song and several others with considerable skill. Newcomer Clooney displays a most promising singing talent in her rendition of "You Got Class" as she urges "the oldest chorus boy" to realize he can succeed. She also develops the lyric song, "When You Love Someone."

But Ms. Clooney does not contribute much as a co-star for Hope. She will go on, however, to achieve a stage presence in her work on the big screen and on her television show in the late '50s. Also, the acting and singing of Tony Martin and Arlene Dahl remain only passable in this film drama. In short, Hope shines, but he has very little support. Hartmann's evaluation of his last work for Hope is accurate. *Here Comes the Girls* should have been a comedy with a few musical elements. In the early script version by Ed and Hal Kanter, producer Don Hartman praised them for the creation of "the best Bob Hope comedy ever written." Ironically, the results became only a good Hope movie.

One year later, in 1954, Paramount released a Hope vehicle that did not stress song and dance routines, a type of spice often used in the comedian's movies. *Casanova's Big Night* became one of the most lushly colorful pictures of Hope's career. This period piece depicts the golden age of ornate living in Venice during the Eighteenth century. When Aldous Huxley visited Hollywood, he viewed the lavish sets of *Casanova's Big Night*. The famous novelist and critic remarked, "I wish I could do something like this." Hartmann was amazed that a British novelist of his distinction would marvel at a popular art form that so contrasted with Huxley's literary world.

Using one of the most tightly structured dramas Hartmann and Hal Kanter fashioned, Hope had the good fortune to play opposite Joan Fontaine. Paramount employed the actress in her best comic role. Ed had scripted one of her first leading roles with the 1937 work, *The Man Who Found Himself.* Ms. Fontaine became a star with her demure heroine roles in such '40s films as *Rebecca* (1940) and *Jane Eyre* (1944)—both serious parts. Film critic Bosley Crowther, in an April 19, 1954, *New York Times* review, gives her credit for playing a comic character but does so with sarcasm as he describes her co-starring role with Bob Hope: "Joan Fontaine as a grocery merchant whom the tailor's apprentice [Hope's role] really wants, clatters and bangs along with him, smirking and giggling all the way." Crowther errs in his recollection of "giggling" because Fontaine never had such a role—even in comedy she maintained a certain dignity and authority that she imparted to the serious characters in her films.

In this same 1954 review, Crowther gives Hal Kanter and Ed Hartmann "their modest due" because "fast gags and likely complications such as the locale of Venice might provide are worked to their fullest advantage. (Item: the scent one breathes while riding a gondola—'Canal No. 5.')"

The column space this long-time *New York Times* film evaluator allots to *Casanova's Big Night* belies his acerbic tone. He neglects to report some of Hope's physical comedy in two elaborate routines. As an imposter, Pippo, Casanova's tailor, is forced to duel with a professional swordsman. First of all, he stashes his sword under the banquet table only to have it retrieved by a blackamoor court boy with whom Pippo wants to get even. Much of the comedy develops from the tailor's quirky way of dueling, which perplexes the fencing champion. Francesca, by Fontaine, tries to help Pippo with an attempt to conk the professional from behind a curtain. The tailor gets twisted around as he tries to bob and weave away from the thrusts of the challenger. However, the strike by Francesca pushes Pippo forward, and a lucky thrust of his sword brings an end to the champion and the match.

Another delightfully humorous sequence develops when Pippo needs to appear in disguise before the dignitary and ruler, The Doge of Venice. Hope gets to do another version of a dowager, sort of a "Charlie's Aunt." He even gets the Doge to dance with him and, of course, twists and stomps on the monarch in his awkwardness. And in the cavorting, the padded bosom of the dowager keeps slipping down.

While this 1954 movie usually avoids in-gags with topical allusions, it has two sketches that imitate a device used in the Road Pictures starring Hope and Crosby. In a prison scene, Pippo spews forth a monologue as he agonizes about his fate. An interruption

Screenwriter Hartmann's daughter Susan meets a
comical, bogus Casanova on the set of
Casanova's Big Night (1954).

From the collection of Edmund L. Hartmann

from a prisoner brings a plea by Hope for continuing his best chance
to act—a bit used in many Road Pictures. As a conclusion to the
picture, Pippo is about to be executed with a downward swing of
the ax. The ax stops with a freeze-frame special effect. Hope breaks
character and speaks to the movie audience announcing that
Paramount wants him to die. The comedian then shows his version
of the film. He knocks down the executioner with his own ax
and kills a bevy of soldiers standing by—obviously escaping the fate

the studio desired. He polls the audience to see if they want this heroic ending, and, to his disappointment, he receives a negative response—they wish him dead.

Not only does this comedy employ the deflating of an ego, but it uses the presentational stage technique of having the actor relate directly to the audience. The humor created by this gimmick may have lapped over from the risible departures used in the Hope and Crosby radio variety shows. Then, it seems, writers incorporated this presentational comic device in the 1940 *Road to Singapore* and continued it with the 1953 *Road to Bali.*

Comedian Hope's performances in his many films profited richly from a co-starring actress with a comedienne's flair. Joan Fontaine, fortunately, assisted him well in *Casanova's Big Night,* as did Lucille Ball in *Sorrowful Jones* and *Fancy Pants.* Hope did not have such support with his seventh and final film written by Hartmann. In the 1953 *Here Come the Girls*, Arlene Dahl and Rosemary Clooney were singers who portrayed women without humorous characteristics.

5 Some Hits and Misses

When asked why he didn't write the sequel, *Son of Paleface*,[1] Edmund Hartmann simply replied, "They didn't ask me." This 1952 resurrection used similar characters but without a tight, smooth-flowing plot line. *Son of Paleface*, starring Bob Hope, Jane Russell, and Roy Rogers, did not achieve the financial success of its precursor, however, some rank it above the original.[2] The excellent performance of Hope as a hapless Harvard son of the inept dentist, "Painless" Potter, makes it a hit. That is, a hit of sorts. Gag writer Frank Tashlin tried to take over as a scriptwriter and director, but he didn't have the story writing skills of Hartmann, who held the 1948 story line to a tight design. Also, Tashlin, of Warner Brothers Porky Pig cartoons—as a fledgling director of live-action features—couldn't obtain the best acting from Jane Russell and Roy Rogers. While it would be unkind to say Roy's horse Trigger appeared to have more theatrical presence than these two actors, Russell and Rogers should have had line coaches to train them on their delivery. Seasoned director Norman Z. McLeod, who directed such Hope films as *Road to Rio* (1947), *My Favorite Spy* (1951), and *Casanova's Big Night* (1954), revealed his skills in working with actors in *The Paleface* as well as pictures with comedians W. C. Fields and Danny Kaye. This director also had such seasoned screenwriters as Ed Hartmann, Hal Kanter, and Jack Rose, to mention a few of the writers McLeod used for his films.

These three and many others were both story and gag writers. As Hope's career progressed into the '60s he seemed to get harnessed with less-skilled writers and directors, a downward trend that started in the '50s. Of the post-war films, the 1947 *Where There's Life* employed one of Hope's strongest writers, Melville Shavelson, who helped Bob write his 1990 biography, *Don't Shoot, It's Only Me*. *Where There's Life* develops into one of Hope's intrigue films, somewhat like the precursors, the 1942 *My Favorite Blonde*, and five years later in 1947, *My Favorite Brunette*. The machination design of *Blonde* develops as a spoof of Alfred Hitchcock's *The 39 Steps* with German spies. *My Favorite Brunette* becomes a lampoon of the detective genre. *Where There's Life* bases its intrigue on insurrectionists who try to assassinate the heir to the throne of a small European country called Barovia. Comedian Hope, of course, is Michael Valentine—the man who might be king if he lives through the ordeal by escaping the villains. The complicated plot depicts the revolutionaries of Barovia throwing a knife at Valentine, aiming a gun from an adjacent building, sabotaging an airplane to destroy him, drawing lots among the seditionists to choke him with a noose, plus an elaborate chase to capture him, dead or alive. An initial plot line has an angry New York policeman trying to make sure Valentine marries his sister. This persistent character, Victor O'Brien, shows William Bendix as a colorful addition that gives humorous variety to *Where There's Life*.

Audiences of the '40s flocked to see one of their favorite radio comedians in a movie. Bendix, a soft, comic version of Archie Bunker, is a blue-collar ship construction riveter, a radio character originated in the mid-'40s. The popular sitcom, *The Life of Riley*, formed the basic character to complement Hope's Valentine. The lumbering, easily confused character meets the lubricious, excitable one. Some of Bendix's best moments occur when he has trouble comprehending a complicated turn of events. Victor O'Brien, in *Where There's Life* says with disgruntlement, "What a revoltin' development." It is a stock comic utterance he used in many episodes of the radio and television series, *The Life of Riley*.[3]

Bob Hope has a much different sort of humorous character—a desperate, manic person fearing destruction by enemies and invasive protectors who dog his every step. When one of the protectors from the little European country that wants him to take the throne as king gets a fatal knife in the back, he tries to explain to the police. He cites all the threats on his life that appear too fantastic to be believed. The chief at the police station says, "Send him to Bellevue."— meaning, of course, the sanitarium in New York City for extreme "mental" cases.

In this posed shot for *Son of Paleface*, it would appear
Bob won and wed Jane Russell while Roy Rogers
stayed with his faithful Trigger.

From J. C. Archives, Inc., photos

Hope adds another dimension to his skills as an actor. In *Where
There's Life* he provides nuances of fear in an odd, whimsical manner.

The ending of this movie doesn't quite gel. The struggle to get
Valentine married to Victor's sister seems to be cut from the resolution. The leading character, Michael Valentine, favors a woman from
Barovia who has officially pursued him to become king. Hope kisses
Swedish actress Signe Hasso for the curtain and urges the audience,
with a turn to the camera: "Go home. You've seen it all." Hope gives
a nuance to the line, which has a double meaning—that is, some
sexual connotation.

What some fans or critics might call a less-effective level of an
intrigue comedy was released in 1949 as *The Great Lover*. The title,
naturally, does not befit comedian Bob Hope's character. He depicts
a scoutmaster returning with his crew of teenage "Boy Foresters"
who become his nemesis. Inept Freddie Hunter has little ability to

control them—the boys dominate and look after him by insisting that he avoid any activity they think is a sin. Freddie also falls into the clutches of C. J. Dabney, a card shark who bilks him with intentions to kill him. Dabney is played by an accomplished British comedian, Roland Young, noted for his handling of the character, Topper, in three sophisticated comedies of the '30s and '40s. Hope thereby meets another type of comic villain—an apparently meek little fellow who is actually a con man and a killer. Roland Young illustrates how he can create a character that deals with a complicated, supposedly superior comic villain. Hope's naïve luck helps him survive. And Young shows a persona that ranges 180 degrees from the simple, amiable portrait that William Bendix develops in *Where There's Life.*

The plot mover happens to be Young. In the initial scene, the audience sees Dabney strangle a man who received a big win in a crooked game of poker through the manipulation of the supposedly meek con man. Naïve Freddie becomes his next associate and helps fleece a rich person via the card game. Duchess Alexandria (Rhonda Fleming) and her father, the Grand Duke Maximillian (Roland Culver), become the targets for Dabney's shifty, double-dealing poker scheme. The winning hands go to Freddie, who becomes utterly amazed that he is suddenly having such success. Dabney then sends the innocent dupe to get change for a one hundred dollar bill. By chance, Freddie asks Jack Benny (as himself) if he has change. Jack produces a jeweler's magnifying eyepiece to see if the bill is authentic. While he doesn't have any money to accommodate Freddie, he tries to slyly slip the bill into his own pocket. Hope grabs the bill from Jack and moves away, not sure of who he has just met. He says, "No, he wouldn't be traveling first class." This is in reference to a running gag of Benny's parsimonious disposition. In this comedian's radio and film appearances, a number of jokes are made on what a skinflint he is with his servant Rochester, a black comedian who appeared with Benny in all the performance media. This type of cameo became a device whereby a number of well-known entertainers appeared briefly—especially in the Road Pictures.[4]

The leader of the Boy Forester group, Stanley (Richard Lyon), develops into another controlling person who becomes a constant, obnoxious dominator of Freddie, who accuses Stanley of the weaknesses of smoking, drinking, and chasing women. All three sins, according to the recited code of the Boy Foresters, should be avoided. Freddie gets caught periodically by the vigilant gang of teenage

Bob takes a bath to spruce up for a possible date
with Jane in *Son of Paleface*.
From the collection of Donald McCaffrey

prudes. As indicated, Hope portrays the opposite of "the great lover." Fleming, as the Duchess, doesn't care for Stanley at first, but when she exposes Dabney as a murderer she almost becomes a third victim. Stanley shows his mettle by rescuing her from the strangler. At the end of the movie he begins to march his scouts away from the Duchess after he tells her he wasn't of her class. She stops him and proposes. He accepts.

The intrigue comedy, *The Great Lover*, does prove to be almost equal to *My Favorite Blonde*, *My Favorite Brunette*, and especially *My Favorite Spy* (1951). Hope and Young turn in superior performances.

Part of the problem rests with both the plot and characterizations. While Hope is effective as the inept leader of the Boy Foresters, the part doesn't have the dimensions of Peanuts White, the inadequate vaudeville clown who is pressed into government service as a double agent and notorious spy. This is partly the result of the well-developed plot and characterization by screenwriters Edmund L. Hartmann and Hal Kanter.

Another comedian, Mickey Rooney, gave some spice to Hope's repertoire of pictures. Their 1953 *Off Limits* remains entertaining when seen today, but has a rather routine "I've seen this before" quality. The stock plot has Rooney playing a self-confident lightweight boxer, with Hope as the handler of a promising pugilist. *New York Times* reviewer A. Weiler had something to say about the design of the movie:

> If it is not precisely hilarious all the way it is not the fault of the comic and the covey of capable guys and dolls who are earnestly mocking the military police and prize fighters in this wacky caper, but of the story, which is thinner than an undernourished flyweight.[5]

Evaluator Weiler gives Rooney a plus when he writes that the actor "is fine in a subdued role, which finds him floundering and helpless unless Hope is in his corner." It remains as one of Mickey's enactments that does not have him "chewing the scenery." Most of his acting exists in the world of big comic hams.

Even Hope is subdued, as if director George Marshall controlled any humorous but overstated remark that might have helped the picture. Hope always had the ability to produce the right shading for comic exaggeration. This becomes evident when women flock to him. His character loves the attention, and he has the charm of a likeable con man. However, it becomes an overbearing situation, and he joins the army and trains to be in the military police division.

In the service he meets Herbert Tuttle (Rooney) who knows Wally (Hope) is a boxing manager and trainer. Herbert insists, "Take me. Train me." "Herby," as he is called, proves to be an excellent fighter, but he must be constantly coached by Wally's instructions from ringside. In addition, Herby's Aunt Connie dislikes boxing and wants her nephew to give it up. With a likely sexual double meaning, Wally asks her, "What about wrestling?"

Eventually, Connie, played by Marilyn Maxwell, stops protesting her nephew's obsession to be a prizefighter. As if sprinkled into the plot without much logic, Marilyn and Bob sing "All About Love" as he dances. Earlier, Bob and Mickey sing a duet about their army positions, "It's Best to be an MP," as they walk about town. The composer and lyricist team of Ray Evans and Jay Livingston probably handled these songs, but the principles, Hope, Maxwell, and Rooney receive credits as "songwriters." Finally, the plot returns to the eventual success of manager Wally and Herby as they win against the navy prize-fighter. At the fade-out,

The show-topping dance of Eddie Foy (Hope)
and George M. Cohan (James Cagney)
in *The Seven Little Foys* (1955).

From J. C. Archives, Inc., photos

Connie and Wally embrace on a train because they are on their honeymoon.

As a drastic switch in his career, the comedian handles a serious role with the 1955 *The Seven Little Foys*. Of course, the biographical part of a real life song and dance man, could be natural for Hope, a man who started his career in vaudeville. However, Eddie Foy had a dark side that appeared to be an enigma for a person who entertained many people during his career. Two screenwriters, Jack Rose and Melville Shavelson, conceived the idea that Hope would be able to handle the biography film of Eddie Foy. And both wanted to handle positions on the picture that would be a first for them: Rose offered to produce the film and Shavelson wanted to direct it.

Bob agreed with the plan of the two screenwriters. In his book, *Don't Shoot, It's Only Me*, he states: "I've made lots of pictures with producers and directors who didn't know what they were doing. This is just the first time they had the guts to admit it."[6]

With Hope's 100th birthday on May 29, 2003, and his death shortly after, one of the most interesting clips from *The Seven Little Foys* was presented on TV repeatedly, showing Hope as Eddie Foy and James Cagney as George M. Cohan. At the Friars club, the song and dance pair exhibit a duel of their hoofing talent on top of a long dining table.

One of Eddie's real-life offspring, Charley Foy, narrates the film, and writers Shavelson and Rose give a sharp edge to his reminiscence, usually avoiding sentimentality. While the scenes are a product of the authors' imagination, there exist many moments where Bob indicates he could handle serious dialogue. When agent Barney Green (George Tobias) suggests he take the seven children on the stage as actors and singers, he gets Eddie Foy a top New York theater, the Palace. Aunt Clara objects, and she argues with Eddie that he should remain a single act. She wants to take care of the children. He says they will play the Palace even on Christmas.

CLARA: I leave.

EDDIE: You've been leaving for fifteen years. I haven't seen the back of that dress yet.

CLARA: You will see it now. I go.

EDDIE: Okay. I'm not going to beg you. I'll catch up with you at New Rochelle.

CLARA: Not New Rochelle. I go to Italy.

EDDIE: That's fine with me. But it's tough on Italy. I'll buy you a one way ticket.

As this confrontation dialogue shows, Eddie as played by Hope, uses vivid, strong sarcasm—a trait that the real Eddie Foy evidently had in abundance. The characterization in the picture also depicts the sharp tongue he used to control his seven children. As they are almost taken away from him and given to the care of Aunt Clara, Hope exhibits another side of Eddie. He directs his apologia to the judge:

> EDDIE: I'd like to save all of us a lot of time. I want to plead guilty. I laid a pretty big egg in the fatherhood racket. I only tried it because I knew their mother would want me to. I owed her that much. Judge, I don't know anything but show business. I've been on the stage all my life. I didn't think there was anything wrong in wanting my kids up there with me. If I were a carpenter I'd bring them up as carpenters and nobody would drag me into court. Maybe your father was a judge. That's all I know. A song and dance man. . . I want you to know this is the longest speech I've given without getting a laugh. (Excerpt from the movie, *The Seven Little Foys*.)

That last line would ordinarily be given with the adept, comic flip Hope had in his repertoire. It isn't that way at all—it is as somber as the rest of his delivery.

With skilled underplaying of his explanation, the comedian displays the fact that a person noted for a gift that induces laughter can also gauge his emotions to bring an audience almost to tears. Comedians such as Jackie Gleason, Bing Crosby, Red Skelton, and Ed Wynn also proved they could act in both comedy and serious drama for film and television.

While the use of underage children on the stage and in motion pictures during the career of Eddie Foy did not cause much of a legal stir, the custody battle and the suitability of children as actors could be questioned. The court scene provides the climactic portion of the movie. To find a loophole in the law, Eddie calls for a demonstration of two girls to sing and two boys to dance. Foy asks the judge if what the children do can be considered entertainment. The judge agrees to Eddie's definition of a loophole in the law. Obviously, the children are awkward and only provide a novelty act for the audience, but they are too cute to receive boos from the crowd. They bump into each other and stray from the dancing line when they have their initial performance at the Palace in New York. Eddie discovers the youngest hiding in a picnic basket, pulls him out, and says he should be as brave as the rest of his siblings. A good part of the humor develops when it becomes evident that the herding of the seven is like trying to herd cats.

With the speech before the judge to apologize for being an inadequate parent trying to raise his children, Eddie develops a dimension of sympathy. However, his ego and ambition to succeed on the Broadway stage show him neglecting both his wife and his offspring. In the early part of the film the movie audience witnesses his drive to be and remain a headliner in vaudeville. This obsession pushes him to avoid women. At the time he meets his future wife, Madeline, he declares he must do a single—referring to marriage in show business terms. He utters a line that might have come from a W. C. Fields movie: "I'm not interested in dogs, women, and children in that order of importance." In all of Hope's pictures, the comedian couldn't muster up such an abrasive, obnoxious character in a brilliant way that creates dark comedy. Yet some critics who know about Foy's faults think the 1955 depiction of his life was a whitewash.

One explanation of this anomaly could be that Hope presents the talent of Eddie Foy in such a fashion that makes him admirable. Any follower of the performance arts must admire such adeptness. Some of these thespian abilities shine in the following scenes: (1) He barges into his future wife's classical ballet routine as a comic tramp and burlesques her movements with strange hops and shuffles. While he at first does this impromptu because her act becomes overextended when he is due to go on stage, this take-off becomes a hilarious skit in his repertoire. (2) The Italian ballerina Madeline Morando has the sophistication that prompts her to observe, "You are refreshingly vulgar." In a repartee that proved to be Hope's forte, he responds: "I knew I'd get to you." This, naturally, has the banter and wit that helps with a twist of character self-depreciation. (3) An unusual singing-in-the-rain song when Hope sings vaudevillian Bert Williams' famous "Nobody." The lyrics reflect a cynical view of not being accepted: "I never done nothing to nobody. And until I get something, sometime, I don't intend to do something for nobody, no time." (4) When Eddie finally gives in and proposes marriage to Madeline, she wants to declare it to all who are in her ballet class in Italy. "Do you want me to sing Pagliacci?" This becomes a selfish action since he wants to use her in an act she has abandoned. (5) All the children develop the toughness of their father. Consequently, Eddie and the seven children never become objects of sentimentality.

Most of the critics held *The Seven Little Foys* in high regard. To them, it was a hit. Also, the fans liked Hope even when he played a character with a dark side. The success of so many of the actor's pictures produced a loyal following. But, two movies that followed, in 1956, *That Certain Feeling* and *The Iron Petticoat*, ended up as duds. Teamed with an actress not known for the comic touch, Eva Marie Saint, Bob struggled with an adaptation of a Broadway play, *The King of Hearts*, in which he played a "ghost" cartoonist for a popular comic-strip artist played by George Sanders. Hope, known for his nervous, even neurotic, humorous characters, produced two amazingly weak pictures. Unfortunately, *The Iron Petticoat* did not evolve into a hit like *Ninotchka*, the 1939 film with Greta Garbo and Melvyn Douglas. In a similar plot, a Russian woman (played by Katherine Hepburn) gets involved with American Air Force officer, Bob Hope, and the results received weak or even bad notices from the critics.

The next year in 1957, Bob recovered his reputation with another serious biographical attempt. This time he played the colorful playboy mayor of New York City, James J. Walker. *Beau James* gave Hope another success with an essentially non-comic role. In the '50s the actor starred in three superior humorous works that gave him critical and popular acclaim, *The Lemon Drop Kid*, *My Favorite Spy*, and *Casanova's Big Night*.

Many lighter moments in *Beau James* explain the qualifier "essentially" serious and can be applied to *The Seven Little Foys*. The portrayal of Jimmy Walker shows him confronted with two basic conflicts: First, the estrangement in his marriage with his wife Allie Walker (enacted by Alexis Smith) because of his affairs with women, especially Betty Compton (played by Vera Miles); Second, Jimmy's inability to relate to the New York political party machine. Because he neglects the mayoral office and doesn't attend to the corruption developing in many of the city's departments, there could be an inner conflict not easily detected. Walker's happy-go-lucky disposition provides a mask to cover much of his distress. Hope must have been cast in this role because in the bulk of his career he gave forth a positive image. In short, he often offered the audience a very likeable fellow in the roles he created.

Beau James depicts the climb to become mayor of New York City. As a state legislator, Walker had some political experience that gave him credentials for the position. But he was also a person with charisma. He had some show business credentials and even wrote a romantic song with the lyrics, "Will You Love Me in December as You Do in May." And he can perform such a song and loves to sing "Manhattan." Walker, as a real-life person, held the post of mayor of New York City from 1926 to 1932. The corruption that surrounded him would eventually bring him down. And of course, his private life would also leave its mark.

A concluding paragraph in a *New York Times* review touches on Walker's fate and the effective performances:

> Considering their rather deferential assignments, Miss Miles, as Betty Compton, Miss Smith, and Darren McGavin, as the Mayor's secretary, are surprisingly convincing. Mr. Hope's hero is a likable fellow unquestionably. Maybe it doesn't matter that a personable, capable man, in the country's second toughest political post, became "the city's heart" instead of its conscience. According to "Beau James," it doesn't.[7]

This film does have some wisecracks that do have a relationship to Bob Hope's flair for impromptu humor. At least this becomes his delivery of the material that was scripted by Melville Shavelson and Jack Rose. Naturally, this had been done adroitly, displaying the talent developed in his vaudeville and radio days.

For example, when Walker joins a parade of policemen he notices that one of their horses is quite a beautiful animal. Jimmy wisecracks, "That horse. Stop showing me up." Shortly after this someone from curbside tells him to fight the malfeasance investigation. He says, "If I go, the town goes with me." This probably is a joke directed at all of the corrupt people hired by the Tammany Hall political cronies who pushed him into the position of mayor. Or it could be interpreted as recognition from many of his admirers that he was "the city's heart." At the court inquiry he defends himself brilliantly:

> I was told that if I stood up here in this room and swore that no favors were given or expected for this generosity given to me it would sound like *Alice in Wonderland.* Maybe it does sound like fantasy for a man to declare himself both a politician and an honest man. But your Excellency is a politician also... I've given most of my life to a political career. I've been at it so long I've grown attached to it. I like being mayor of New York much as my father thought I would. If there was a scintilla of doubt in my mind or yet in my heart about the honesty, about the accomplishment and the affection that went with it. If there

were any doubt about my public, official record, as mayor of that big city I would not be imposing on your generosity in allowing me to plead my own case. I say it here with an easy conscience and the knowledge within myself that no matter whether misunderstood or not—I did the best I could. . . I never did anything wrong. But doing nothing is not enough. I should have done a few more things right. (Excerpts from the movie, *Beau James*.)

Walker gives this apology in a court and in a baseball stadium. He admits that he had neglected his responsibility to New York. This apologia has a much different context than the one Hope delivers in *The Seven Little Foys*. There exists one similarity in the two performances, however. Hope employs a low-key approach, an understatement in his acting. And this illustrates how a comedian can handle a serious role so effectively. The character change develops from an enactment of an entertainer first and a lawyer next. Again, this shows the range of Bob Hope in depicting two divergent biographical persons. Some critics would have liked to see more such serious dramas from a person noted for his humorous portrayals. Both *The Seven Little Foys* and *Beau James* were two hits of the '50s.

Two films produced in the last portion of the decade did not fare so well. *Paris Holiday* (1958) and *Alias Jessie James* (1959) indicate the fading quality of Hope's career in films.

With two leading comedians who might be considered the most popular talents of their own countries, Hope from the United States and Fernandel from France, the performances of the famous actors alone might have guaranteed success for *Paris Holiday*. However, both comedians' careers in films were on the wane. Once famous actors, they now remained superior entertainers in the memory of the audience when they had once existed at the pinnacle of the comic world. Ironically, they were both born in May 1903, and at the age of 54, a year during the production before the release of *Paris Holiday*, they did not have the best material. Hope tried to take over with a story credit and with the role of producer.

Some portions of this 1957 film during production the year before had potential—such as the first meeting of the two comedians. Hope, as Robert Hunter, is shown walking down the elaborate stairway of an ocean liner. A spontaneous outburst of clapping comes from a room below him. He beams with a big smile, thinking the crowd recognizes him as a well-known American actor. To his chagrin, the adulation has been focused on Fernandel, who has been descending the stairway behind him.

In the second scene of *Paris Holiday*, Hope exhibits his skill as the fall guy left out of the scene. As Fernandel signs autographs he routinely gives Hope one since he is holding a letter, although it is not intended for the French comedian's signature. Finally, they meet and the Gallic actor wonders if he is a standup performer on the boat. Indignantly, Hope corrects him, "I'm a passenger first class. Deductible."

Through a translator, Fernandel is told that Hunter is a famous American comedian. The Frenchman calls him "Bobbie" and starts feeling his noted ski-slide nose—a subject for humor in many Hope movies—especially the Road Pictures. Bob implies the strange features of his rival, "That comes straight from the horse's mouth." (From the movie, *Paris Holiday*.)

The two comedians soon become symbiotic pals, and his French friend shares his adoration of beautiful women. Hope meets two with opposite dispositions: Ann McCall (Martha Hyer), a rather aloof belle, and Zara (Anita Ekberg), a sexy spy with voluptuous breasts. When Zara presses her nearly- Mae-West anatomy against Robert Hunter and asks for a match to light her cigarette, he sweats out, "Any closer and you won't need one."

Hope's ever-faithful covey of writers furnish him with some "zinger" gags, however, the main writers, Edmund Beloin and Dean Riesner, create a stew that remains so complicated it is hard to follow. But Hope, who developed the story, may have contributed to the case of too many cooks spoiling the broth. The climactic sequence involves a chase instigated by spies trying to get a dramatic script with secret codes. Fernandel tries to save Hope by lowering a rope ladder from a helicopter. Thereby, we see Robert Walker clinging for his dear life as obstacles in the way threaten to knock him from his precarious perch. All of this develops into a poor Mack Sennett device that a twelve-year-old boy or girl might enjoy, but is less appealing to more sophisticated fans.

Probably the most unusual cameo to ever appear in a Hope movie occurred when the casting director (or Hope) decided to use the famous U.S. director, Preston Sturges, for the part of a French playwright named Serge Vitry. Since he received a portion of his education in France and moved back to that country in 1949, he could write and speak the language fluently. Vitry (Sturges) asks Hunter if he has the background by winning Oscars in America that would give him credibility to play the role in his intense drama: "How many have you won?" It becomes a joke on Hope because the comedian received honorary Oscars but none for acting. Sturges (like Hope and Fernandel) plays himself in this short role that proves he had solid acting ability as well as superior skills as a playwright, screenwriter, producer, and director. This cameo role of Sturges proved to be one of the more illuminating portions of *Paris Holiday*.

The 1959 *Alias Jessie James* seemed as if Hope tried to replay some of the comic Westerns that were created in the past, especially *The Paleface* (1948) and *Fancy Pants* (1950). Critics point to one portion of the movie that seems fresh and innovative—the climactic shoot-out. In many Westerns the hero takes on a legion of outlaws and disposes of all of them. So, Milford Farnsworth thinks that he is a hero by an impossible feat of wiping out the villains. The camera, via editing, reveals he has the support of many "guns" picking off the enemy. The army of hiding assistants includes cowboys, sheriffs, hired avengers, and heroes or heroines of the Old West. Many of the cameo actors appeared in television series of the late '50s or in earlier feature Westerns. Each aims his or her gun and kills one of Farnsworth's foes. The feature Western protagonists who appear in cameos are Roy Rogers, Gene Autry, and Gary Cooper. The television stars of Western series that were so popular in the '60s were: James Arness of *Gunsmoke*, James Garner of *Maverick*, Fess Parker of *Davy Crocket*, and Hugh O'Brian of *Wyatt Earp*. Others who assisted in the demise of the outlaws were such unlikely allies as Jay Silverheels (Tonto in *The Lone Ranger*) and Bing Crosby (who would appear in the 1966 remake of *Stagecoach*). This shoot-out sequence remains a classic "Oh, look who that is."

The mundane plot shows Hope as Farnsworth the insurance salesman who persuades Jesse James to take out a life insurance policy of $100,000 and then has to make sure he doesn't die or his company will be bankrupted. Jesse James tries to get Farnsworth to impersonate him so he can collect the money. While the picture *Alias Jesse James* has some moments to its credit, Hope and his supporting cast leave much to be desired. Wendell Corey, for example, seemed "long in the tooth" or just so weary that his supposed comic villain is lackluster. This last Hope film of the '50s became a miss. Some works in the '60s had merit, but the golden years of the film comedian were evaporating into a decline. Few great stars knew when it was time to retire, but Bob Hope would struggle through the '60s and score some hits when he moved to television. Audiences still loved this personable, adroit actor who conquered all the media.

6 *Neglected and Underrated Movies*

The success of many of the films labeled "Big Broadcast," "Broadway," "Follies," or "Melody" generally begat another variety movie. The 1938 *Thanks for the Memory* did not become a sequel of *The Big Broadcast of 1938*. When Hollywood's Paramount Studios would grind out many pictures a year, the hit song of this Big Broadcast variety show created another movie using the song title, "Thanks for the Memory," in which Bob Hope and Shirley Ross sing and reflect about a former romantic affair.

While this film has another hit song (by Hoagy Carmichael and Frank Loesser) rendered by Hope and Ross, "Two Sleepy People," it is not a variety show or musical. The movie, *Thanks for the Memory*, comes closer to a sophisticated comedy with the plot of a struggling author who remains at home as his wife (Shirley Ross) goes back to work as a model. Problems develop when they accuse each other of infidelity. The script comes from a stage play by the famous playwrights Frances Goodrich and Albert Hackett, who also had a number of screenwriting credits. The pair adapted their play, *Up Pops the Devil*, to the screen in 1931. This earlier film version featured Carole Lombard and Norman Foster in the lead roles that were played by Shirley Ross and Bob Hope in the 1938 *Thanks for the Memory*. Part of the comedy is developed by some high-living incorrigibles who are interrupting the normal lifestyle of Hope and Ross. Some of the cast, such as Charles Butterworth, Hedda Hopper, Roscoe Karns, and Jack Norton, add color and comedy to the film.

In the opening scene, Hope, as Steve Merrick, and Shirley Ross as his wife, Anne Merrick, are having a conversation about all the "leeches" that are frequenting their home. Steve observes, "You know Anne, between you and me that mob is getting slightly on my nerves. Day and night they join the Merrick's hospitality. Why, there are so many people practically living here, it's almost like a Federal Housing Project."

The Merricks have Great Depression financial problems, some of it exacerbated by the demands of the human parasites. It is evident when the landlord comes for the rent that Hope is playing one of his favorite roles as a con man. When a delivery boy comes to the door with a collect package, Steve asks the landlord, played by Edward Gargan, to pay. As landlord Flanahan pulls out some bills, Hope takes one and gives it to the boy demanding payment. Steve blithely says, "Keep the change." Flanahan is flustered because Steve affects a pleasant air and Anne supports him with the same sweet disposition. In fact, the whole problem of the back rent shows Steve and Anne affecting words laced with honey. The landlord joins them with a similar air, but one that has a sarcastic tinge. Steve is still able to get $10 from the owner of the apartment by assuring him the IOU will be honored. However, Steve cannot swindle the janitor when he delivers a package of cleaned and pressed shirts because Steve has bilked him too often. The janitor is played by Jack Benny, the "comic servant" for both radio and motion pictures, Eddie "Rochester" Anderson.

When the gang of leeches arrives, it is evident that the genre being created is one that flourished in the '30s and '40s on both stage and screen. *Thanks for the Memory* evolved into a sophisticated comedy with a wealth of humorous situations and witty lines. Much of this can be traced to the work of Frances Goodrich and Albert Hackett, prolific writers for the media. These two collaborators were noted for adapting the witty comedy of the Dashiell Hammett Thin Man series plus many other works.[1]

The group of freeloaders consists of the queen bee of the group Polly Griscom (Hedda Hopper), George Kent (Roscoe Karns) and his obese, 16-million-dollar wife (Laura Crewes), cynical Biney (Charles Butterworth), and the quintessential drunk (Jack Norton), who wanders in periodically and elicits a statement like, "Who's that?" All of the crew, except the drunk, Bert Monroe, and George Kent, overflow with pretension even though they seem to have no dignity in their constant sponging of liquor, food, and even clothes off the Merricks.

Shirley Ross in her second movie with Hope,
Thanks for the Memory (1938).
From the collection of Donald McCaffrey

Even being married to a millionairess doesn't work for George. He mopes around and complains that his wife is forcing him on an allowance. When kind-hearted Anne returns to her modeling job, she gives George money. He moans at his plight and says, "People who are foolish enough to get married should stay that way."

Steve tries to finish his novel but must become the househusband in the process. A great deal of the humor develops as he dons an apron and tries to cook. He overdoes the quantity—possibly to account for the entrance of the hangers-on to his household. Even using cookbooks doesn't work. He is eventually humiliated by the black janitor who laughs at his attempts to be what he eventually calls himself, when he is about to leave Anne—"the man of the house." This situation evolves into a series of ludicrous incidents that can be classified as a reversal of roles. There is a similar comic switch when George becomes dominated by his wife. Often in comedy dramas, this device develops with the normal positions of the male and female exchanged to achieve zany results.

Also tied to this sophisticated genre are the misalliances between couples—the alienation of affections and the real (or merely assumed) infidelity. Steve gets linked to a dizzy Southerner named Luella, a comedienne Hope employed in vaudeville and radio skits.[2] She enters, very disturbed: "I wonder if one of you boys could help?" She has a bat in her apartment. Steve mocks her accent when she diphthongizes "I'll just diahie." Cynical Biney, to a degree, imitates her accent: "No woman dies when there's life in her body. Get your gun, Steve." While Luella fears that the bat will get in her hair, Steve soon has Luella figuratively entangled in his hair. This happens at the same time he believes his wife is having an affair with the potential publisher of his novel, so he decides to pursue the rather batty Luella. All marital strife comes out before the perpetual intruders when the two women get into a mild catfight. Steve reveals his feelings of inferiority when his wife tells Luella that she pays for Steve to take her out on the town:

> STEVE: Shut up will you! All right, tell them, tell them all. She buys my food, she buys my clothes. She pays the rent. To make a long story short, she is the man of the house. Now everybody knows it.
>
> BINEY: It should stay that way.

Ever the pessimist and sponger, the wit and detachment of the hard-nosed Biney show one of the keys to the genre. While some domestic elements are part of the risible nature of *Thanks for the Memory*, much of the plotting and clever dialogue shows the predominance of a sophisticated dramatic work. Credit should be given to playwrights Frances Goodrich and Albert Hackett, plus screen adapter Lynn Starling. This proves to be one of the best of the "neglected and underrated" motion pictures.

Steve and Anne finally get away from their Bohemian fast-living friends and Steve finishes his novel. The revelation that Anne is pregnant brings the couple together. In a somewhat strained reprise

Steve sings "Thanks for the Memory" and Anne, touched by the sentiment, joins him in the song. While some critics think this is a minor movie in the Hope repertoire, an evaluator with a historical perspective and a fresh examination of this film could develop a revisionist view. *Thanks for the Memory* has been neglected and underrated—almost a lost work. Other sophisticated genres have received more attention, and there may have been so many of this type of film that it has been overlooked.

It shows either the comedian or Paramount trying to make a match with Shirley Ross. Actually, the pairing with Martha Raye in three pictures seemed to be bringing results, but a lighter, romantic comedy may have been the order of the new direction. Bosley Crowther reviewed this film, calling it "among the pleasantest of the year's light romantic comedies."[3]

Bob's next co-starring role with Shirley Ross was the 1939 *Some Like It Hot*, which had a secondary title, *Rhythm Romance*, so as not to be confused with Billy Wilder's 1959 movie of the same name starring Jack Lemmon, Tony Curtis, and Marilyn Monroe. In this film, there is a frequent role executed by Bob in many of his movies—a professional entertainer in a routine and lowly position. In this plot he is a smooth-talking barker for a sideshow in Atlantic City. On the boardwalk, Gene Krupa and his band are used by management to attract potential customers to the various activities for the concession and entertainment stands. Krupa appeared previously with Benny Goodman's Orchestra in films, but with his fame as a spectacular drummer he started his own group in the "Big Band Era." And Gene finally received an acting role in *Rhythm Romance* or *Some Like It Hot*. Tied to popular culture history is the fascinating fad of jitterbug dancing. Scenes in this movie show this craze of youth in the late '30s into the '40s. When the entrepreneur of the boardwalk, Stephen Hanratty, witnesses the large crowd of couples dancing to Krupa's band, he realizes he must take advantage of the situation to lure the youthful crowd. The definition of "jitterbug" gives an apt description of the dance: "A jazz variation of the two-step in which couples swing, balance and twirl in standardized patterns and often with vigorous acrobatics."[4] In a jitterbug scene the viewer can witness the woman, usually thin and petite, almost thrown away from the male partner—over his head and under his spread legs. It is, indeed, a vigorous exhibition of acrobatics. In a sense, such moments, with the Gene Krupa group playing, produce some characteristics of a cult movie. While Hope was a skilled dancer he never attempted the jitterbug with Shirley Ross. In fact, the actor is too busy playing one of his likeable con men with many humorous touches. As Nicky Nelson, he runs a wax museum on the boardwalk. As a fast-talking barker, he also tries to be an agent for Lily Racquet (the Shirley Ross role), who is a singer looking for work. He also wants to promote the Gene Krupa Band. Actually he is a pretender of many talents who has trouble paying the rent for his wax museum.

The original title *Some Like It Hot* refers to the jazz motif of this Hope movie. There is a special perspective to this film. The work exists somewhere between a neglected and underrated film with Bob Hope. The comedian may have thought it was not one of his best works, and this would be true. However, there is a consistency in the character he portrays. It is one of his best con man portraits. This may be related to the source play, *The Great Magoo*, by two formidable playwrights; Gene Fowler, noted for the biographies of such luminaries as John Barrymore and Jimmy Durante; and Ben Hecht, the prolific playwright and screenwriter. Even though Lewis Foster and Wilkie Mahoney, the scripters who adapted the play to film, may have been pushed into creating a rather typical and routine musical, the character of Nicky Nelson did provide meat for Hope's acting.

In *Some Like It Hot*, Hope's Nicky Nelson makes the mistake of trying to gamble with Hanratty for a ring his girlfriend, Lily, gave to him. Unfortunately, Nicky throws the losing "snake eyes" with the dice. Lily finds out that Hanratty has the ring. This, of course, causes a falling out of their relationship and the boss, Stephen, moves in, taking Nicky's place.

Paramount believed that this comedian and his partner in a romantic relationship would strike gold at the box office as they did with their song in *The Big Broadcast of 1938*. Hope writes a song that Ross performs with the Krupa band. While the song, "The Lady's in Love," becomes a hit in the movie's plot, it does not become the real-life success of the two previous pairings of Hope and Ross, "Thanks for the Memory" and "Two Sleepy People."

A wrap-up of the complications in *Some Like It Hot* involves the manager and boss of all Atlantic City boardwalk entertainment giving up his pursuit of Ms. Ross. Not only does Hanratty give Hope the object of their affection, Ross, but he also promotes the comedian to an important position as emcee on the boardwalk.

While it may be a matter of taste, Hope's comedies that can be classified as musicals do not seem to weather well with time. However, sometimes there are only a few songs that do not matter enough to interrupt the continuity of the story. Stanley Green developed a listing of Hope's musicals that tends to classify movies that include only one or two songs as a musical. As a result, over half of the comedian's films are catalogued in his encyclopedia in this manner.[5] Hope's first picture, *The Big Broadcast of 1938*, has been classified as a musical, but it has many skits and plot elements of a variety show. However, there are six musical portions so it could be classified in the genre. *The Paleface* (1948) has three songs, but screenwriter Ed Hartmann never considered it a musical. His screenplay for Hope in 1953, entitled *Here Come the Girls*, did not meet with his approval because it was not intended to be a musical—he wrote the script as a straight comedy drama. Music was added later. Green includes all seven of the Road Pictures as musicals. *Road to Rio* (1948), however, seems to be the only film with enough music to fit the classification.

The powers that be at Paramount found a new romantic attachment for Bob: the lively Paulette Goddard. She had played the gamine in Charles Chaplin's *Modern Times* (1936) and had a role in *The Great Dictator* (1940). When she co-starred with Hope in *Ghost Breakers* (1941), both actors moved into the ranking of "box office gold" for the studio. In 1941, their *Nothing But the Truth* utilized a pairing that worked once more. The source for this picture came from two previous versions filmed in 1920 and 1929 that had been adapted from a 1916 play that employed an effective farcical plot. Hope plays a stockbroker who enters into a bet of $10,000 with his business colleagues, which requires him to tell the truth and nothing but the truth for 24 hours. Comedy comes from the negative revelations he has about his friends and even his girlfriend, Gwen (played by Goddard).

The fourth version of this popular comic idea emerged in 1997 with Jim Carrey, who is arguably the leading actor in this mode. In *Liar, Liar* the scriptwriters Paul Guay and Stephen Mazur change the basic plot considerably by switching the Hope character of the 1941 version from stockbroker to lawyer. Also, some fantasy enters this latest version when the character's five-year-old son realizes his father is a liar. His birthday wish is for his father to tell the truth for 24 hours.

Jim Carrey's mentor is Jerry Lewis, and both actors are inclined to over-acting. While some Hope detractors believe he makes sure he is the star of any film (which is seldom a valid criticism), Hope knew from long experience in all the production media that understatement and restraint produce some of the most effective humor. Unfortunately, it is difficult to find the 1941 version of *Nothing But the Truth* to compare the performance of Hope with the 1997 Carrey enactment in *Liar, Liar.*

In 1947, Paramount used its stars (and extras) to develop a hodge-podge called *Variety Girl.* Since Bob Hope and Bing Crosby have more time with a variety of routines than other leading actors, the picture's lobby posters showed them dressed up for a song and dance. While I refer to *Variety Girl* as a "hodge-podge," it has been neglected as a revue picture. There is enough "Do you know who that is?" to stimulate the younger fans of the '40s films. The basic plot is forwarded by Bing Crosby as he meets a would-be talented singer Catherine Brown, played by Mary Hatcher. He is practicing his golf shots on a grassy part of the Paramount lot when he hits a ball and strikes Hatcher's rear. He apologizes and they engage in a conversation about her talent as a singer—a talent much like such sopranos as Deanna Durbin and Kathryn Grayson. Bing then gets a talent scout to give Hatcher a screen test. A young, handsome DeForest Kelly—who became more widely known as the Starship Enterprise doctor "Bones" on the television series *Star Trek* and the feature films of the Star Trek crew—enacts the scout's role. When Kelly leaves with Hatcher, Bob Hope meets Bing to criticize how he is practicing his golf club swing. In the process they exchange insults:

Bob asks Bing, "How's your golf?" Bing replies, "In the seventies." Immediately, Bob takes a crack at Crosby's age: "I know. But how's your golf? You are looking good lately. Have you changed embalmers?" Bing says "Shall I beat you to a pulp with my Oscar?"

This last comment, of course, was a crack at Hope's never having won an Academy Award for acting although he did receive honorary awards.

For a final song and dance number executed by the pair, the insults continue. Much of their routines were similar to those they used in the Road Pictures and in their appearances in early '30s vaudeville.

About two-thirds into the film revue, Bob takes over as master of ceremonies; a role he perfected in vaudeville and a position he played in his first feature film, *The Big Broadcast of 1938*. The location of a series of songs and sketches takes place in what is called the "Variety Club." Paramount Studios had a theater where stars performed live in similar songs and sketches for charity. Screenwriter Edmund L. Hartmann told me in an interview how he admired Hope as emcee in

Variety Girl for the film and the stage review at the Paramount Theater. Of Hope's emcee role in the stage presentation Ed remarked:

> I saw him do an entire benefit for the Variety Club when we were about to do the film *Variety Girl*. And he knew nothing about who was on or anything else. He had no rehearsals. All adlib. Paramount Theater—jammed. He walked in at the back. There was a man waiting for him with a list of the cast. He took that list, walked out on the stage and you would have thought he rehearsed that show for six weeks. He was so at ease, he was so funny, he was so wonderful in introducing those people. He was completely in charge of the entire evening. He was fantastic.

Hope, in many ways, could be called a "natural" emcee, and he contributed this function in many of his pictures. In *The Facts of Life* (1960), Bob even did a burlesque of an amateur emcee who thought his jokes were very funny. His co-star, played by Lucille Ball, portrays a sophisticated suburbanite who thinks he is crude and a bore. Hope's winning ways with an audience gave him a start that you might say made him a natural. In this movie, Bob lampoons the role of emcee—an art in itself since it became a forte of his life-long profession. The comedian had years of vaudeville and radio experience that helped him to perfect this art long before he was hired to act in feature films for Paramount in 1937.

The final production number of *Variety Girl* gives both Hope and Bing the lead-in song and dance routine with a song called "Harmony." The insults fly:

BING: (singing) If you keep saying I'm too fat.

BOB: (talking) I'm a rat.

BING: (singing) And if you don't like the way I croon.

BOB: I'm just a goon.

Crosby complains that if he's not okay—Hope chimes in by singing "What we need is plain old harmony." Then they sing a duet and dance in compatible movements—in harmony. Hope then goes tit-for-tat by singing how Bing might think his jokes are bad, and Crosby replies (in rhyme), "What a cad." And, naturally, the reference to Hope's ski-slope nose comes into play. Soon, the cast of what seems to be the whole Paramount roster of actors joins in with the song "Harmony." And it is a joyous group of such important actors showing that Paramount was second only to MGM as having many of the favorite stars of the time. Paramount had bits, songs, and sketches for several of the big stars, including Gary Cooper, Allan Ladd, Veronica Lake, Dorothy Lamour, Burt Lancaster, Ray Milland, Barbara Stanwyck, directors George Marshall and Cecil B. DeMille, and many more. One of the ironies of the plot of *Variety Girl* develops for the would-be star soprano, Mary Hatcher. She becomes a fictional star named Katherine Brown in the movie, but as one of the Paramount discoveries, Hatcher made only three more features in the '40s and a final movie playing Maid Marian in a pilot film intended for television entitled *Tales of Robin Hood* (1952).

When *The Iron Petticoat* was released in 1956, there were enough critics and general moviegoers who remembered *Nintochka*. This 1939 movie, directed by Ernst Lubitsch and starring Greta Garbo and Melvyn Douglas, became a hit because audiences found that the famous actress Garbo, who was noted for her serious dramas in film, was amazingly adept at comedy. Garbo plays Ninotchka, a serious Russian woman commissar who eventually becomes fascinated with Parisian fashions and falls in love. Publicity for the film uses the catchy announcement: "Garbo laughs."[6]

An MGM Press Book for *The Iron Petticoat* included an advertisement for newspapers and television that displayed cartoon caricatures of Hope with his ski-slope nose and Katharine Hepburn with her firm jaw and distinct expression of lips and teeth. The ad sets forth such hyperbolic statements as "The FUNNIEST PAIR in pictures!" and "HILARIOUSLY TOGETHER FOR THE FIRST TIME."[7] Most of the press book copy relates incidences that happened during the filming of *The Iron Petticoat*. While there are some differences in the plot from *Ninotcha*, the Lubitsh film with Garbo and Douglas has all the elements of the sophisticated comedy, a type of work often used by the famous German-born director.

The Iron Petticoat has more of the intrigue type of comedy that fits the humor of Hope and for the actor first considered for the part, Cary Grant. Grant was not available, and Bob got the role of Captain Chuck Lockwood. Katherine Hepburn, as Vinka Kovelenko, is a pilot like Chuck. The two pilots are united as a result of the U.S. government giving Captain Lockwood the assignment of using Vinka for propaganda purposes and converting her to the "American way." Turning to the press book synopsis, some of the humor comes from the clash of cultures and ideology:

> Although at first Vinka, who has not deserted, tries to swing Chuck to the Soviet ideology, she gradually falls for him—and for black lace lingerie—and is arrested by Russian agents as a traitor.[8]

As is indicated in this description, two things are evident: The Russian woman is enamored with what Soviet's consider "decadent" capitalistic values, and she falls in love with a man who does not believe in the Soviet way. In this respect, *The Iron Petticoat* has the certain romantic comedy plot of *Ninotchka*. The arrest of Vinka leads to the intrigue of the hero attempting to rescue his heroine.

Internet reviewer Hal Erickson sees this Hope and Hepburn picture as a neglected and underrated work. The two may not be "The Funniest Pair in pictures," he comments, but they work very well together.[9] Strong, effective acting will often save a movie. This retrospective examination sees enough merit in the work to rank *The Iron Petticoat* as an ignored film. The initial reactions were not positive, probably because the popularity and quality of *Ninotchka* as a similar film took away from any successor.

One of the most heated controversies developed with one of Hope's films. It sparked contrary reviews by interested critics and fans alike. Appearing in the movie theater in 1966, *Boy, Did I Get a Wrong Number* employed screenwriters George Kennett, Albert E. Lewin, and Burt Styler. This trio of writers had the skills to write for television sitcoms but seemed to have problems sustaining a comedy feature for the usual length of an hour and fifteen minutes to an hour and a half. Arthur Marx, the son of Groucho, wrote screenplays for Hope and it could be he had an unfavorable relationship with the comedian. In an unusually vitriolic, self-proclaimed "unauthorized biography" he wrote:

> The plot of *Boy, Did I Get a Wrong Number* had to do with a real estate agent who, while trying to phone his wife, accidentally becomes involved with a knockout runaway actress. It wasn't much of a script, and the reviews it received helped to explain why Hope was having such a difficult time getting financing and distribution of a story my collaborator, Bob Fisher and I had sold him.[10]

Marx was referring to the next year's Hope movie, *Eight on the Lam* (1967). The biographer, who also tried to evaluate Hope's film remarks about the fact that *Boy, Did I Get a Wrong Number* didn't have "much of a script." This became a boomeranging criticism of his own *Eight on the Lam.*

Both *Boy, Did I Get a Wrong Number* and *Eight on the Lam* received the critical label of "BOMB" in Leonard Maltin's 1999 guide to movies and videos.[11] Maltin shortly dropped *Lam*, but kept *Number.*

Some screenwriters who have written biographies, and Arthur Marx is the best example, have legitimate complaints that Hollywood powers-that-be change the work of the writer as often happens. However, as a biographer, Marx gratuitously sets forth opinions with little or no proof. When he provides proof it is of a personal nature—such as personality conflicts rather than any artistic problems with the script, directing, and acting.

But writing is not the only problem that these two movies possessed. Acting and directing had some important negative affects on the central premise of the comic plot. It is possible that George Marshall did not have the directorial power he once had to handle a weak script and whip it into shape. He was, nevertheless, handling screenwriters in the '60s who did not have the skills of the older screenwriters, such as Don Hartman, Frank Butler, Hal Kanter, and Edmund L. Hartmann. But Marshall had lost some of his creative powers. How much was Hope to blame? Like Marshall, Hope doesn't have the same sparkle in these '60s works as he did in his '40s films, but Marshall's use of Phyllis Diller and Jonathan Winters doesn't gel with Hope's still-breezy style. Both Diller and Winters were at their best as standup comedians. Too often they could not handle the ensemble style of acting that is critical to a unified production, either on the stage or in films.

Phyllis Diller appeared in three Hope films in the '60s. The first, *Boy, Did I Get a Wrong Number*, shows Diller as a supportive domestic, and she repeats the role in *Eight on the Lam.* For her third film, *The Private Navy of Sgt. O'Farrell* (1968), her strident attempt to be an ugly but humorous character goes even more awkwardly bizarre. Rather than being an asset to Hope's films, she became a liability. She may have been encouraged by director George Marshall in her first film. From my viewpoint, an unnamed *Variety* reviewer made a mistake when he stated:

> George Marshall's direction sparks events in proper perspective, wisely allowing his characters to go their separate ways in their own particular styles.[12]

This is a rather strange evaluation, because most comedy movies should have a consistency and a pattern of acting styles, or they could become a chaotic mish-mash. The only time this seems to work in Hope's movies is the revue and musical films. At times, the leading character in a comedy might have a different style than the subordinates or supporting players. For example, W. C. Fields had a flamboyant demeanor that contrasted with some of the actors supporting him; nevertheless, it fit the character that Fields established. Actually, Hope proved to be a team player and adapted to the cast and this particular type of comedy film.

Biographer Lawrence Quirk sometimes ventures into the criticism of acting, often without specific support for his observations, as when he evaluated *Boy, Did I Get a Wrong Number*:

> At least his early co-stars, beautiful as they were, were also reasonably talented actresses, but anyone who sat through five minutes of *Number* could see [Elke] Sommer wasn't in the league of, for instance, Madeleine Carroll. But dumb beauties were Hope's cup of tea in the mid-Sixties. Even in the comedienne department and with the notable exceptions of Diller, Lucille Ball, and Martha Raye, Hope rarely sought out skilled performers who might outshine him.[13]

From my own evaluation, Quirk undercuts his whole argument when he includes Diller as an accomplished comedienne alongside Lucille and Martha. Diller is in the class of standup comics who perform well in solo performances. She does not seem well assimilated into the same movie with Hope and the other players. She steals scenes from Bob with her ruckus behavior. If Hope didn't realize this was happening, his previous perception of his remaining in concert with such women as Paulette Goddard, Lucille Ball, and Martha Raye must have waned with age. He worked with these actresses at least three times, as he did with Phyllis Diller.

Quirk scores to a degree when he says Sommer doesn't have the skills of Madeleine Carroll, who complemented Hope in *My Favorite Blond* (1942). However, this British actress does play it pretty straight and in the fashion of such American actresses as Paulette Goddard, Jean Arthur, and Carole Lombard. There are no specific demands on Elke Sommer for witty remarks or simple verbal jokes. Her comedy comes from humorous situations, and she becomes a central part of the plot.

Sommer handles the role of a sexy French star who becomes tired of showing off her physical charms in bubble baths. As an actress with dreams of a higher status in her profession, she hopes to have a meaty, serious role in Hollywood, only to find she must continue as the queen of soapsuds. Her director shoots the scene, but Didi (Sommer) rebels. Jumping from the tub, covered with bubbles, she grabs a robe, rushes to her car, and speeds off to a hotel in Rocky Point, Oregon. A real estate agent named Tom Meade (Hope's role) tries to phone his wife and accidentally gets the hotel room where Didi is hiding out from her studio and director. So, this is the title for the basic plot—*Boy, Did I Get a Wrong Number*. This exclamation, which probably needs suitable punctuation, indicates the danger Tom might inherit from a wife who has the fury of a Grecian Harpy for helping out this curvaceous star. In the phone conversation he said he would keep her identity secret and bring food to her since she might be recognized if she went outside the hotel. He even lets her stay in his private cabin. He receives help to avoid his wife's suspicions of infidelity from their maid, Lily (Phyllis Diller). When both Tom and Didi are in the cabin, Lily hops on a motorcycle and speeds to warn him that his wife has decided to visit the family retreat. Now, both maid and husband try to hide the voluptuous bathtub star.

This entire machination smacks of warmed-over nineteenth-century French bedroom farce. Consequently, humor comes more from the situation than the cleverness of the lines in the screenplay. For example, Didi complains that she has had no food since yesterday. Hope says, "You poor undernourished kid"—a joke that has a mild satirical twist since she has more than ample curves. Even Tom's son looks at a picture of Didi and observes, "They're not real." Most of the anatomy gags become tiresome since there is too much repetition of this one joke. One of the lamest refers to Didi's status as a star as "the biggest things since bathtub rings." This doesn't make very much sense as a joke for Hope. His banter with Diller is somewhat better as he wonders why his wife is not back from her beauty salon appointment:

TOM: What are they doing to my wife that takes so long? Teasing her follicles?

LILY: Beauty parlors! Yuk! I do my own. (She cups her hand on her frazzled hair.)

TOM: That's why we couldn't find the eggbeater.

The joke about women producing a hairdo as if it is a rat's nest appeared about fifty years ago, but the ever-returning styles that go out of fashion make this a valid gag.

There are shades of the silent screen slapstick comedy in *Boy, Did I Get a Wrong Number.* For example, Lily dashes on a motorcycle in what the silent age called "The Rush to the Rescue," as she warns Tom that his wife is coming to the cabin. Didi also takes sleeping pills and passes out. Tom and Lily try to hide her in a bed that folds into the wall only to have it pop open. They then attempt other places in and near the cabin. And when the police think Tom has murdered Didi by throwing her in the lake, they start procedures for dragging for her body. Tom steals a police car and a comedy chase develops with all the mishaps that do seem old hat.

It is possible that more examples of the exchanges between Tom and Lily prove that it is viewed as a better film today than originally thought in 1966.

Journal evaluators of Hope's films in the '60s found his comedies lacking in the quality that they claim the actor once had. Some of the public from the turn of the century (2000 to 2003) seem to want their humor broad, simplistic, and full of slapstick. Defenders of *Boy, Did I Get a Wrong Number* are young fans who probably find films by Jim Carrey, Dean Martin and Jerry Lewis, Abbott and Costello, Phyllis Diller, and perhaps the Three Stooges very funny. To these fans the broad humor of these comedians is very appealing. They might find sophisticated, romantic comedies too tame to be humorous. A person needs only to check the Internet Movie Database for user comments about *Boy, Did I Get a Wrong Number.* Four out of five reactions are favorable and might be considered naïve. The following excerpts are on the rhapsodic side: "This is the funniest movie I've ever seen"; "In my opinion, Bob Hope and Phyllis Diller were destined to work together"; and "If your family is a fan of Nick at Nite, then this movie should delight them." There are five pages of reactions with only one that is distinctively negative. However, these opinions show that there is an audience for such simple, robust comedy movies. It is, of course, a matter of taste.

Biographers Quirk and Marx do make their accounts of Hope's ego as influencing his decline in the '60s, but this concept seems to relate more to his choice of the women actresses. Occasionally, these biographers will show bad blood developing between male actors during the shooting of a picture, and they seem to think these relationships negatively influence the final quality of the movie.

This may be so in a few of Hope's works, but what about the more positive results? A sympathetic relationship, for example, existed with Crosby and Hope starting in some of their vaudeville acts in the early '30s that carried into seven Road Pictures. Obviously, they were compatible and took turns in the limelight.

Even when Hope encountered the aggressive Jackie Gleason in *How to Commit Marriage* (1969), if any rivalry of egos might have prevailed during the shooting of the film, it didn't appear in the quality of the two acting together. It became one of Hope's better pictures of the decade.

Occasionally, Bob may have strayed from fitting well into a movie cast and become disconnected from the cast when he played a cameo role. Actually, he used more cameo actors in the Road Pictures than he ever appeared in a cameo. Only five of his fifty-seven features can be classified as cameo appearances: *The Greatest Show on Earth* (1952), *Scared Stiff* (1953), *Showdown at Ulcer Gulch* (1956), *The Five Pennies* (1959), and the *Muppet Movie* (1979). Two examples of these cameos show there is understandable neglect of guest appearances.

Both Hope and Crosby appeared in the next-to-final scene of *Scared Stiff*, a remake of the *The Ghost Breakers* (1940), starring Hope and Goddard. The stars this time are Dean Martin and Jerry Lewis. The heads of Bing and Bob seem to be attached to skeletons in the haunted castle. This frightens Martin and Lewis and the comedy duo run away—an end gag that is not very significant by today's standards of humor, but such exchange of comedy team cameos were used in the '40s and '50s. Bob appears with the Muppets briefly as an ice cream vendor who serves Fozzie Bear an ice cream.

The most effective cameos were executed by Bing Crosby in some of Bob's films. At the end of *The Princess and the Pirate* (1944), Bing saunters in as a common sailor and takes the princess away from Bob. And a much darker comic bit is used in *My Favorite Brunette* (1947), which shows Crosby in a cameo as the executioner in a prison registering dismay when Hope is declared innocent and Bing doesn't get to execute him. The gag writers in the '40s were more skilled with this type of humor.

Hope's last feature film and starring role, in *Cancel My Reservation* (1972), has some of the domestic misalliance of *That Certain Feeling* (1956) and *Critic's Choice* (1962). In *That Certain Feeling*, for the first time Eva Marie Saint plays the part of Hope's wife, who becomes estranged because he cannot stand the pressure of his position as a cartoonist. His wife thinks he is weak and a coward. In *Cancel My*

Reservation, Saint has a reversal of roles as an assertive wife wanting to co-host Hope's television show, driving him away from her. *Critic's Choice* employs a playwriting wife who is married to a newspaper critic who insists that he must review her drama on the opening night's premiere. All three of the comedy films deal with a plot of a humorous estrangement of a husband and wife. In short, they are about a misalliance that gets resolved as all romantic comedies have since the Roman playwright Plautus and the English dramatist William Shakespeare created similar comedy conflicts.

Not every fan of Hope's films finds his last feature appearance a failure. Those who admired his work from the past tended to forgive a script that didn't help Bob, the comedian who had become an icon. I viewed *Cancel My Reservation* on television about ten years ago and found the work a mediocre Hope movie. Revisited in 2004 and a viewing of other '60s motion pictures of the comedian's last eleven works showed that it may all be relative. It is understandable that anyone who remained a fan of his comedies would find some facets of the work enjoyable. Nevertheless, critical, journalistic reviews were not favorable:

> "Cancel My Reservation" is adventure comedy—or, more accurately, murder comedy, in which, Bob Hope, as a big-time Eastern TV personality, has to prove his innocence to a small-town Arizona sheriff (Keenan Wynn) and at the same time patch up his marriage (to Eva Marie Saint) and solve the mystery so as to save his own life. It is an extremely busy movie, with more action than insight, and a method of exposition that seems to consist mainly of voice-over wisecracks.[14]

While there is a tendency to blame Hope for this last, 1972 movie that shows a decline in the quality of his films, some of the diminishing effectiveness comes from the writers of the script, Bob Fischer and Arthur Marx. The voice-over narration includes gags that do not give Hope as a TV celebrity enough jokes to sustain such an accounting of events that take place to put the protagonist in jail.

The initial point of the writer's dramatic, inciting incident presents a scene of the local sheriff and his deputy racing in their car to put Hope (as Dan Bartlett) in jail for the murder of a Native American woman from the reservation. In confinement, Dan narrates via voice-over to explain how he came to Arizona. In part, he needs a vacation from the stressful existence in New York as a TV comedian with marital problems.

Two examples show the rather affected, self-conscious humor of the screenwriters:

> DAN: The fellow who said people need people obviously was never stuck in the Long Island Parkway in rush hour. (Shots of a long line of cars with some trying to switch lanes plus the honking of horns) [It was] the mating season for barracudas.
>
> SHEILA: (Turning to dialogue in the car) Why do we have to use the Parkway?
>
> DAN: It's cheaper than getting shock therapy.

Dan finds the body of a Native American woman in his room in an Arizona resort. A return to voice-over narration follows:

> DAN: (In a tone burlesquing the private eye TV series.) With a bullet hole in the back, the blood, and the fact that she wasn't breathing, I assumed she was dead.

These examples of the gags Hope uses in *Cancel My Reservation* seem to be influenced by the flood of situation comedies in the early '70s. While they may be considered acceptable for the small box screen, they are not up to the quality of the dialogue used in many of Hope's features in the '60s.

Evaluator Roger Greenspun, for the *New York Times*, concentrates on a type of plot that Hope's writers used for the comic murder mystery and spy humorous thrillers of the '40s. Even with topical updates on the rights of Native Americans, women's liberation, and the sexual revolution, scripters Marx and Fisher are not as innovative and fresh as previous writers for Hope had been. Jay Cocks, film reviewer for *Time*, also mentions the attempt to use topical references as jokes. This critic ridicules the protest of women destroying their bras during the women's liberation movement. Trapped in a cave Hope fashions a bow by a stick and Eva Maria's leopard-skin brassiere to send a message for someone to rescue them. Eva Maria remarks, "I'm certainly glad I didn't burn my bra."[15] Evaluator Cocks thinks this is very cheap humor that belongs on "sniggering sitcom stuff."[16]

Nathan Rabin, on the Internet, presents a more positive note when he used a heading "Films that Time Forgot" that fits the theme of this discussion and does more than say, "view it." With an exclamation mark he declares: "Buy it!" This critic finds the intrigue effective with Hope entangled in "a series of comically compromising positions."[17]

It should be noted that Greenspun and Cocks are 1972 contemporary examinations, while Rabin's evaluation is retrospective and written June 6, 2001. Much of the late work of Hope in films does need a revisionist perspective.

Part of the reason two variety motion pictures, *Rhythm Romance* and *Variety Girl*, remain obscure is certainly tied into the taste of music and humor changing throughout the years—in fact, decades. How many people have a fondness for the big band era jazz beat of the drummer Gene Krupa? Or the romantic melody, "The Lady's in Love?" Some people, even the youth obsessed with the latest musical mode, find something different from the past that has unusual dimensions. Of course, seniors occasionally have the nostalgia to purchase a video with the stars Hope and Ross in *Rhythm Romance* (or *Some Like it Hot*, the original 1939 title)—and naturally, the music of yesteryear. The same can be said for *Variety Girl*. There are so many of the Paramount stars in the picture and the roles of Bob Hope and Bing Crosby have an important function for the variety show format. The success of the re-release of VHS and DVD versions of the more prominent Hope movies mean that much of these neglected and underrated works will be available. More standard motion pictures like the 1938 *Thanks for the Memory*, the 1941 *Nothing but the Truth*, and the 1956 *The Iron Petticoat* are more obscure; however, the trend to release more Hope movies does not seem to wane—as long as audiences find something new about something old in their life.

The impetus to explore the total range of Bob Hope's films started when the comedian reached the age of 100 and accelerated with his death the same year, 2003. This study has shown that 1960s works such as *The Facts of Life*, *Road to Hong Kong*, *I'll Take Sweden*, and *How to Commit Marriage* stimulated more interest in the movie contributions by the comedian. This reminds me of a movement in the '60s to explore the contributions of the comedians of the silent age of comedy cinema. An audience evolved who found a new experience in viewing the masters of this neglected mode of cinema with the television showings of the feature films of Charles Chaplin, Harold Lloyd, Buster Keaton, and many other comedians of the teens and '20s. It may be that other comedians besides Bob Hope will be recognized for their contributions to twentieth century comedy films.

7 The Rocky Road to Exotic Worlds

Fans of the Road Pictures of Hope and Crosby enjoy the unusual humor and a film series full of carefree nonsense. Or should the billing be Crosby and Hope, like most other duos of this sort, with straight man first, then comedian? There is also no doubt that such an entertaining conglomeration of in-jokes, farce, song and dance, fantasy, exotic worlds, and buddy comic banter evolved from the provinces of vaudeville and humorous radio programs of the recent past. These influences would reemerge in the birth and continuation of television.

The strange format of the Road Pictures became very popular in the '40s. Hence, seven movies developed in the series: (1) *Road to Singapore* (1940), (2) *Road to Zanzibar* (1941), (3) *Road to Morocco* (1942), (4) *Road to Utopia* (1946), (5) *Road to Rio* (1947), (6) *Road to Bali* (1953), and (7) *Road to Hong Kong* (1963).[1] As is evidenced here, the first five pictures in the series were created in the '40s, and the last two were created almost as if they were afterthoughts. It should be realized that both Bob Hope and Bing Crosby handled many other assignments for Paramount during the entire span of the Road Pictures years.

The initial dip into the buddy world of two people on a journey, *Road to Singapore*, was slated for George Burns and Gracie Allen or Fred MacMurray and Jack Oakie.[2] But the idea didn't appeal to Burns or MacMurray. Eventually, Paramount producer Harlan Thompson detected promise in the talents of good friends Bob Hope and Bing Crosby for the roles in this type of movie. Screenwriters Don Hartman and Frank Butler designed a tight story for two men who didn't care a hoot about their futures. Hope (as Ace Lannigan) and Crosby (as Josh Mallon) both escape from the confines of forced or prearranged marriages.

Ace's relatives in the United States demand that he marry a woman he had been dating; and Josh's father insists that his son take over the family business and marry. The writers developed a running gag to get the bonding buddies out of difficult predicaments: The two men face each other and start playing patty-cake. Their foes are confused about grown adults engaged in a child's game. They are then astonished when the patty cake climaxes with Ace and Josh throwing punches to the unsuspecting foe's jaw in the middle of the horseplay. In order to get away from their adversaries, this running gag is used by the duo four times in this Road Picture and occasionally in the sequels.

To provide romantic rivalry between the comrades, Dorothy Lamour is added to the mix in *Road to Singapore*. Besides her beauty, Lamour brings song and dance to the work. While she is not effective as a comedienne, Dorothy, as Mima, a native of Kaigoon, elicits humor by ordering the men to do various tasks in their rented house, a native dwelling. While they flee from women in their homeland, they become captive in Singapore. Therefore, the basic formula for the Road Pictures germinated into full bloom even in the first movie: (1) Escape from the homeland to an exotic world. (2) Adversaries emerge, even in the duo's world of presumed refuge. (3) Conflict develops between the buddies for ego dominance and rivalry for the affections of a woman. (4) A climactic fight, chase, or simple escape ensues. (5) One of the men gets the woman. Of course, slight variations develop.[3] In *Road to Singapore*, the buddies each experience an escape from the same woman only to experience trouble in paradise.

Hope did capture the affections of the woman in his pairing with Martha Raye in his late '30s films. The women in the road series would change his character's fortune for good or ill—generally the results were negative for Bob. The female (Raye) and male (Hope) comics in these '30s films would embrace at the fade-out for *Give Me a Sailor* and *Never Say Die*. In the Road Pictures, Bob becomes the fall guy for Bing and often is shut out when the crooner walks off with Dorothy Lamour, or even two women in *The Road to Bali* (1952). In the fourth of seven Road Pictures, *Road to Utopia* (1946), Hope marries Lamour, a variation on the formula.

In the second pairing of Bob and Bing, *Road to Zanzibar*, the conflict between the buddies increases because Bing's character becomes a full-blown con man. As carnival "connivers," Bing gets Hope to perform dangerous stunts: acting as the human cannon ball, sitting in an electric chair with a supposed lethal charge going through his body, and struggling with an octopus and later, a gorilla. The initial scene shows Bob as Hubert "Fearless" Frazier supposedly being shot from a cannon. He crawls out from under the cannon just as a dummy substitute for Hubert accidentally catches fire and flies overhead into a tent. When the dummy substitute for "Fearless" crashes into a circus tent, it burns down and the pair must flee from the law for this mishap.

In Road to Singapore (1940), Hope and Crosby are poised for
the running gag of patty cake to distract the enemy.
The gag moved from picture to picture.

From the collection of Donald McCaffrey

The escape of Hubert and his pal, Chuck (Crosby), eventually leads to their safari across Africa and on to Zanzibar. During the trek they are joined by two women, Donna and Julia, played by Dorothy Lamour and Una Merkel. A battle of the sexes ensues as the men vie for Donna's attention, a plot device used in most of the seven Road Pictures. To complicate this essentially farcical design, the women manipulate the men to further their own objectives. Consequently, this creates comedy by having the two females as superior con artists, almost surpassing the "master of deception" Chuck Reardon. Such elaborate complication seems to delight fans and some critics who admire the convoluted lampoon of "cult classics". Not all are equally amused, however; for example, Internet All Movie Guide evaluator Hal Erickson complains: "Like the earlier *Road to Singapore*, *Road to Zanzibar* sticks too closely to the script and plot to allow these inveterate ad-libbers Hope and Crosby free rein."[4]

Herein lies the lack of background for those who imagine the best lines of the comedians were ad-libbed. A good actor-comedian handily delivers jokes as if they were spontaneous. Vaudeville and radio had writers make the wisecracks appear to flow out of the mind of the comic, as if gifts from the gods. Screenwriters Frank Butler and Don Hartman are to be commended for offering an intriguing series of scenes and sequences that hold up and appeal to even present-day audiences. As the Road Pictures progress from one sequel to another, the writing quality begins to fade to a degree or perhaps the novelty wore off. Furthermore, wisecracks do not a comedy-drama make. Humor more often exists in innovative complication and when laughable moments spring from the characters, the actions, and emotions of the comedian and clown.

If you want a verbal gag, *Road to Zanzibar* employs one with Hubert in the carnival act of sawing a woman in half to gain money for the foursome's boat passage. Chuck asks him if he knows how to do it. Hubert says, "If I don't one of us will go back half fare."

But when the hapless voyagers get captured by cannibals, basic humor evolves when Hubert has to fight a gorilla, and when the pair executes the running gag of patty cake and socks two natives during their escape. The writers have an innovative bit that shows the cannibals entering the game by patty-caking and delightfully hitting one another. It is basic slapstick humor, but it sells with the audience. Screenwriters Don Hartman and Frank Butler certainly were instrumental in creating the basics for what most critics call the best of the Road Pictures, *Road to Morocco*. This film has a perfect blend of intrigue, and the gags hold sway. The buddies, Bob and Bing, as

Bing is puzzled when Dorothy Lamour seems to prefer Bob in
the third Road Picture, *Road to Morocco* (1942).

From the collection of Donald McCaffrey

Turkey and Jeff, become shipwrecked off the coast of Africa. Needing
money, Jeff, ever the manipulator, sells Turkey into slavery. Later,
Jeff finds his pal has been employed by the Moroccan Princess
Shalimar, (Dorothy Lamour), who needs to marry Turkey. She has
learned by prophecy that her first husband will die and she can then
go on to procure another husband. Complications develop when she
falls in love with Jeff. Eventually, the pair counters the efforts of a
villainous sheik Kasim, played by Anthony Quinn, who has an ar-
rangement to marry the princess. While this development seems
rather melodramatic, the situations are exaggerated to achieve a
humorous, almost silly tone.

What may seem silly to some viewers today is the deluge of presentational, facing-the-camera-head-on, delivered jokes. That is,
comments often are referential—commenting on the situation
unfolding in the comic drama. For example, when Hope and Bob
ride a camel and sing, "We're off on the Road to Morocco," they are
mugging toward the audience by looking into the camera lens. The
first portion of the lyrics even has a comment on the plot:

We're off on the road to Morocco / This taxi is tough on the spine
Where we're goin' / Why we're goin'

How can we be sure / I'll lay you eight to five
That we meet Dorothy Lamour / Off on the road to Morocco
I hear this country's were they / Hang on 'til the end of the line
I hear this country's where they / Do the Dance of the Seven Veils
We'd tell you more but we would / Have the censor on our tails.[5]

When there is an apparent disconnect regarding how easily the pair escaped from a net, Turkey wonders, "How did we get loose?" Jeff looks toward the audience, "Don't tell 'em." When they try to use the favorite patty cake routine to escape, before they can throw a punch, the villain Kassim knocks their heads together and throws them down. Turkey remarks, "That gets around," a referential remark alluding to previous pictures as if to say Quinn saw them do it in another picture.

Even camels talk in *Road to Morocco*. "This is the screwiest picture I've been in," mouths one camel. Later, when people are fighting and chasing each other, a camel disparages humans, "Glad I'm a camel." Another, apparently male, camel delivers the joke, "I'm glad you're a camel too, Mabel." Much of the fighting and chasing has the spirit of play as Jeff and Turkey thwart the Moroccans by giving them a hotfoot or jumping around and hiding as if it all becomes a child's game.

In the final scene both men and the two women companions are on a raft in New York harbor after another shipwreck. Out of the blue, Hope expresses his agony in wild despair. Jeff points out that they are now safe. Turkey objects to being interrupted and stops emoting. "You had to open your big mouth. I might have won an Academy Award."

In cold print such goings-on might appear as errant nonsense. Nevertheless, the performances in this picture, as guided by director David Butler, are nearly impeccable. Bing Crosby remains suave and conniving, underplaying the man who would sell his friend into slavery. Hope's character protests his treatment by just about everyone in the picture. Again, just slightly overstated with comic perspiration. It probably is the pair's best performance, each complementing the other's comedic style.

Appearing on screen just after the end of World War II, the 1946 *Road to Utopia* is sometimes considered superior to *Road to Morocco* by some fans of the Road Pictures. It might be considered second to *Morocco*—arguably, of course—it depends on your taste.

The fourth of the Road creations, *Road to Utopia* (1946), has more topical and reflective jokes; it might be considered too much a product of the times. There could be more to enjoy for the senior citizen raised on the early '40s pictures. And, there is one line in the film that tells what this land of utopia is. It refers to striking it rich by discovering gold in Alaska. That, supposedly, gives a person utopia.[6]

Until a recent viewing of *Utopia*, I remembered this movie for one incident that I thought was one of the duo's best gags. It is tied to the character of Bob Hope as Chester Hooton, a bit of a sissy in a land of He-Men. The pair of buddies enter a saloon in Alaska, and they order drinks. Bing, as Duke Johnson, says, "Give me two fingers of rotgut." Asked what he will have, Chester gives a surprising request, "Lemonade." Met with disapproving stares he adds with a lower, rough voice, "In a dirty glass." Hope's timing and inflection produce a solid laugh.

A referential gag produces a camera look from Chester when he gets to kiss Dorothy Lamour. She portrays singer Sal Van Hoyden, who is really an heiress looking for the map that will lead to a gold mine. After a satisfying kiss, Sal looks at the camera, at the same time looking at the audience, and says, "The picture can end now."

Hope tries to cover his mistake of ordering a glass of lemonade in the tough Alaskan bar in *Road to Utopia* (1946).

From the collection of Donald McCaffrey

To complicate the plot with other reflective jokes in the picture, Robert Benchley serves as narrator. He appears occasionally to comment on what is happening. In the '40s, Benchley was a noted humorist in both print and the screen. He appeared in a series of short films and also a few features. His shorts often show him giving wry lectures that misfire when they are meant to inform.[7] Only a few of his inserts in *Road to Utopia* seem to add to the movie. When the saloon chorus girls do a variation on the can-can, a small insert of Benchley, looking toward the movie audience, appears in the upper left of the screen. In a half-leer he tells the audience that now the movie is getting somewhere.

In one of the many plot diversions, Chester and Duke are being drawn along in a dogsled. They see Santa Claus and his sleigh in the woods. The Jolly Old Fellow asks them if they want something. "We are not children," they reply. Santa rides off and it is revealed that he has two beautiful girls among his gifts. Painfully, the buddies wail at what they have missed and act like very young children. While this is not very funny, it is tangential to the movie. Fans of the period, and even today, like this sort of nonsense.

Like the talking camels in *Road to Morocco*, there is a talking fish and bear. The bear complains that they let a fish talk, but not him: "To me they won't give one stinking line." It is not clear how such humor got into the script, but it is possible that some gag writer (or writers) who created film shorts in the '40s with animated talking animals was hired for what was considered a novelty in this decade. Screenwriters Don Hartman and Frank Butler didn't give their talents to this work.

Whoever did the in-jokes for *Road to Utopia* did manufacture one that resonated. As Bob and Bing ride along on a dog sled, they see a mountain that looks just like the opening studio logo. Sure enough, the stars appear over the mountain and the word: "PARAMOUNT" appears. Hope observes, "Looks like bread and butter to me."

The most innovative song develops as the comrades sing "Put It There, Pal" in a friendly, rollicking tune with a handshake. As a counterpoint to the lyrics, insults are exchanged in pleasant but mocking tones of "pal." Such is the private war of insults that came from vaudeville to radio; a staple for all comedians at the height of the verbal airwave period.

The plot, despite the many diversions, does hold the picture together. Two villains chase buddies Chester and Duke to force them

In the final scene of *Road to Utopia*, Hope's character marries Dorothy and they grow old together. Bing appears in the final reel.

From the collection of Donald McCaffrey

to give up the gold mine map. And two women, Sal and Kate, want the map as well. In the resolution of the film, Duke (Bing) does not get the woman. This is a switch from the prize usually being awarded to the slick member of the buddies. However, Chester gets the woman, Sal, and they are married. Years later when they are older, they receive a visit from an elderly Duke with two young women on his arms. Duke then meets their son, who is a dead ringer for the young Duke (Bing Crosby). While this may seem to be a bit risqué for the time, Hope gives the camera a look and explains, with tongue-in-check: "We adopted him."

One year later, *Road to Rio* (1947) appeared as the fifth of the seven Road works. Screenwriters Edmund Beloin and Jack Rose incorporated some elements of the formula used in the series. Bob and Bing earn their living by bilking others as entertainers; Bing dominates Bob and uses him as the fall guy; they get in trouble with the law and need to escape; they meet a woman they both wish to court or seduce; they find themselves the possible victims of villains. Even so, the formula seems more like the Bob Hope non-road movies of the '40s, when he is chased by criminals or spies. The screenwriters and director, Norman Z. McLeod, employ a tone and mode that reflects such previous Hope pictures. Much of it is in the character and actions of the villains. Gale Sondergaard plays Lucia's (Dorothy Lamour) conniving aunt. Aunt Catherine works her skills as a hypnotist to force Lucia to marry a man she doesn't desire.

And Aunt Catherine employs two henchmen to ward off the comrades, who are also trying to prevent the marriage. Naturally, Hot Lips (Hope) and Scat (Crosby) manage to outwit the thugs. As a variation on the patty cake routines of previous pictures, Hope and Bing merely sock the villains and run. In another variation, the pair teaches the thugs their patty cake routine, and they delight in the child's game and sock each other unconscious. Hope tells the audience, "That's what they get for not seeing our pictures."

There are not as many referential gags in *Road to Rio*; and, to an extent, this is a blessing. Why? The action and intrigue produce a shock-treatment effect for the audience, and today's viewers might not be receptive to some of these aside remarks. Hope starred in two 1942 movies, *My Favorite Blonde* and *They Got Me Covered* that had a more straight-forward intrigue development that might be an easier plot to follow and could be a plot to involve the audience. Additionally, these two films used spy and crime plots.

How does *Road to Rio* rank with all seven? Most critics find it a minor work, but it does have entertainment value. The last part of the film has Bob and Bing forming a band to provide passage on a ship where they have been stowaways. Ever the con men, they enlist a trio of entertainers, the Wiere Brothers, who only speak Portuguese, trying to pass them off as an American band with Hot Lips and Scat as the other two members of the group. The three are taught a few stock English phrases, like "You're telling me," "This is murder," and "You're in the groove, Jackson." These idioms of musicians and the young set of the '30s and '40s therefore get sprinkled incorrectly into their conversation.[8]

Eventually, Lucia is rescued and, as in *Road to Utopia*, Hope "gets the girl." In the fade-out scene, Scat looks through the key-hole to the couple's room and witnesses Hot Lips using hypnosis on *her*. He may have learned this from the hypnotic skills of the villainess aunt, and this may have been the way he charmed his wife originally.

The 1952 *Road to Bali* proved to be an improvement over *Road to Rio*, even if writers Frank Butler, Hal Kanter, and William Morrow go back to many earlier in-jokes and employ a man in a gorilla suit for wild slapstick laughs. Odd as it may seem, this sixth Road Picture is the only one filmed in color. It helps, since *Bali* has striking native dress, an exotic environment, a production number with quasi-ballet, and a variation on Balinese ritual dances.

As in many Road Pictures, Hope as Harold and Crosby as George make their living as entertainers, this time in Australia. Similar to

As entertainers, Bing and Bob perform a Scottish song
and dance in *Road to Bali* (1952).

From the collection of Donald McCaffrey

the duo's 1940 *Road to Singapore*, they must escape to a foreign land to avoid marriage. Also as in previous films, they need to find the right woman, and of course, it is Dorothy Lamour, this time as the Balinese Princess Lalah.

Naturally, there are villains who are out to dispatch Harold and George. A conniving prince hires the pair for a deep-sea diving expedition for treasure. George tricks Harold into believing he will be a hero if he embarks on the dangerous search for a cask of valuable jewelry; but his prize for the dive is Princess Lalah, who warns him of the giant squid that attacks divers. By some miracle, Harold escapes from the tentacles of the creature. As a poke at the illogical or missing plot element in the Road Pictures, the pair often reflects on how they have freed themselves from confinement or even death. In a fantastic turn of the plot, a gorilla, who has lost her mate, embraces Harold, and as he escapes her hairy clutches, they are captured by natives. The two men and the gorilla receive a tranquilizing blow with tube darts.

Hal Kanter said he was praised by head screenwriter Frank Butler: "He read the pages I had already done, told me that my sight gag—Bing and Bob escaping a gorilla, dive into opposite ends of a hollow log and emerge from it on opposite ends—was one of the best he ever read."[9] This chase scene did not appear in the film, however, as can be witnessed on the DVD of *Road to Bali*. Kanter reported that Crosby read the script and said, "Funny, but a little chase-y, no?" So, he and a fellow writer took some of the "chase" out of the script.[10]

One innovation by the team of writers, Butler, Kanter, and Morrow, involved a variation of the patty cake routine, which doesn't work in this picture either. The natives seem to have seen other pictures in the series, so they duck and the Hope and Crosby duo knock each other out.

A volcano on the tropical island brings the picture to a climax. Flaming portions of the set begin to collapse with the eruption. In the chaos of the fire that consumes the native huts, Harold tries to be the hero by rushing in to save Princess Lalah. In one of the standard role-reversal jokes, the princess carries him from the burning hut and dumps him on the ground.

In the last scene of *Bali*, Princess Lalah chooses George. Harold, wanting to get a girl from the magical basket that produces sexy women instead of cobras, plays the Indian flute. Wiggling up from the basket is Jane Russell in one of the more provocative costumes she might wear in a musical. With a tight-fitting body suit and a wide brim hat, it is very similar to the sexy attire she wore in

Con man Crosby has Hope demonstrate a personal flying
machine in *Road to Hong Kong* (1962).

From the collection of Donald McCaffrey

The Son of Paleface (1952). Russell wears this same type of sexy
costume as she sings a new version of "Button and Bows," rescued
from *The Paleface* (1948). Jane chooses Crosby and the women
walk off, arm in arm, with the con man of them all. Hope protests,
"Hey, wait. What are you going to do with two women?" With a
suave, cool, double-meaning, Crosby says, "That's my problem."
Bob calls for members of the studio audience and his agent to help
him get a woman. He tries to push the animated "THE END" designation on the screen out of the shot as the scene fades. As intriguing as this burlesque of a South Sea island picture is, it is a potpourri.
Evaluator Lawrence Quirk writes:

> *Bali*'s script was a mélange of all other elements of previous Road
> pictures. Bob and Bing are again cheap vaudeville entertainers; again

they run away when two girls want to marry them; again they run into Lamour on a South Sea island where she's seeking treasure, this time in an ocean. This was used as the framework for the usual quota of funny, and barely funny gags. *Bali* depended on guest star cameos more than other Road films (except for the subsequent *Road to Hong Kong*). (*Bob Hope: The Road Well-Traveled*, p. 121)

Quirk continues by mentioning Jane Russell and an inserted scene showing the role for which Humphrey Bogart received an Oscar in *African Queen*. "Bogey," as he was called, pulls his boat through a weed-clogged water passageway with a rope. It is a strange intrusion in the movie that has some of the type of in-jokes used by the French new wave in the '50s and '60s.[11]

As previously mentioned, a plus in the picture were production numbers such as the ballet variation of Balinese ritual dances, and the use of Technicolor helps to position *Road to Bali* for a critically superior rating. It is certainly a handsomely mounted Road Picture production; there are numerous elaborately staged song and dance sequences.

Critics and fans of a popular series often see some fading on the quality of an idea that has worn thin. In some respects, this does happen with most sequels. The last of the Road Pictures, *Road to Hong Kong* (1962), previously had been labeled as hackneyed and uninspired. I was amazed that the work holds up as well as most comedies of the period. Part of the problem is one of taste and a re-alization of what was popular in the early '60s. Spy melodramas were the rage. Sean Connery as James Bond appeared in *Dr. No* the same year as *Road to Hong Kong*. This was one of the many spy movies and novels that found a ready, eager audience. Furthermore, people were fascinated by the possibility of space travel as far back as the birth of movies. The wonderment increased when astronaut Alan Shepherd took the first American flight into space in 1961, a year before the movie was released. Thus, *Hong Kong* ended up as a spy-space travel spoof, a variation for this last of the Road Pictures.

The characters written for Hope and Crosby, however, still ad-hered to the Road formula. The eternal con man role of Harry went to Bing, the weak bungler part of Chester was assigned to Bob. Another throwback to earlier plots is the pair's itinerant vaudeville gig that starts the movie, but in this work the routine is just before the open-ing titles. They try a confidence game that gets them in trouble with an audience. Flim flam man Harry wants Chester to dress in a space suit with a motorized propeller on his rear-end to demonstrate to a crowd that they can own a personal flying machine. Chester crashes and ends up in the hospital. The scene with Harry urging his supposed pal to handle the flight has some of the best Bing and Hope buddy banter with the character of Chester finally giving in. Harry explains to Chester he is the brain and his bilked pal is the brawn. In the hospital the argument continues as Chester complains about how Harry treats him. He notes in a put-down how Harry is attired in an overly crazy quilt suit coat. Looking into the mirror at his injuries, Chester moans, "Give me a stick. I'll kill it." *Hong Kong* illustrates how the rapid-fire banter of the buddies continues with much of their old skill, even if each, especially Bing, appears to be aging in this last Road Picture.

Sexual double entendres are sharper and more risqué with the entrance of a young Joan Collins. This might indicate that someone in casting thought Dorothy Lamour might be looking as old as Crosby; so Dorothy, who maintained the lead female role in the previous six pictures, gave way to Joan. However, Lamour has a cameo and a decent duet with Bob, "Warmer than a Whisper." Lamour's autobiography indicates that being given a mere cameo angered her.[12]

The spy-spoof aspect of the complex plot develops when Chester goes to Tibet in order to regain his memory, which he lost from the crash of his personal flying-suit. The information that a cure can be found in Tibet comes from an oddball Indian physician enacted by Peter Sellers. Four years later the British comedian would portray another, even wackier doctor in a cameo for the 1966 *The Wrong Box*.

Cured by a potion from the Grand Lama during his visit to Tibet, Chester becomes something akin to an idiot savant. A formula for a powerful rocket fuel becomes stuck in his brain. Sinister spies out to conquer the world, played by British actors Robert Morley and Walter Gotell, get hold of Chester and Harry and test space travel by using the duo instead of apes for the flight. Why? It seems better than losing the apes on such a dangerous mission. Because they are surrogates, the pals get locked in a feeding machine and are fed bananas and milk. Restrained, bananas are shoved into their mouths and milk is squirted on their faces. In an ineffective attempt to wipe the mess off their faces, a roller sponge comes down after each feeding to cause more agony. The writers, it would appear, tried to use the famous "factory feeding" machine so brilliantly employed by Charles Chaplin in his 1936 *Modern Times*. In what comes close to a satire on industry's attempt to keep workers on the assembly line during lunch, Chaplin's use of this elaborate gag has some depth and inspiration. In *Hong Kong*, it is merely a joke and not satirical in context.

Eventually, Chester and Harry escape the spies. A chase develops under Morley's leadership because he plans to destroy the world and travel to another planet with the new rocket fuel. Innovations on the standard climactic pursuit only become different from a reference to the motion picture medium. Almost caught by the spies, Harry looks into the air and calls for special effects. With a stop camera effect, suddenly Harry, Chester, and Joan Collins as Diane appear in Hong Kong Chinese garb. Dorothy Lamour appears as herself as a singer in a play. This referential exchange produces a gag:

DOROTHY: I'd better hide you.

CHESTER: From the crooks?

DOROTHY: (With an expressionless lack of inflection) From the critics.

Of course, it is one of her best lines in her diminutive role. Fortunately, Lamour displays one of her noted talents: she sings one of the few solos in the movie, plus a duet with Hope.

A fight with the spies becomes an added element to the climactic sequence as the trio, Chester, Diane, and Harry, carry the fight to the rocket ship. Launched into space, the two men and woman land on a planet where they are marooned forever. Harry and Chester decide to share Diane, each having her three days a week. The question comes up: "What do we do on Sunday?" Chester says dryly, "Everybody rests."

Road to Hong Kong thereby produces the raciest gag of the whole series, reflecting the changing mores and humor ushered in during the '60s. It became easier to get such sexual allusions in a picture because the censorship code had been loosened much earlier in the '50s.

Hong Kong has more guest cameos than any of the Road Pictures. Lamour and Sellers appear on screen longer than other cameos. What is referred to as "the Italian invasion" features the abrupt entrance of Dean Martin and Frank Sinatra, who immediately grab Diane. They are dressed as astronauts from the planet Plutonlum and become the victims of a cry from Harry for special effects as

Martin and Sinatra are suddenly whisked up into space. David Niven, in the briefest cameo, is in a ten-second shot as a monk in Tibet. Jerry Colonna gets a literal walk on and off. Although not clearly identified, most of the people who appeared in cameos had become so prominent and famous they could be readily recognized at the time the film was released.[13]

The evaluation of *Road to Hong Kong* requires extra consideration because the film is one of the most complicated in the series. It even has an Internet critic, Richard Scheib, who declares it has the highest quality of the road movies. With the qualifier "arguably," he wrote: "Despite it being a decade before they had made their previous *Road* movie, *Hong Kong* is arguably the best of the series." He supports his "best" rating citing Peter Sellers, calling his cameo a "hilarious, mercilessly paced sequence." Also, he likes the abundance of "meta-fictional" gags. (To be found in "external evaluations" linked to the movie *Road to Hong Kong* entry from the Internet Movie Database.)

If others might give the picture a higher rating for this use of strange transitions and metamorphoses, you would almost think the writers Norman Panama and Melvin Frank were influenced by *Alice in Wonderland* or *The Wizard of Oz*. I will explain it this way: this Road Picture was a precursor to the *Monty Python* television series and movies. Put another way, the Road Picture has become a separate genre of comedy. It is the thinking person's Abbott and Costello or Martin and Lewis.

How are the Road Pictures similar to the *Monty Python* film creations? *Road to Hong Kong* possesses almost all the characteristics of the British movies without some of the dry, obtuse humor of the English comedians. For example, the use of nonsequiturs in *Monty Python* sketches on television and in features are characteristic of *Hong Kong*. It is announced: "And now for something completely different."[14] Of course, it is the same thing. Irony exists as a staple of the Road Pictures' comedy. "How did we get out of this situation?" This question not only exists as an "it does not follow" joke, it also works as a referential gag in the movie medium. *Monty Python* is filled with self-referential comments on the skits when something in the performance might seem like a lame excuse for comedy. For example, a monstrous weight comes crashing down to wipe out the routine. In prison, Bing wonders if people would arrive at the movie theater in the middle of *Road to Morocco* and laments, "They missed my song."

Road to Bali even borrows from a Marx Brothers movie, a sort of double referential jest: In *Horsefeathers* (1932) Groucho looks at the camera and says, "Listen, I have to stay here, but why don't you folks go out to the lobby for a smoke until this thing blows over?" As Leonard Maltin writes, "Hope turned to the audience and commented, 'He's going to sing, folks. Now's the time to go and get your popcorn.'" Twenty years later a similar humorous line is delivered using the Groucho device in *Road to Bali.*[15] In-jokes abound in both the British and American creations.

Fantasy punctuates the live sketches of *Monty Python*, especially with animation conceived by Terry Gilliam: a naked woman's arms fall off, or a naked woman flies in the air; a pompous man in nineteenth century attire has a lecture of complete nonsense and is exterminated by a huge foot crushing him. Some of this type of whimsy is injected in the Road Pictures as visions. Dorothy Lamour materializes out of the sand in *Road to Morocco* and joins Bob and Bing in a song, "Moonlight Becomes You." *Road to Utopia*, as described earlier, shows Bob and Bing traveling in a dog sled with a mountain in the background. A transformation develops to reveal the Paramount studio logo, a mountain with a crescent of stars. Of course, the last of the series, *Road to Hong Kong*, has the final scene on a planet called Plutonlum, where a special-effect-on-command pulls people into the sky.

Many of the jokes created in *Monty Python* and the Road Pictures are politically incorrect—especially sexual allusions. The British television series deals with sex using more specifics and odd variations on sexuality: A man dressed as a woman in a sketch seduces an official inspector who comes into "her" house. Many scenes in the American road series have comic seductions by the character Dorothy Lamour portrays but are essentially discreet. Bob Hope plays a character who loves the female attention but is usually being duped by the female. Hope's wolf barks and tiger growls in his encounters with women do have some lustful connotations. Bing and Bob wake up thinking they are holding hands with Dorothy in *Road to Bali*. Instead they find they are holding each other's hand. It happens to be a gag used by Harold Lloyd in *Grandma's Boy* and goes way back to the silent comedy, in this case 1922, and probably was a comic bit from even earlier, in vaudeville. The pair gets angry at each other as if they have performed an indiscretion of homosexual proportions. But an act of even greater disgust for the men occurs in *Road to Morocco* when the comrades try to kiss a vision of Dorothy

Lamour. As the vision pops out of sight, they end up kissing each other on the lips. Actually, such jokes seldom are used throughout the series, though its predecessor, the *Monty Python* television series, has many homosexual jokes. For example, one of the few songs by the actors features a comic inversion using a rousing song that seems to be the macho nature possessed by the Canadian Mounted Police. Instead, the lyrics reveal male homosexuality, a switch from a presumably masculine occupation.

One final inversion of values develops by tasteless sequences in both television and feature films of the *Python* group: poking fun at a group of mentally deficient men trying to play soccer. It obviously was intended to be dark or black comedy. Among American comedians, Jerry Lewis seems to use this type of humor by depicting a moron. Hope may play a bumpkin and a not very bright character—but never a mentally disabled person.

The roles played by Hope and Crosby in the Road Pictures do have a warmth that makes them appealing. Both enact their roles with enthusiasm. It could be said there is little variation in their personalities from movie to movie, and that they handle the same personas. Bob Hope has more comic variation of character in his other features than in the Road Pictures. Bing Crosby plays a suave, straight-man character to Hope's duped comic role that does not change from film to film. The two actors, however, displayed considerable range in other films. Crosby did play serious roles in *Little Boy Lost* (1953), *The Country Girl* (1954), and the 1966 version of *Stagecoach.* Bob Hope also appeared in serious parts with *The Seven Little Foys* (1955) and *Beau James* (1957).

Some critics are in error, however, when they argue that the Road Pictures lack design. Because a big ladle of fantasy and referential jokes intrude in a way that appears to be a potpourri without a plot, an unnamed reviewer of *Road to Rio* in the *New York Times* wrote:

> If this synopsis sounds sketchy, it's only because the story doesn't matter anyway. For the script merely serves as a means for getting a pair of impecunious musicians driven out of one state after another by irate husbands and boy friends until they are cornered, forced to stowaway on a Rio bound steamer and meet up with a beautiful senorita and her problems. All that matters really, is that "Road to Rio" is fairly well loaded with laughs. (February 19, 1948)

While Bosley Crowther, the critic that reviewed most of the Road Pictures, became accustomed to the formulaic approach employed by the writers, directors, and actors, he couldn't quite realize the design. If the works in the series became too plot-oriented, as many of Hope's other films were, there would be little attention to the many diversions. How else could the in-jokes on the media, the fantasy, the running gags (from series episodes to the next picture), and buddy banter be realized by the creators? In fact, Crowther lauded the strange diversions in *Son of Paleface* (1952) the sequel to *The Paleface* (1949). This *New York Times* critic viewed a similarity in the discombobulating allusions he liked and judged most of the Road Pictures favorably.

Most of the Road movies do have some excellent moments that make them enjoyable, rivaling our present day comic features. Much of it can be credited to effective screenwriting, acting, and directing. All three of these aspects seem seldom to gel in many recent comedies.

Finally, which Road Pictures seem to be lasting films with appeal to today's evaluators? For different reasons, I see four "on the road" adventures as superior works and rate them in this order: *Road to Morocco, Road to Utopia, Road to Hong Kong,* and *Road to Bali.* Critics most often praise *Morocco* and *Utopia,* citing these pictures' consistency in writing, directing, and acting. If there is a kind of silliness in their plots and gags, these two still have the appeal to the thinking person's love of innovation that is common to an *Alice in Wonderland* and *Monty Python* nonsequitur–type of fantasy world. Also, some humor is created like a running gag—in-jokes that carry through from one film to another. This becomes true of the sixth, *Road to Bali,* and the seventh, *Road to Hong Kong,* if you apply a revisionist evaluation. These two, the last of the Road Pictures, possess rich, fresh material that show the writers still have innovation in the 1952 *Bali* and then, ten years later, in *Hong Kong.* Actually, most sequels tend to fade out due to repetition and lackluster performances. The Road Pictures defy the clichés of a tired genre. The Hope–Crosby performances seem to have a life of their own that make them enjoyable decades after the final theatrical release in 1962 of *Road to Hong Kong.*

8 Fade Out on Movies: The Fade In of the Small Screen

Contrary to the view of many evaluators of Hope's films, he did receive some popular acclaim for a few of his '60s works, plus kudos from critics who examined the films decades later. Some of the revisionist opinions may have been influenced, however, by the poverty of comic writers in the twenty-first century. The last of the Road Pictures in 1962, *The Road to Hong Kong*, shows the comedian holding his own in a major motion picture. The same could be said for the 1960 film, *The Facts of Life*. Hope appeared in this humorous, almost satirical exposé of sexual yearning in the suburbs. Melvin Frank and Norman Panama, the same writers who would create *Road to Hong Kong*, sold this work to the studio. *The Facts of Life* has co-star Lucille Ball as a sophisticated suburbanite woman who engages in all the activities we now associate with the "soccer mom." She and her husband are the kind of couple who associate with "the country club set" to maintain their status among their peers in suburbia. Therefore, the label of the movie as a satire—or, at least, a sophisticated comedy—has some basis.[1]

Miss Ball co-starred with Hope in the 1949 *Sorrowful Jones* and the 1950 *Fancy Pants*. Her third pairing with him proved to be an asset to *The Facts of Life*. In this movie's affluent society, many people, especially women, experience boredom. At first Lucille, as Kitty Weaver, finds Bob, as Larry Gilbert, too much of a showoff at various social functions. But when a group of these suburbanites plans a Mexican resort vacation, they become attracted to each other. The plot becomes a satirical version of British director David Lean's

Brief Encounter (1945), the romantic story of two married people falling in love. Naturally, *The Facts of Life* plays footsie with infidelity.
It becomes a comic drama that could be characterized as a bedroom
farce. To provide humor, the starstruck lovers confront many obstacles
in the attempt to consummate their physical desires.

They first become attracted to each other when no one else in
their group is able to go deep-sea fishing for marlin on a chartered
boat trip. Larry (Hope) helps Kitty (Miss Ball) in landing a 150-
pound marlin. This event leads to their surreptitious adventure into
infidelity. Their attraction becomes so strong they almost kiss, only
to get interrupted. She sneezes again and again—as if some allergy
suddenly consumes her. When they come back from the vacation,
they make further attempts to meet. Kitty calls him under an assumed
name when he is engaged in a business conference. Since she has a
meeting as a volunteer with the Community Chest, he answers the
phone with a faux pas: "Hello, how are you, Miss Swift. How's
your chest?" The others in his meeting already know he is talking
to a woman, so Larry quickly corrects himself, "Your community, I
mean—your Community Chest." Another time, they go out for a private meeting of drinks and conversation. Larry pushes Kitty, who has
gotten drunk, to go to a motel where he suggests, his brain rather dim
from alcohol, that they register as Mr. and Mrs. G. Washington. This
pseudonym gives the writers a number of opportunities to develop
one-liner jokes. The cynical, worldly motel clerk notes when he sees
"G. Washington" on the registry: "You come from good stock." Asked
where their room is located, the clerk says, "It's the one next to the
cherry tree." Kitty wants some coffee, so Larry drives out, late at
night, only to get lost. She gets tired of waiting and calls a cab because she thinks he's not coming back. Finally, Larry arrives to find
her gone. The acid-tongued clerk offers an explanation to where she
has gone: "To tell you the truth, George, I think she went back to
Mount Vernon."

The use of sharp wit by a minor character, in this case the hotel
clerk played by Robert B. Simon, actually originated with the screenwriters of the '30s and '40s. There certainly were authors in those
two decades who possessed the talent for sophisticated humor, witnessed in the *New Yorker* magazine and the Broadway stage.[2]

The many other attempts by Larry and Kitty to hold secret meet-
ings result in a rather complex bedroom farce. Suffice it to say that
every effort to find a place for their love affair turns into a comic
disaster. But "all's well that ends well," as Shakespeare put it, and

the would-be lovers end up back with their mates. Larry and Kitty dance once more when their suburbanite neighbors have a New Year's party. They say good-bye to each other jokingly as Mr. and Mrs. G. Washington.

Those fans and critics who contend that only the '40s films of Bob Hope were successful should thus look more deeply into the total repertoire of his movies. The fade to black did not totally occur in the '60s.

The next, and his fourth and final film with Lucille Ball, *Critic's Choice* (1962), did not have the merit of *The Facts of Life*. Hope's role is as a stage drama critic, Parker Ballantine, and the plot revolves around a husband versus wife situation. Parker's newspaper reviewer profession clashes with his wife's ambition to be a playwright. The source for this Hope and Ball film was a Broadway hit with the same title. All three of the previous pairings of the comedian and the comedienne became hits. With effective, witty dialogue,

The characters played by Lucille Ball and Bob struggle to consummate an adulterous affair but are thwarted by many obstacles in the 1960 *The Facts of Life*.

From J. C. Archives, Inc., photos

plus the talents of Bob and Lucille, an evaluator might think the fourth movie would have captured the audience easily. It could be that the basic dramatic material doesn't match the talents of these two superior actors. First of all, the role of Parker Ballantine doesn't fit Hope. This Broadway critic offers little to make him a sympathetic character. Some of Ballantine's sarcastic remarks could have been handled more effectively by another comedian—even though Hope did execute lines of this nature in *The Seven Little Foys*. In *Critic's Choice*, the character of Ballantine delights in the task of writing a negative review, but it pains him to give a positive evaluation of a new play.

Angela Ballantine, Parker's wife, gives the finished play to her husband for his suggestions. Parker complains, telling her that the dialogue remains awkward and that her work is that of an amateur; he insists that it shouldn't be produced. To his consternation, Angela procures both a well-known producer and an egotistic, eccentric director. This young, womanizing Broadway director, Dion Kapakos, played by a young Rip Torn, has more comedy potential. Torn actually gives an excellent, humorous performance. He fits the part, and he would go on to create many character roles in his long career.[3] The character of Dion provides a second conflict for Parker. The director also acts as a "play doctor" and spends many nights with Angela to whip the drama into shape for opening night. Critic Ballantine finally decides he must review his wife's play. And he writes a negative review. He should have bowed out and let someone else take over. Since there is no clear indication that the play presented proved to be a weak drama, the husband shows an excess of integrity and should have taken the option of another reviewer—and his paper does have another drama reviewer. Nevertheless, Parker gets into Angela's good graces because he makes sure that her sisters (the play's subjects) attend opening night. A good deed for sure, but hardly enough to counter his bad review. Thus the film version of *Critic's Choice* ends with a hanging ending. Did the play's run overcome leading newspaper critic Parker Ballantine's bad review? It remains a puzzling ending, and this is in part responsible for *Critic's Choice* being the only unsuccessful movie featuring Bob Hope and Lucille Ball.

Odd as it may seem, Lucille doesn't seem to work as well with Bob as she does with Rip Torn. She could have been weary of the part assigned her. With Hope she almost plays a straight part. She gets to perk up in her scenes with Torn. Jack Sher, who adapted the movie from the stage version, did much better work in collaboration with other screenwriters to produce inventive scripts for Bob Hope and others. The screenwriter proved his skill, particularly for the Hope and Hedy Lamarr picture *My Favorite Spy* (1951). Sher continued as a co-author with A. B. Guthrie Jr. to create the acclaimed Western *Shane* (1953).

Although a pure speculation, if Hope and Torn had reversed roles, the movie might have been a hit. Naturally, Hope would not have cared for a supporting role, but as a con man/director he might have been perfectly cast.

When Lana Turner and Bob Hope appeared together in the 1961 *Bachelor in Paradise*, there was quite an age difference between them. When he was cast with Lucille Ball, who was eight years younger, the age difference doesn't show. In her 40s, however, Turner seemed much younger than Hope, in his late 50s. Nevertheless, actor Bob as Adam Niles attempts to seem younger for the part he is playing. And, most of the time, he can pull off the deception. An Internet commentary by Hal Erickson gives a brief and well-stated basic plot summary, complete with some of the entanglements:

> Bob Hope was in the first stages of his cinematic decline when he starred in *Bachelor in Paradise*. Hope plays a "romantic expert" who is contracted to write an expose on the sexual habits of suburban California housewives. For research purposes, he moves into a subdivision called Paradise.... Much to the dismay of the men in the community, all of the gorgeous young wives gravitate to Hope—especially Paula Prentiss.[4]

Since Lana Turner as Rosemary happens to be one of the few single women in Paradise, Adam finally captures her affection. However, as in many romantic comedies, a misunderstanding develops. Some of the lines attributed to writers Hal Kanter and Valentine Davies show that they didn't write the best material for what was meant to be a witty comedy. In the following exchange, the couple expresses their independence, and Adam Niles attempts to be clever:

> ROSEMARY: I came out here to tell you what a despicable person you are.
>
> ADAM: You might get an argument. I'm very fond of me.

Hope skillfully executes the humor of a man who thinks he is witty; therefore, the interplay of human folly does bring laughs.

Kanter, in an autobiography of his professional work as an author, indicated that Bob told his radio and television writers not to "sprinkle" gags in the script for *Bachelor in Paradise*—an instruction Kanter appreciated.[5]

Jack Arnold's direction of *Bachelor in Paradise* seems labored, but the film still probably achieves the position of one of the best of the '60s, for Hal Kanter was one of the top Hope script authors. As a director, Arnold had struck a lucky chord by creating a hit with the 1959 *The Mouse That Roared*. Of course, this film had the services of one of the best British comedians, Peter Sellers, in the leading role. When he turned to directing Hope in *A Global Affair*, he has less flair. Arnold actually worked as an eclectic filmmaker, and he earned more audience and critical acclaim when he directed science fiction films in the fifties, such works as *Creature from the Black Lagoon* (1954), *This Island Earth* (1955), and *The Incredible Shrinking Man* (1957). However, Arnold's directing might have been only half the problem. Hope did not have the best writers in the '60s, and his last solid efforts for this decade remain *The Facts of Life* and *Bachelor in Paradise*. Only one screenwriter, Charles Lederer, had the experience of writing comedies going back to the '30s and spanning into the '60s. Arthur Marx and Bob Fisher as screenwriters were relatively new to the profession.

A Global Affair has a rather novel premise—that is, for a Bob Hope movie–although the theme has been almost done to death in recent movie comedies. Hope is Frank Larrimore, a bachelor who gets stuck raising a baby. As a computer specialist for the United Nations, Frank has an abandoned baby placed in his arms by a woman guide, Michele Mercier, who has discovered the infant. Frank's position as computer specialist doesn't exempt him from having to take the child. After all, as the security chief indicates, Frank must handle the situation because he once gave a speech on helping children. As the good deed is thrust upon him, Frank complains, "They don't allow children in my apartment—only dogs." Until now, the plot smacks of situation comedy without the possibility of becoming a sentimental one. When he purchases an animal carrier for the baby, it appears that sentimentality might not creep in. When the baby starts to cry in the carrier as Frank tries sneaking into his apartment, Frank tells the baby, "Don't cry. Just bark a little." So far, so good. Then, however, the plot design begins to slide downhill. The apartment supervisor gets suspicious, as does Frank's potential mate, Lisette (Michele Mercier), when women from all over the world start to visit him, wanting to adopt the baby.

Taking advantage of the movement to a more open U.S. society of the '60s, humorous sexual innuendo develops as women flock to his apartment. Especially effective though somewhat heavy-handed humor transpires when a female Russian official named Sonya outdrinks Frank by consuming glasses of straight vodka. One of the better lines in the film has Sonya saying with a deadpan look, "It is very difficult to seduce me." This remark fits her assertive nature and cool disposition. Very much the exception to the personality of Sonya, Yvette, a French woman, invites Frank to have an affair and, scantily clad, climbs into his bed. Unfortunately, Lisette catches Yvette in his apartment and storms out, very disgusted with Frank. Eventually she learns he is not guilty, and the misunderstanding is resolved. Frank goes before the United Nations and declares he will keep the little girl and find her a mother. Of course, he will marry Lisette. They kiss as the picture dissolves into "The End."

As described above, there exist some risible scenes in *A Global Affair*, yet situations develop that lean heavily toward sentimentality. The same year, 1963, Hope's humorous character in *Call Me Bwana* provides him with a much meatier part—that of a rogue. Of the many films I have evaluated, roles that contain some elements of a picaresque person suit him best. In *Bwana*, Bob has the traits of a con man and a rascal—in short, a picaresque character. As Matt Merryweather, he wishes to be an explorer and guide for the Dark Continent, Africa. His only knowledge of the land comes from the gleaning of reports in some diaries of a deceased uncle.

Probably the most inventive gag in all of *Call Me Bwana* occurs in the second scene of the film. All the décor gives the appearance that Matt lives in Africa. A black servant also has the dress of an official from that region. Merryweather goes to the window and opens the curtains to reveal, not the jungle, but the skyscrapers of New York and the sounds of the city traffic. Matt, listening to the horns and sounds from cars, remarks, "Oh, those jungle sounds." Comedies ever since the silent period have used such revealing gags—a switch and surprise much like the last line of a joke.

The first scene shows the U.S. and Russian governments worrying about finding a capsule, coming back to land in Africa from the moon. This inciting incident provides the motivation for Merryweather to be hired by his government to lead an expedition. We know from the exposition delivered in the second scene that he has an obsession to be a guide from the notes on Africa from his uncle. In his apartment we see a portrait of his uncle, who wears a pith helmet and has a huge mustache. It becomes a joke, because we can see that the relative's photo is an altered one of Hope.

With the potential established for an effective, humorous film, the script Hope is saddled with remains very weak. There is an attempt to work the situation into a James Bond burlesque. Matt eventually ends up traveling through space in a rocket capsule with a Russian spy, enacted by the voluptuous Anita Ekberg. James Bond usually ends up with a beautiful woman who has switched sides under the charms of the British spy. Early in the movie, a joke on Ekberg's prominent anatomy is delivered when she is photographed from the waist to the head. "I know of no other woman in the world who is so well equipped for this mission," a Russian official tells Luba (Ekberg). Naturally, she also has super intelligence, being a professor of anthropology at a state institution. Dr. Ezra Mungo, another Russian spy, allows the British comedian Lionel Jeffries to turn in an effective job with his fuzzy characterization. He almost steals certain scenes away from Hope.

The safari becomes a trek with all kinds of obstacles. This is so because Merryweather cannot handle the job as guide. Some gags work, and some gags don't. Even Hope's nose comes into the picture: a baby elephant grabs his ski-slope protuberance as if it had found a mother. But much of the invention of the screenwriters, Joanna Harwood and Nate Monaster, becomes labored and sometimes just silly. The long scene in the jungle, when Hope plays golf with the real-life Arnold Palmer, might have employed a few ad-libs. Instead, all we learn from this diversion is that Hope can really swing a golf club. Also, somebody creating *Call Me Bwana* tried to inject this type of surrealistic non sequitur, and this was conceived well by the Road Pictures screenwriters and acted well by Hope and Bing Crosby.

Even in the '60s, climactic sequences in movies relied on the chase, the rush to avoid detection, and the fight between adversaries. Although *A Global Affair*, with its sentimental roots based on an abandoned child, did not have the thrill-related climax, *Call Me Bwana* does. This humorous adventure in Africa overdoes nearly all three of these elements, however, with the rush to avoid detection as the major one. A fight between the Russian spies and U.S. agents emerges when the space probe is discovered being worshiped by natives as some sacred object from the sky. The spies steal the capsule, load it on a truck, and speed off. They don't realize Matt and Luba have gotten into the probe. Matt and Luba start pulling levers and buttons within the capsule, activating the rockets. This results in the truck being pushed down a treacherous African road and launching off the road into the blue, and then coming down for a landing to career wildly like a scene from an ancient Mack Sennett comedy. The space cylinder occupants push another button, and it soars away from the truck and flies into the air. Like his spoof of James Bond, Hope kisses Ekberg in the capsule as she lies in a prone position—a Bond-type tryst in a boat or space capsule for the climax of the film. At the end of the movie, the two have married, and it would seem as if they have a baby crying in a nursery. Evidently, it must be time for the six o'clock feeding. Their baby, finally shown to the audience by means of another revealing gag, happens to be an elephant. Hope turns to the camera: "You're wrong. We adopted him."[6]

In the hands of other screenwriters and director, *Call Me Bwana* might have been an effective lampoon of the Bond spy series. In fact, one of the authors, Johanna Harwood, has credits as a scriptwriter for *Dr. No* (1962) and *From Russia with Love* (1963). When three or more writers execute a work, it can be difficult to determine what contribution each makes. The material could have worked, but the results degenerate into an awkward piece that gives only a little enjoyment.

On the other hand, the 1965 *I'll Take Sweden* possesses an almost satirical edge that affords more enjoyment than *Call Me Bwana*. The picture contains some characteristics of the beach party pictures of the '60s designed for teenagers. A genre for the decade, some '70s and '80s motion pictures also show college-aged men and women on riotous spring breaks. Another variation, *National Lampoon's Animal House* (1978), proved so popular that similar and divergent National Lampoon pictures continued to appear from the early '80s into the mid-'90s.

When Tuesday Weld and Frankie Avalon are cast with Bob Hope in *I'll Take Sweden*, it is almost certain the audience is in for a feature dealing with the conflict between generations. Tuesday has the part of JoJo, and Frankie plays Kenny Klinger. Hope is the father and apparently feels responsible for preserving JoJo's virginity. To break up the romantic notions between his daughter and Kenny, Hope, in the role of Bob Holcomb, manages to get a transfer to Sweden. As you might guess, JoJo falls for Erik, a young Swedish man. Holcomb has a change of heart. He begins to feel that Kenny has a better personality than Erik. So Dad sends for Kenny to claim his daughter. Much of this plot seems typical and a cliché of the time, only rising above teenage comedy with a slight amount of risqué humor. The latter develops more fully when Bob finds a woman his own age, Karin.

For *I'll Take Sweden*, critic Howard Thompson takes over for the usual reviewer, Bosley Crowther, with a very negative evaluation:

> The picture is an altogether asinine little romp, laboriously eking out a winding trail of sexual innuendoes, with some pasted-on backgrounds of Sweden and much mad rushing in and out of bedrooms. And it couldn't be duller or more obvious.[7]

While I would not give such a scathing review of this movie, it remains a weak, torpid example of the best that Hope gave us from the '40s through the very early '60s. Thompson overstates his objection to sexual innuendoes, however. Double entendre has always been a vital part of the theatre since the Greek drama. Also, the "mad rush in and out of bedrooms" does not indicate lascivious behavior in the mode of the French bedroom farce. Father Bob merely tries to find JoJo and Erik before they have a sexual encounter, making a mad dash from room to room and with a hotel passkey, interrupting older couples who may be in bed but are not engaged in coupling. They are as innocent as JoJo, who tells Eric she will not go to bed with him. On the other hand, Karin and Bob check into the hotel with anything but chaste intentions. Karin recognizes the father's attempt to control his daughter as pure hypocrisy:

BOB: She's here—with Eric.

KARIN: Where are you going?

BOB: To stop her.

KARIN: From what?

BOB: Well, she's about to do the thing you're about to do. And that's a terrible thing for a girl to be doing.

KARIN: That's a fine thing to say to me.

BOB: I didn't mean it like that, Karin. I, I,... You're much older.

KARIN: Older!

BOB: No. No. I didn't mean it that way, either. What I meant—she's much younger.

Hope, as Bob Holcomb, embraces the comic frustration with some of his flair from the '40s and '50s movies. He stumbles over his words, trying to check the anger of the person who would be his future wife. Director Frederick De Cordova guided a variety of comedians for television sitcoms: Jack Benny, Burns and Allen, The Smothers Brothers, and Fred MacMurray. De Cordova paced this climactic scene with the mastery he had achieved in television and feature films. The above dialogue's innuendos between Hope and Dina Merrill produces some solid laughter. Also, the premise of *I'll*

Jack Benny moved to filming his sitcom shows while Hope moved to live and taped variety presentations.

From the collection of Donald McCaffrey

Take Sweden becomes a novel one. It has some similarity to a nine-teenth-century French farce and the risqué Restoration British comedy such as *The Country Wife* by William Wycherley. These French and British works of the past often employed a subtle use of double meaning, often with a sexual twist. But much of the dialogue created by the screenwriters of the 1965 film does not have the gift for language of this past tradition. *I'll Take Sweden* only toyed with the moral clashes of the generation gap and the gap between a liberal Sweden and the more conservative, Victorian code of America. It was certainly a significant concept for the satire of hypocrisy, but unfortunately screenwriters Nat Perrin, Bob Fisher, and Arthur Marx were not up to the difficult task.

The postulated risible idea for the 1967 *Eight on the Lam* has no high literary slope to climb. It remains a simplistic concept; no chance of a satire in a fluffy family situational comedy. At least the authors of *I'll Take Sweden* tried to be satirical. Once more a widower—this time with a covey of seven offspring—Harry Dimsdale (Hope) in *Eight on the Lam* learns that he is about to be accused of reworking his books as a bank official to pocket $10,000. Rather than attempting to exonerate himself, he becomes a fugitive. The whole family, Harry and his brood, start out on a trek that presents many situations with potential for laughter. The babysitter, Golda (Phyllis Diller), and a dim-witted policeman, Jasper (Jonathan Winters), attempt to follow the family. Screenwriters Bob Fisher, Albert Lewin, Arthur Marx, and Burt Styler show how four cooks can spoil the broth. Also, someone in the scripting crew or casting department, the director, or the producer decided to use the two stand-up comedians, Diller and Winters, to serve as low-class clowns.

To produce a complicated stew, the writers of *Eight on the Lam* introduce Ellie (Shirley Eaton) as a close friend of Harry's. Since Ellie has taught some of the children, she goes on the journey as a tutor and a rather cool sex object for Harry. Thus, two women get grafted into the plot—Golda the manic babysitter and Ellie the former teacher and sophisticated tutor. The story line gets so convoluted that much of the motivation for the twists and turns remains merely a puzzle for almost any reviewer.

As Hope's film career faded, so did the talent of his gagmen, who had almost all their writing credits from limping sitcoms. And there seemed to be a shortage of writers like Hal Kanter, Ed Hartmann, and Frank Butler who had true story-telling ability. As far as the gags created in *Eight on the Lam*, it seemed as if most were retreads and often lacking in inventiveness. For example, Golda desperately looks for some food for the gluttonous Jasper. Not only does she feed him dog food, but he eats it from the dog's dish, clearly labeled "Pogo." When a picture of Harry is shown to a filling station attendant, he remarks, "I'd know that nose anywhere." Many times in his previous movies, Hope's ski-slope had been used as the subject for a gag, and, again, the climactic chase sequence had been used before with a variety of vehicles. This time they are golf carts. If any innovative gags had been injected into this crazy dash, the writers and the director could be forgiven.

Part of the problem with this last part of *Eight on the Lam* may be the fading talent of George Marshall. He had directed a superior Hope picture, *Monsieur Beaucaire*, in 1946 and the excellent *Fancy Pants* in 1950. However, his last two of seven films for the comedian were close to being the proverbial bombs of his very long career. As indicated, the chase scene using golf carts became a weak cliché. This resurrection of chase sequences ended in a weak imitation of what Buster Keaton,

The master of assault comedy, Jackie Gleason meets his match in Hope's last effective comedy, *How to Commit Marriage* (1969).

From J. C. Archives, Inc., photos

Harold Lloyd, and Charles Chaplin could achieve in the '20s. These comedians could build this portion of a picture to produce more and more laughable gags—from a snicker at the beginning of the chase sequence to a howler at the peak of excitement. By the '60s there existed a resurgence of interest in such comedies. Unfortunately the execution of this type of humor proved to be a lost art.

In the title role of *The Private Navy of Sgt. O'Farrell*, Hope's performance fares better than in *Eight on the Lam*. In this film he returns to the con man character, an enactment that earned him previous success. But Bob seems to lack the spark of even his early '60s efforts. In short, he seems to be tired of it all. It may be that he felt saddled with director Frank Tashlin and an ineffective plot by writers Robert Fresco and John Green. Using the basic material that relates the story of Dan O'Farrell's attempts to find a sunken ship loaded with beer for the soldiers, director Tashlin takes credit for crafting a script with this thin, frivolous thesis. Maybe he should have given his story creators full acknowledgment so they could take the blame.

The plot of the movie continues with Dan's realization that, if men can't have beer, they need women to bolster their morale. Since they are on a desert island in the Pacific Ocean, they are now only an occupying army. O'Farrell celebrates the arrival of a cargo plane that is expected to be loaded with women nurses. Out steps the man-hungry Nellie Krause (Phyllis Diller) from the plane's door as Dan sings "Welcome Pretty Ladies." Stand-up comedian Diller puts on her ugliest appearance, with a hatchet jaw and hatchet laugh. She strikes a flamboyant attempt to be sexy—with an extended leg that remains more awkward than alluring. Director Tashlin doesn't seem to hold her overstatement in check or, perhaps, believes she is funny when unrestrained. The same can be said for the comic villain, Lieutenant Colonel Roger N. Snavely, as created by ham actor John Myhers. Director Frank Tashlin started directing and writing animated cartoons. He worked best as a gagman for *The Paleface*, one of Hope's outstanding pictures. His directing of popular comedians Jerry Lewis and Danny Kaye shows how he allowed such actors to tear a comic passion to tatters. Such humorous hyperbole may appeal to some in the audience, but Diller and Myhers soon become annoying to the discerning evaluator.

Fortunately Bob Hope, after thirty years of feature work from *The Big Broadcast of 1938* through his many years on the stage, radio, and television, knew how to moderate the level of his acting to make his appearance in *The Private Navy of Sgt. O'Farrell* an appealing performance. In the concluding sequence the army base personnel believe that Dan O'Farrell died while defeating a Japanese submarine crew. The navy captures the Japanese as they try to escape in a lifeboat. As Dan approaches the island in his own inflatable lifeboat, he hears a loudspeaker announcement memorializing his death and exalting his heroism. "I'm not dead," he says, as if he doesn't quite believe it. Then a comic revelation shot shows that he has in tow the huge Japanese submarine. The scene has shades of a similar shot from Buster Keaton's *The Navigator* (1924), when the silent screen comedian attempts to use a tiny rowboat to tow a mammoth ocean liner that is adrift. Director and screenwriter Tashlin creates an improbable gag, which could be labeled fantastic, a type of joke that Keaton avoided. His hapless little fellow can't move the ship.[8] As the final scene comes to an end, all the people in the army camp say adieu to Dan and his lovely bride Maria, played by Gina Lollobrigida, a woman Dan met long ago.

As almost the last hurrah of his film career in *How to Commit Marriage* (1969), the comedian sometimes executes his role in a low-key fashion that almost plays it straight to Jackie Gleason's role as the flamboyant entrepreneur of '60s rock bands. Critic William Robert Faith's book, *Bob Hope, A Life of Comedy*, applauded this film:

> The film traded heavily on that rivalry and was riddled with insult humor as only Gleason could fire it off. It was the next to last movie Hope attempted and it had considerable polish, largely owing to Norman Panama's rewriting and direction. The picture suffered unfairly from critics' comparisons with more modish comedies being turned out by Mel Brooks and Woody Allen. The irony, of course, is that both Brooks and Allen owed a debt to Hope's film style. Both traded on Hope's comic persona but Brooks added more sex and Allen's situations were darker.[9]

Faith is perceptive in his view, but Panama certainly tried to be with the times. Here was a comedy that dealt with divorce, illegitimate offspring, fans following an Eastern guru, oddball rock bands, partners sleeping together without being married, and even a brush with the swinging scene of the period. Granted, the treatment was not as blunt as Brooks and Allen, but it still tackled the more liberal contemporary mores. The film contains, at least, a lampoon of the fashionable trends of the '60s.

Complications develop. The two fathers become rivals because of the possible union between their children. The daughter's father, Frank Benson (Hope), and mother, Elaine (Jane Wyman), obtain a divorce. While they are no longer married, the whimsical, funny situations have a ring of the swinging world of the '60s. They develop new relationships and meet in a nightclub run by Gleason, playing the role of Oliver Poe, a rock band sponsor. Oliver relishes putting Frank against the wall with his putdowns:

OLIVER (observing the "split family" with dates): Well, well, well. One big happy family.

FRANK: You're too funny for one man. You ought to subdivide.

OLIVER: I don't get it. You with him and you with those. I mean her. That computer sure got screwed up when it made that date.

FRANK: How would you like to step outside?

OLIVER: I certainly would.

FRANK: Well, please do so we can breathe again.

OLIVER: I'm getting out of here before I punch a senior citizen right in the snoot.

FRANK: Back up, Moby Dick. How would you like to have your flab parted in the front, too?

In this exchange, both characters prove to have the skill to call it a draw. Oliver pokes fun at Frank's divorce and choice of a date. When he says "you with those," he refers to the airhead blonde with her large breasts proudly displayed in a low-cut dress. Frank then insults Oliver with three fat jokes.

Critic Faith does point out that Gleason handles insults with considerable skill. In this scene, Hope matches his expertise. One trick, however, shows Hope outmaneuvering him. This happens toward the end of *How to Commit Marriage*. Jackie often plays a bragging, self-assured know-it-all who wins by his own aggression, even if he may be a bore or a fool. Gleason, however, does not have the gift of mimicry. Hope can assume a number of impressions—often on a comic level. In *How to Commit Marriage*, Hope imitates an esteemed guru who many admire and follow—a trend of the time. Comedian Professor Irwin Corey enacts this role in the film, using his usual distorted logic with an exaggerated vocabulary that is merely a string of nonsense. Hope, as Frank, dons similar garb, with a huge mustache and beard to do a credible impression of the guru. Impersonating The Baba Zaba (Professor Corey's guru), Frank gives a speech to the audience where his daughter and her boyfriend are seated to receive wisdom. He urges the couple to take their out-of-wedlock baby and get married.

Naturally Frank and his wife Elaine are reunited, and the young couple will get married. Again, happy endings are achieved after many complications—typical of comedies throughout the ages.

How to Commit Marriage obviously developed in an effective way that some evaluators have not remembered. After all, not all of Hope's movies toward the last of his career were weak creations. Successes may be due to director Norman Panama, who scripted some of the best Hope vehicles, *Monsieur Beaucaire*, *Road to Utopia*, *Facts of Life*, and *Road to Hong Kong*. He may have rewritten some of the script to make it at least an interesting bowing out for Hope in his fruitful world of the cinema. Television, more and more, became the focus for comedians in the '60s, and naturally the screenwriters and directors got into the act.

Before he took the plunge to have his own show on television, Hope became a guest on such shows as Ed Sullivan's 1949 *Toast of the Town*. According to Bob Hope's biography on his website, www. BobHope.com, the comedian's formal entrance as a television actor occurred on Easter Sunday in 1950. Called *Star Spangled Revue*, Bob hosted guest stars Douglas Fairbanks Jr., Beatrice Lillie, and Diana Shore.[10] This use of prominent show business personalities would become a format for many television shows for decades to come. The small box entertainment had become the casket in which vaudeville was buried. A reflection on what had happened was one of Hope's frequent self-disparaging jokes about his performances in a range of media. An accurate quote appears in *Bob Hope: My Life in Jokes*: "Of course, you all know what television is. Remember vaudeville dying? Well, you're looking at the box they put it in."[11]

Bob's "formal debut" in the 1950 *Star Spangled Revue* had the comedian enter all dressed up in a tuxedo, hat, and cane. His monologue started with, "The reason I'm wearing this outfit is the fact that a lot of performers die on television. If that happens to me, I want to be prepared for it."[12]

One of Hope's "Comedy Hours," sponsored by Frigidaire in 1951, the early days of his television shows, came across as one of his better specials. Bob presented many talented entertainers. Some in the lineup were Sid Caesar, Imogene Coca, Frank Sinatra, Eddie Cantor,

Ed Wynn, Jimmy Durante, and Faye Emerson.[13] Like the popular stage shows of the nineteenth century, a series of sketches, song and dance, plus stand-up comedians—even an occasional billing of high-society ballet or opera—might become one of the turns on these shows. Before the advent of cable television, the audience often received basic network entertainment that had almost a faddish, sometimes boring deluge of the same type of programming. In the formative days of television, however, some excellent shows were witnessed. Live variety shows with highly talented actors existed next to live dramatic series such as Playhouse 90 and Kraft Television Theater. Some of these early efforts provided a wide range of prestigious drama to audiences in the more populous parts of the United States. Eventually, the genres of the Western, mystery, situation comedy, detective and crime series became the staple of the medium.

From all historical evidence, though, Bob Hope would settle into the variety show format. For example, the Colgate Comedy Hour became a haven for stage, radio, and movie actors. Such luminaries as Bob Hope, Eddie Cantor, Dean Martin and Jerry Lewis, Fred Allen, Abbott and Costello, and Jimmy Durante played an important part in making that five-year series successful. Like a stage vaudeville show, comedians contributed to the hour-long program. On March 30, 1953, Hope's part of the program had him doing a burlesque of "Buttons and Bows," the hit song of his 1948 *The Paleface.*[14] While it may seem as if this take-off on the Academy Award song did not follow the tradition of television comedy using topical material, the 1952 *The Son of Paleface* was recent in viewers' memories. Of more importance, "Buttons and Bows" enjoyed a repeat performance from *The Paleface* in a saloon scene in the '50s film sequel. Performers of this hit song were Hope, Jane Russell, and Roy Rogers. This use of guests on variety shows would carry over into television situation comedies, Westerns, and socially significant dramas, although there exist so many different types of entertainment on television it remains difficult to determine influences.[15]

One of the basic problems with the variety shows created by the leading comics probably developed from the nature of the creation. The skits and songs remained the material of the times, without long-lasting impact.[16] Hope's films do have contemporary references—especially the Road Pictures—but the stories created by the writers of the day had enough detachment from the temporal taste to ensure that Bob's pictures will live on and be enjoyed.

9 Through the Decades with Hope's Films: 1934 to 1972

In the '30s, Hope had important or leading roles in seven two-reel shorts and seven features. Bob developed a formative humorous character for his films that evolved in the Broadway musicals and his radio programs. The persona would slowly come to an early fulfillment, moving from the short movies to the features.

For the 1934 two-reeler *Paree, Paree*, Hope created the amorous young man trying to impress a woman. He attempted to keep the youthful image of a man pursuing a beautiful woman when he was a fifty-year old in the 1961 *Bachelor in Paradise* and the 1963 *Call Me Bwana*. He remained somewhat successful in this attempt to be youthful; more so than Bing Crosby, who was beginning to show his age, as he pursued Joan Collins in *Road to Hong Kong* (1962). In truth, Bing was only two years older than Bob, but illness made him look much older in that movie, the last of the Road Pictures.

In another two-reel film, *Calling All Tars* (1936), Hope displayed his slick, very youthful thirty-three-year-old persona. Here he added the con man that would be one of his lasting portraits in many pictures, such as two features in the thirties, *Give Me a Sailor* (1938) and *Some Like It Hot* (1938) (renamed *Rhythm Romance*). This added characteristic—the bilker—combined with his attempt to capture the affections of a woman remained two of his main traits throughout his career. In the retitled film *Rhythm Romance*, Hope as the protagonist dupes others but has the entrepreneur of the boardwalk entertainment snookering him—a type of reversal comedy that makes the comedian a more complex character. And the Road Pictures has

Crosby winning the woman at the end of the movie, except for in *Road to Utopia* when Hope marries Lamour and Crosby is literally left out in the cold, in Alaska. The running gag of the Road Pictures shows Bing outwitting Bob at just about every turn of the plot.

From 1934 to 1972, many aspects of the entertainer grace Hope's movies. The early two-reel, *Paree, Paree*, for example, has all the requirements of a musical, with both songs and production numbers. Bob's first feature, *The Big Broad cast of 1938*, possesses songs and skits. In the '30s, the 1938 *College Swing* and *Rhythm Romance* continue many of the traditions of the musical. In every decade except the last Hope picture in 1972, the comedian appeared in musicals. And he often served as master of ceremonies for this genre. In *College Swing*, however, he received the role as a tutor for Gracie Allen to prime her to pass a college examination tied to her inheritance.

Probably the most diverse motion picture character the comedian created was the hypochondriac in the 1939 *Never Say Die*. Some critics think that Hope in such a role was not effective. Bob Thomas remains the chief critic of this persuasion.[1] The risible applies to almost all deviant human behaviors, including hypochondria and even insanity. Taboo subjects for our culture lie in aberrant sexual behavior of the pedophilia and necrophilia, so only the rare stand-up comic would attempt such a joke. Much later in 1956, Hope would develop the role of a psychologically disturbed cartoonist in *That Certain Feeling*. While it remains mild humor about a weakness, it did not seem to fit the popular persona that attracted both critics and fans. It might be said that both evaluators and the general public are rigid in what they expect from Bob Hope. *Never Say Die* actually had some elements of social satire.

The 1939 *The Cat and the Canary* became a successful "Dark Old House" filled with mystery, intrigue, and some tricky plotting that furthered the fame of both Hope and Paulette Goddard. It would lead to a more effective sequel with the same co-stars in the 1940 *The Ghost Breakers*. Nevertheless, *The Cat and the Canary* cannot be overlooked. Besides establishing the co-stars with a status they had not enjoyed before, director Elliott Nugent artistically creates the threatening atmosphere early in the film from shots that fit the genre. The climax moves from the comedy lines Hope provides to nearly the art film level:

> The shadow of a crouching man thrown hugely on the wall, to dissolve into the shape of a cat, then vanish. The "real" monster which inhabits

the passages under the house is a hideous creation, a gangling stalker in long robes whose stiff hulking walk is made all the more terrifying by its speed.[2]

This illustrates that the comedian would embrace almost any genre and use his type of innovative humor that would give it a fresh turn. In the '40s films, there evolved an actor who would embrace the gamut of film modes. This decade displayed a very active popular comedian engaged in nineteen features as the star. The second most prolific period followed in the '50s, with fourteen features.

The '40s decade started with the 1940 *Road to Singapore*, which proved to be a distinctive genre. Bob Hope and Bing Crosby were unaware of this breakthrough, but the Road Pictures have never been successfully imitated or continued as a separate genre. Bob and Bing's chemistry explains part of this achievement; however, there were also the writers and directors who could pull this type of movie into a particular form and taste that made the sequels successful box-office films for Bob and Bing. The majority of the Road Pictures were released in the '40s *Road to Singapore*, *Road to Zanzibar*, *Road to Morocco*, *Road to Utopia*, and *Road to Rio*. Only *Road to Bali* (1952) and *Road to Hong Kong* (1962) were created in subsequent decades.

Already mentioned is the '40s *The Ghost Breakers* and its relationship with the end of the '30s film, *The Cat and the Canary*. As a sequel, it employs almost the same plot but adds one of the best black comedians in the movie business, Willie Best. He almost outshines the acting of Hope as a droller by a more subtle fear of ghosts, often depicted with overstatement by black comics in the '20s and '30s. This specific mode, the Dark Old House, would not be used again by Hope, but a remake of *The Ghost Breakers* would be made starring Dean Martin and Jerry Lewis, named *Scared Stiff*. Ironically, with screenplay doctoring Lewis became the scared stiff surrogate for Willie Best, the black comedian. In Jerry's mugging of an Anglo-Saxon version of Best, Willie came off as more acceptable and funnier. Also, very few remakes or new versions are superior.

The '40s were war years, and Hope handled both military service films and spy comedies. There were two concerned with the activities of soldiers. *Caught in the Draft* (1941) proved to be more popular than *Let's Face It* (1943). This '41 feature shows Bob trying to avoid the draft because his character nearly faints at the sound of gunfire.

All efforts to avoid the draft do not work, and he ends up as one of the bumbling recruits in the army. Similar mishaps rain on Abbott and Costello when they are drafted in *Buck Privates* (1941), released only five months before Hope's *Caught in the Draft*. While Bob only did one more military picture in the '40s, Bud and Lou were such a box-office success that they did two films using different branches of the service during the same year, 1941—*In the Navy* and *Keep 'em Flying*—or, in another obvious way to put it, the team just ground out two more features that year so Universal could get the money. Paramount was not that greedy and didn't make another military film with Hope until 1953, *Off Limits*, where he would be in competition with Dean Martin and Jerry Lewis. In the '50s they made three of this genre, *At War with the Army* (1950), *Sailor Beware* (1951), and *Jumping Jacks* (1952). The latter film refers to paratroopers, and Hope's *Off Limits* has Bob paired with Mickey Rooney, showing them as Military Police on patrol. If the film had proved a hit there might have been a sequel with a new comic team, but Bob and Bing were firmly established with Road Pictures. Besides, Rooney was such a ham Hope probably couldn't team up with him.

Two later celluloid creations, *The Iron Petticoat* (1956) and *The Private Navy of Sgt. O'Farrell* (1968), became examples of a type of service comedy. The '50s film with co-star Katherine Hepburn could be classified as a cold war effort, with some effective acting by both Kate and Bob as pilots and officers. The 1968 military service work has the comedian on a Pacific island base, trying to provide his men with beer and nurses. This movie requires the audience to suspend its disbelief that a sunken ship of beer has released cans full of beer that will float with ocean currents. It also requires a suspension of disbelief that a manic Phyllis Diller is a funny nurse as she mugs her way through every scene.

Comedian Bob Hope had competition when it came to the military service movie. As early as 1948, Red Skelton appeared in a very laughable comedy, *A Southern Yankee*. Granted, it was about the Civil War, however it had spy, combat, and melodrama plotting that linked with the traditional genre. In 1955 Hollywood filmed a version of the stage hit *Mister Roberts*, with a box-office enhancing cast of Henry Fonda, James Cagney, William Powell, and Jack Lemmon. Many of these wartime movies, like *No Time for Sergeants* (1958) and *Stalag 17* (1953), enjoyed a wide audience as stage dramas and film comedies. Strange as it may seem, an audience existed for such fare long after World War II, the Korean War, and the Vietnam War ended.

One of the best illustrations of the "long after the time" military comedies is the Korean War period's military action of the Mobile Army Surgical Hospital movie called M*A*S*H (1970), directed by Robert Altman. In its plot and acting, it became a service comedy masquerading as a satire. While it seemed to be a fresh approach with a strong dose of black comedy, it had all the elements of enlisted men and officers (in this case mostly physicians) rebelling against a repressive military bureaucracy. This is standard fare for most humorous depictions of military life. It is much like the tone and plot of *Mister Roberts*, *No Time for Sergeants*, and Hope's *The Private Navy of Sgt. O'Farrell*. Furthermore, these military service films formed the basic plot for the popular television series—almost as long running as the many television Westerns that appeared in the '50s and '60s.

Different comic modes would, as is evident with the military genre, cross over from decade to decade. This would happen with a type of movie Bob Thomas classifies as "The Comedy Adventures";[3] however, he defines the genre too broadly, including such intrigue films as the spy movies and *The Ghost Breakers* (an intrigue Dark Old House film) starring Hope in the '40s. The adventure film needs a more narrow range, such as the Western or the costume comedy— like Bob's swashbuckler movies. One of the first in this category developed when Paramount loaned the comedian to MGM for *The Princess and the Pirate* (1944). This creation proved to be a delightful romp for Hope. He would prove his itinerant actor character as the great pretender—a role that shows the comedian at his best. In the costume or period movie, he often becomes a dissembler to avoid detection of his humble status, such as a barber posing as a great swordsman in *Monsieur Beaucaire* (1946), and a tailor who takes on the role of his master as a great lover in *Casanova's Big Night* (1954).

When the United States went to war in 1941, the spy humorous work developed—usually directed against Nazi Germany's saboteurs operating in America. A take-off from the Alfred Hitchcock *39 Steps*, a film called *My Favorite Blond*, with the leads Hope and Madeleine Carroll, had the intrigue expected from the genre. Bob gets pulled along as Madeleine escapes from the spies. He is the hapless comic victim of treachery by the manipulations of German agents Gale Sondergaard and George Zucco. An even more raucous, but not as well crafted by writers Frank Fenton, Harry Kurnitz, Lynn Root, and director David Butler, picture released the same year— *They Got Me Covered*. Once again, Hope delivers a portrait of a bumbling, cowering man. In this intrigue movie he shows a more negative side—a fired correspondent who has stolen another reporter's story about a Nazi spy ring operating in New York. Otto Preminger plays the role of the head of this treasonous gang. By a great deal of luck and oddball manipulation, Bob brings the group in for prosecution by the law. All spy pictures prosper at the box office when the country is at war or experiencing a cold war.

In the early 50s, Hope would play a double role as Peanuts White and as Eric Augustine in *My Favorite Spy* (1951). Producing quite a contrast in characterization and displaying the comedian's versatility, the former is a nearly talentless burlesque clown, the latter, a notorious, international spy. Once more, the intrigue of this type of comic drama makes it one of the favorite films for Bob's fans. The plotting nature of this genre develops widespread appeal. However, the downside of this mode is that it is limited to the times of war or the cold war. Screenwriters Edmund Hartmann, Jack Sher, and Hal Kanter, with director Norman Z. McLeod, generated a tighter, easier moving production of *My Favorite Spy* than the two other spy dramas that featured Hope as a star in the '40s.

Another type of intrigue drama with a lampoon mode featuring the comedian employed a burlesque of the detective movie in the 1947 *My Favorite Brunette*. Bob, as a struggling baby photographer, is mistaken for a famous detective by a client, enacted by Dorothy Lamour. Hope gets involved as a private eye and ends up in a sanitarium with mentally deranged members of the institution played by Lon Chaney Jr. and Peter Lorre. Mystery, naturally, is an important part of the plot, just as it was part of the design in the comedian's earlier Dark Old House films, *The Cat and the Canary* and *The Ghost Breakers*, and in the spy films. But there is no pretender detective in these films—the protagonist is merely an amateur. The detective lampoon has a more widespread life than the spy spoof. For example, Buster Keaton produces an excellent would-be detective in a series of elaborate dream sequences in *Sherlock, Jr.* (1924). Hope's *My Favorite Brunette* did not, however, spawn similar works for the comedian.

A wider application of the Western farce evidently sprang from the outstanding success of Bob's *The Paleface* (1948). Three works of this genre became a part of Hope's repertoire, *Fancy Pants* (1950), *Son of Paleface* (1952), and *Alias Jesse James* (1959). All four of these Western spoofs have the comic protagonist (Hope) engaging in a deception of character. In other words, he is a pretender who is laughably inadequate in his attempted dissimulation. In the first, the 1948 work, he tries to be a hero and merely looks foolish when he attempts the pose. *Fancy Pants* developed into a revision of the 1935 *Ruggles of Red Gap*. In this work, he is an actor pretending to be an English manservant. *Son of Paleface* has an Eastern graduate of Harvard deceiving everyone in the town that he has a huge inheritance when, actually, no money exists in the chest owned by his father. Much of the slapstick in the movie seems warmed over from both sound and silent movies. Also, some of the gags have the quality of the animated cartoon. This may be explained by the fact that director and scripter Frank Tashlin was long known as the creator of cartoons for Warner Brothers. The third Western involves Hope as the hapless protagonist, a life insurance salesman, who confronts Jesse James and sells him a policy. Part of the plot device has Bob mistaken for the infamous gangster. While the comedian shows he can still hold an audience, he gets little support from actors such as Wendell Corey who plays the real Jesse James. Bob Hope was one of the few actors who embraced the Western to the point of creating roles in four films that were pleasing to his fans, if not to the majority of the critics.

Long after the sequel *Son of Paleface*, Universal picked Don Knotts to do a '60s version of the original, *The Paleface*. The title became *The Shakiest Gun in the West* (1968). The title depicts the quaking frame and shaking hand of dentist Jesse W. Heywood. It is the key to the weakling played by Knotts. Some of the plot of the original remains, but Don provides a different would-be Western hero than Bob Hope's portrait developed for the risible. Hope plugs away in his attempts to be manly, while Knotts withdraws most of the time into a nervous chicken of a man.

Much like the waning of the military service genre, the Western movie had a long history of serious output; there were many protagonists in the silent days, in the early sound period, and in the final maturation of the genre. In the formative years of cinema, William S. Hart moved from the stage in the East to create the prototype of the Western hero in such films as *Hell's Hinges* (1916). This person was a loner who achieved a goal by means that were sometimes variant with social norms. This traditional portrayal continued down through the decades, and many actors followed the model established in this infant period of cinema. Examples of those actors who followed with some variations are Randolph Scott, Joel McCrea, John Wayne, Gregory Peck, and Clint Eastwood. Most of the standard and sometimes labeled "classic" Westerns are serious dramas, and a short list of such works could be *Stagecoach* (1939), *Duel in the Sun* (1946), *High Noon* (1952), *Shane* (1953), *The Big Country* (1958), *The Magnificent Seven* (1960), and *Ride the High Country* (1962). These, of course, are older Westerns that show a variation in subject matter. It is difficult to find as much variation in the comic film. One humorous film that uses a strong woman, played by Jane Fonda, as a leader and a mover of men is *Cat Ballou* (1965), with some characteristics of Jane Russell's role in *The Paleface*. Other comedy Westerns of note are *Support Your Local Sheriff* (1969), *Little Big Man* (1970), and *Blazing Saddles* (1974). All except *Little Big Man* plus an inclusion of *Cat Ballou* are relatively like the fare of Bob Hope's four Westerns. *Little Big Man* has some strong satirical themes contrasting the morality of the "White Man" and the Indian. Actually and maybe to some ironically, the Native American comes out the superior. This is different from *The Paleface* and *Fancy Pants*. Today the comic treatment of this race in these two movies would be considered politically incorrect. This type of humor was, however, typical of the period and existed in the 1968 *The Shakiest Gun in the West*, the remake of Hope's *The Paleface*.

As the comedian, his screenwriters, producers, and directors began to move into the next decade, the '50s, some changes came about. Fewer formula films gave Hope a chance to show his versatility. While it was not clearly realized, the actor achieved more dimension when he tackled two Damon Runyon adaptations released in 1949 and 1951, respectively—*Sorrowful Jones* and *The Lemon Drop Kid*, transcribed to the screen by Ed Hartmann. Bob's depiction of the film title protagonist, Sorrowful Jones, illustrates that a serious side of the personality became possible for actors whose main talent is in producing smiles and laughter. Hope, naturally, has the help of Lucille Ball— probably his best co-performer throughout his career. She becomes more than his match as he throws out jabs to cut down her singing talent. She takes pokes at his stingy nature. And Hope is able to play off the remarks of the child, Little Miss Marker. He is able to handle his relation as a surrogate father with the girl without being sentimental. The film *The Lemon Drop Kid* doesn't provide the same range of emotions. Bob Hope reaches into his bag of comic tricks and does produce some effective moments as he dresses up as an elderly woman to get back the money needed for a home dedicated to older women.

In the decade of the '50s, two essentially serious films show that Hope can act beyond the formula of farce. The two works are *The Seven Little Foys* (1955) and *Beau James* (1957). If a genre could be assigned to these two films, it would probably be "biography." Then again, *Foys* might be called "show business"; and *James* could be labeled a "politics" genre. Regardless of how a person might classify the two movies, the works are based on two living legends. *The Seven Little Foys* has an impressive predecessor, *Yankee Doodle Dandy,* a 1942 motion picture that celebrates the life of entertainer George M. Cohan. James Cagney draws on his incredible charisma to capture the essence of this dynamic performer who wrote songs, plays, and sketches for the stage.

While the persona of Eddie Foy in *The Seven Little Foys* appears to be an effective imitation of the song and dance style of the famous vaudeville comedian of a past age, some of the Bob Hope technique shines through in this excellent impersonation by a present-day actor. This is especially true of Bob's speech before a judge, pleading his case to use his children for skits and songs on the stage.

Biography linked to show business has examples besides Cagney's George M. Cohan in *Yankee Doodle Dandy*. Cinema biographies of popular entertainers such as Al Jolson, Eddie Cantor, Buster Keaton, and other personalities have been attempted with limited success. Larry Parks imitates the famous vaudevillian in the 1946 *The Jolson Story*. However, it was necessary to have Al Jolson dub in the songs, while Parks appears to be executing the phrasing of the lyrics as Jolson would have. Such a device became only moderately credible. In *The Buster Keaton Story* (1957), Donald O'Connor struggles to mime the pratfalls that Buster executed with such finesse and, even with his agility as a dancer, produces a carbon copy of this master of silent screen comedy. And, as if somebody who assigned a title to the life of Eddie Cantor had no imagination, there is *The Eddie Cantor Story* (1953). Here is the worst of the lot. Like Donald O'Connor's performance, the actor did not have the screen presence to match that of Cantor. The impersonator, Keefe Brasselle, came from a nightclub background. Most depictions of these stars of the stage and screen become a whitewash of the actors' flaws. *The Seven Little Foys* attempts to show some of the negative features of Eddie Foy's self-centered disposition. It is to Hope's credit that he does a credible acting job of the portrait.

A genre, the focus of this chapter, is determined by the following characteristics: content, form, and style. Usually there are previous pictures that are similar or even become models for those that follow. *Beau James* seems to be one-of-a-kind—like the 1941 *Citizen Kane*. The content might be the answer. Just like *Citizen Kane*, where could anyone find the real-life model for another William Randolph Hearst for a similar movie? And for *Beau James*, where could you find a real-life model for mayor of New York Jimmy Walker? The political portrait of World War I President Wilson, simply called *Wilson* (1944), doesn't provide this model because this president was exemplary—Hearst and Walker are picaresque, a type of rogue for which there is no equal. Walker, of course, had more of a playboy nature and, as Hope depicted him, a more appealing side than the newspaper tycoon, Hearst. Consequently, Walker is a subject for some comedic elements; Hearst, a subject for tragedy.

Hope was cast effectively as Jimmy Walker since the mayor could compose and sing songs and had a social life tied closely to entertainers. Even more than Eddie Foy, Walker possesses the womanizing flaws of the playboy and neglects his position as mayor. While Jimmy has a law degree with experience in the state legislature, he doesn't evolve into an effective leader and politician. It becomes Hope's most serious role, and it could have been given an Oscar, like Bing Crosby who received an Academy Award for playing a priest in the sentimental *Going My Way* (1944). However, there exists a strong contrast in Hope's *Beau James* if compared with Bing's role. Both *The Seven Little Foys* and *Beau James* employ only a few moments of sentiment and generally avoid the whitewashing of the protagonists. Bob Thomas points out that *Beau James* is essentially a tragedy, and the only one in Hope's long career. Nevertheless, this evaluator notes some of the lighter moments:

> [It] affords Hope one of his most complex characterizations. He plays most of the film straight; when he wisecracks, it is in the Walker manner. Since Walker was a song writer and a sometime entertainer, musical numbers fit into the film with logic. There is a delightful sequence in which Hope sings Walker's hit song, "Will You Love Me in December As You Do in May?" before ethnic groups. He delivers the lyrics in Italian and Yiddish, does a tap dance with a Negro girl in Harlem.[4]

The comedian returned to more formula-type films with *Paris Holiday* (1958) and *Alias Jesse James* (1959), two films that certainly would not be considered Oscar material. A definite change would occur during the '60s. With co-star Lucille Ball, Bob turns in a sterling performance (with Ms. Ball once more his equal) in the 1960 *The Facts of Life*.

We have used the observations of Bob Thomas from his co-written book with Hope, *The Road to Comedy*, because he employs insightful criticism in the second half of the book. And this work was published in 1977, relatively early for this type of evaluation, especially when most biographies or books attributed to Hope were often ghost written from interviews with Bob. Most of the classifications Thomas uses in this book are valid; however, he classifies *The Facts of Life* as a "domestic comedy." The content of the film develops a comic theme that has many elements of darker humor—two married people fall in love with a passionate desire to commit adultery. But difficulties arise with each attempt. This is not a laughable series of situations *within* the family that often produces something like television sitcoms. It is *without* the family and shows a darker side that can be tragic or comic. Many of the lines show a form used in the past, as in the Restoration comedy of the late seventeenth-century *The Country Wife* and this poke at lustful human nature inherited from some of the bawdier moments of Shakespeare's plays such as in *The Taming of the Shrew*. Domestic comedy in the world of television, before *All in the Family*, often had the content, form, and style of the sentimental dramas going back to the eighteenth century. The sentimental drama led some critics of the mode to say: "If comedy can make one weep, tragedy can make one laugh."

One person who viewed a tape of *The Facts of Life* found that the depiction of two lovers who could not consummate their love was nothing to laugh about. By this person's standards, the story was more a tragedy. Such is the difference in taste for comedy that presents a dark side of society. To me, and where I differ with Thomas, the Hope and Ball movie is not domestic comedy but rather sophisticated comedy. To be specific, some of the lines from the film seem like invective from that genre. A suburban group of country club types plans a vacation in the Caribbean, and many drop out, thus leaving behind a couple that would seem unlikely to become united. In her role, Lucille Ball drips with an acid tongue when she, at first, professes a loathing for Hope's character at the thought of associating with him on a vacation: "Six days of old Laughing Boy's enforced cheerfulness." But the couple fall in love, and many of the situations have the nature of the sophisticated comedy of the past.[5]

The 1961 *Bachelor in Paradise* possessed all the potential to be another sophisticated comedy that continued the comedian's new direction. Unfortunately, the picture does not have the same qualities as *The Facts of Life*. Paired with Lana Turner, Hope seems to need the stimulation of Lucille Ball. Lana was in her forties and had never been known for her acting ability let alone her turn of a line to produce humor. Borrowing from the leading character played by Hope in *Facts*, the transfer to a man who thinks he is funny doesn't seem to work in this movie. As effective as he could be working with other writers, screenwriter Hal Kantor doesn't fare especially well with Valentine Davies. Valentine won an Oscar for his Best Original Story. This Academy Award came from his idea for the very popular 1947 Christmas movie *Miracle on 34th Street*. The basic plot of three wives pursuing the role of the bachelor (Hope) has all the complications of Restoration-type wit comedy; nevertheless, the writing and directing could not achieve the high level obtained on the stage in London hundreds of years ago.

The modern stage sometimes attempts the sophisticated stage drama sprinkled with gags that accomplish the whimsical and approach wit. *Critic's Choice* happened to be a hit Broadway play created by a woman playwright who wrote a drama that has a journalist evaluator reviewing his own wife's play. Stage director and critic Walter Kerr in his instructions to playwrights, *How Not to Write a Play*, indicates that a bad concept was to have a drama critic feel obliged to write a review of his wife's play. And Walter's wife became a successful novelist and dramatist. Ira Levin thought he might take the bait and write a humorous drama for the stage for just such a situation. *Critic's Choice* is thus about a Broadway play created by a woman playwright whose husband is a journalist and actually reviews the play. Like the early '60s films with Bob as the lead, this one also shows a movement for the comedian to handle the sophisticated genre. The critic, named Parker Ballantine (Hope's role), seems determined to give his wife a bad review—maybe because he suspects she is having an affair with the director who is resolved to have a solid drama by being a play doctor. A double meaning irritates him when his wife refers to reworking the drama the previous night—"We were at it all night." When he tells his wife he plans to wear his dinner jacket to doll up for a dinner after the opening of her play, she uses sarcasm: "For me? Little old worthless me? You'll spoil me rotten." She uses a southern belle accent to rub in her detestation for his actions. There exists some effective scenes between Hope and Ball, but the film is not as intriguing as the 1960 *The Facts of Life*.

Critic's Choice has many of the characteristics found in adapting a more cosmopolitan drama for the New York stage, with its liberal audience, to the general movie audience. The result is often a "dumbed-down" version of the witty dialogue that once existed in the stage play.

In the 1963 releases of *A Global Affair* and *Call Me Bwana*, Hope seems to be returning to the more standard fare of his past pictures. In *A Global Affair*, the comedian once more, as in *Sorrowful Jones*, gets in a position as an official at the United Nations where he must care for a child—in this case, an abandoned baby. This leads to something akin to the sentimental drama, and the total work doesn't have the energetic movement Hope often gives to a film. *Call Me Bwana* has the vigor of some of the past highly plotted take-offs in the Hope repertoire. It obviously takes its cue from the James Bond spy and space travel features that became so popular in the early '60s. A year earlier in 1962, *Road to Hong Kong* had many of the characteristics of a burlesque of the Bond pictures. In a purposely complicated plot, both of these movies involve treks to other lands, thereby tied to a travesty of the adventure film. Such mechanizations often were used by screenwriters and directors to stretch pictures to obtain the maximum intrigue coupled with laughter. Although this technique became fashionable in the '60s, it was not always successful.

I'll Take Sweden (1965) was developed by screenwriters as a Bob Hope movie that had some success with the sexual mores of Europe, with pokes at strict Victorian morality and some of the hypocrisy that existed in a developing counterculture among the youth rebelling against adults in the United States. The next year, *Boy, Did I Get a Wrong Number*, also played footsie with the sexual liberation that was evolving in that decade. I say "played footsie" since Hope's movies of this period were tame in this respect compared to what would follow as soft core pictures. This development occurred in the late '60s and early '70s. Hope's two films were similar to the French bedroom farce of the nineteenth century. This mode of stage play employed humorous entanglements between a husband and wife, with suggestions of romantic and sexual liaisons. And often these suggestions were mistaken assumptions or misunderstandings and not an intimate relationship the spouse thought to be real.

For some odd reason, the 1967 *Eight on the Lam* became a puree of almost no genre. It became a conglomeration or hash that seemed to go just about anywhere. Yes, it has a man forced to flee from the law, but for no clear reason. The protagonist, Hope as a bank officer, becomes a suspect in a supposed forgery—the person who embezzled money. So he takes his family "on the lam." Mixed into this potpourri are stand-up comics Jonathan Winters and Phyllis Diller, along with two beauties, Shirley Eaton and Jill St. John thrown in to provide romantic objects for Hope, a widower with seven children. Four screenwriters were probably too many for this farcical romp. It would seem each one contributed a sequence, so that any coherence and unity are damned. If any genre could be assigned, it might be labeled a big screen sitcom.

By 1968 the comedian returned to one of his staples from the past— the military comedy, *The Private Navy of Sgt. O'Farrell*. Almost all of Bob's previous service films, *Give Me a Sailor* (1938), *Caught in the Draft* (1941), and *Off Limits* (1953), had better gags and more effective plots. Also, the execution of their roles from the supporting cast, Jeffrey Hunter, Phyllis Diller, and Gina Lollobrigida, didn't help Hope. He returned to his con man role, in which he displayed some of his best acting.

The last year of the '60s produced an acceptable and risible generation gap movie that fit well into the depiction of the attitudes of the time. *How to Commit Marriage* (1969) possessed the considerable talents of Bob Hope and Jackie Gleason. The still popular clowns of the cinema and television seemed to stimulate each other. Arguably the best of the eleven '60s pictures were in the first year of the decade that displayed *The Facts of Life* and in the last year that presented *How to Commit Marriage*. However, if you include the genre that became an inventive, unique type of film in Hope's career, the 1962 *Road to Hong Kong* ranks high. It has become a revisited gem of a neglected picture.

While his last starring role in a feature, the 1972 *Cancel My Reservation*, is set in the Southwest, it relies on its humor from Hope's character as a suspect for murder that could have been set in any location. Nevertheless, some local color does add to its originality. Providing this color is Chief Dan George, who won the New York film Critics Circle Award for the Best Supporting Actor for his role as Old Lodge Skins in the 1970 *Little Big Man*, a movie that became a revisionist view of the Old West. He plays Old Bear in *Cancel My Reservation*, a mystic who has visions that might solve the crime. Hope's wife somehow, probably from watching her detective father, solves the crime and gets her husband absolved as a suspect of the murder of a young Native American woman. Since much of the action takes place on an Indian reservation and Hope's role is a man on vacation in an Arizona resort hotel, the title has a double meaning not always realized by the viewer. Bob's previous mystery film can best be illustrated by the 1947

My Favorite Brunette, when the comedian masquerades as a private detective. Some of the genre's characteristics can be found in Hope's many spy comedies: *My Favorite Blonde* (1942), *They Got Me Covered* (1943), and *My Favorite Spy* (1951).

A survey and classification of the decades of Bob Hope's films from 1934 to 1972 illustrates how the comedian embraced nearly the full range in the humorous genre. One type not classified according to content, form, and style, is the fantasy. It is nevertheless often a part of the Road Pictures, which has been mentioned as almost a genre unto itself. The '60s *Road to Hong Kong* has a final scene on an imaginary planet in space that fits the mold. Fantasy is briefly handled in the 1939 *The Cat and the Canary* and the 1940 *The Ghost Breakers*. For example, in the latter work the ghost of a woman materializes at the end of the film. Obviously, Hope seldom used the comic fantasy, but he and his production creators gave him the gamut of genre. Throughout his long profession as a film actor, he was given the chance to enact a wide range of film types for moviegoers.

10 Assessment: Bob Hope's Legacy

A number of mistaken evaluations of the films created by Hope have been carried on in print by fans and critics. Allegations become widely accepted as fact as mythmakers repeat insistently that (1) Hope plays the same character in all of his movies; (2) Since he came from radio to film and is noted for his phrasing and verbal skills, he was not effective using visual humor; (3) His comedies avoid any risqué jokes—that is, he always has "clean comedy"; (4) The films he created in the '40s and '50s are his best movies and he suffered a downhill slide toward the end of his film career; and, (5) The Road Pictures fade after the fifth of seven works.

First, the range of Hope's portrayals can be traced from movie to movie. In one film he may play the con man, such as his roles in the Damon Runyon film adaptations *Sorrowful Jones* and *The Lemon Drop Kid*. In the Road Pictures he maintains a duped character in opposition to Bing Crosby's con man in all seven films. Hope plays the ineffective pretender in *The Paleface, Son of Paleface, Monsieur Beaucaire, The Princess and the Pirate, Casanova's Big Night*, and *Call Me Bwana*, plus many more movies.[1] In his two more serious films, *The Seven Little Foys* and *Beau James*, Bob imitates personalities from life—most of his other depictions are fictional. Also in this vein, Hope employs burlesque in the creation of a Charley's aunt type of person—a man trying to deceive by dressing in women's clothes and affecting the voice of an elderly woman. Hope creates such roles in *The Princess and the Pirate, The Lemon Drop Kid*, and *Casanova's Big Night*. In fact, when the comedian handles the ineffective pretender material he shows ability with both his verbal and pantomime acting. Part of the idea that he plays the same character comes from a confusion with a style and the actor's persona, as Bob's own personality penetrates his portraits. In short, style over substance. Hope remains versatile in playing a wide range of different roles.

Second, most evaluators believe Hope's risible routines came from his background in vaudeville and radio. This may be a result of what could be remembered (the verbal) and what appeared in print. Vaudeville did depend on mime, and it should be realized that Bob started his stage career as a dancer. Occasionally you see his adept approach to visual humor. For example, in the 1940 film *The Ghost Breakers*, he is a stowaway who emerges from a steamer trunk. In a bent-over position from his cramped space in the trunk, he lopes about the room until he straightens out. It is a dance of agony—comical to see. The same is true of Hope on the drugs given to him by a woman spy in the late '40s lampoon of the intrigue picture, *My Favorite Brunette*. Under the influence of the drug he weaves and staggers, with nearly the pantomime ability of French actor Jean-Louis Barrault in the 1945 *The Children of Paradise*. Fortunately, the comedian knows how to show a man under the influence of a drug. His acting is subtle and does not overdo the action. Probably the best example remains in a climactic scene from one of his superior pictures, *Monsieur Beaucaire*. With a series of bobbing, jumping, and hiding, Beaucaire tries to avoid a master swordsman who forces him into a duel to the death. These examples are only a sample of more recognizable uses of visual humor. Many illustrations of nonverbal facial gestures and bodily movements could also be cited. When Hope encounters a beautiful woman he emits a stock tiger "gurrr" with a curl of his lower lip. His eyes and eyebrows express a range of humorous reactions to many different situations. In fact, many times a simple facial reaction conveys his adept acting.

Third, the cliché or myth of Hope's "clean humor" appears even in his '40s radio days. One example shows how he slipped into the blue humor. I remember reading as a teenager an article about Hope going beyond the bounds of good taste with a sexual allusion. The newspaper article reported that the Federal Communication Council (FCC) had threatened him not to use such humor again. Hope had made a joke about women's skirts getting shorter during World War II, presumably to save material for the war effort. However, the mores of the age might have had women wanting to show off their legs. On his Sunday night program Bob said with his usual breezy charm:

"If women's skirts get any shorter, they will have to get two perma-nents."[2] Of course, the watchdogs of the FCC were outraged, but Hope's undying concern for the war effort by staging comedy vari-ety shows for military bases gave him a pass.

When Hope entertained on military bases he brought one of his radio comedians, such as the manic Jerry Colonna, who helped Bob with the off-color jokes. Naturally, the troupe had beautiful women who could sing and dance in scanty costumes. And often they al-lowed Hope and Colonna to use double-meaning jokes of a provoca-tive nature and, occasionally, a raw sexual gag. His daughter, Linda Hope, collected some of his jokes that reflect almost the full range of his career; however, there seem only a few slightly risqué examples in *Bob Hope: My Life in Jokes*.[3] One mildly suggestive joke refers to the grinds with an occasional bump executed by Elvis Presley: "Elvis is just a young, clean-cut American boy who does in public what everybody else does in private."[4]

Of course, the more important concept on how Hope's humor evolved is in his films. The taste of humor changed more to the blue side in the '60s. As this decade began, Hope united with Lucille Ball for their third and, this time, daringly venturesome sexual comedy, *The Facts of Life*. A passionate desire for a liaison develops between two married couples. The struggle to consummate their affair leads to hilarious scenes in a motel and a mountain lodge, according to evaluator Bob Thomas.[5] Actually, the couple's misadventures re-main in good taste, and there develops an interesting satirical state-ment on the boredom of suburbanites. A similar statement on adult sexual hypocrisy versus youthful sexual freedom is in the 1965 *I'll Take Sweden*. An earlier work, the 1962 *Road to Hong Kong*, ended an old gag about two men sharing one woman on a desert island equally for six days with the punch lines: "What do we do on Sunday?" The reply, "We rest."

When Bob Hope reached his one hundredth birthday, many trib-utes flowed from the pens of evaluators, and he became a featured personality with clips from past documentaries on his life. At that time he was weak and, as people put it euphemistically, "He was sinking fast." This meant he was not as mentally alert as witnessed in his former glory. An earlier interview clip indicated that he be-lieved humor had changed with the times and that we should ac-cept the new, more liberal taste of the public.

Fourth, the mythmakers maintained that the best Hope films were in the '40s and '50s. Maybe the people who generalize about the comedian's successful films would have a valid point if they said his works were more consistently effective in those two decades. When this study investigated some of the films from the '60s and even the earlier works in the '30s with Martha Raye, there were many qualities that Hope possessed in the earlier works as well as in his final films. The 1939 *Never Say Die* had the Preston Sturges touch. As has already been mentioned, the '60s films *The Facts of Life*, *Road to Hong Kong*, and even *I'll Take Sweden* have qualities that make them strong works, even though the comedian's film career was nearing an end.

Fifth, there was never a complete fading of the Road Pictures. In the late '40s, *Road to Rio* did not measure up to all six in the series, but it provided the entertainment that could not count the picture as being weak. The last two, *Road to Bali* and *Road to Hong Kong*, by retrospective analysis, could be rated among the best of the seven Road Pictures.

Whereas Arthur Marx does often praise Hope's skill as a comedian, he seems to relish pointing out some of his faults. He calls Bob's ad-libs "unprofessional" in Broadway musicals: "But despite his unprofessional ways, Hope couldn't be stopped, and audiences appreciated his attempts to wring humor out of lines that weren't very humorous."[6] Again, his ego, Marx thinks, caused Hope to ad-lib because he knew he was better than the material given to him, or he did so if the material didn't work with the audience. This action doesn't respect the playwright and the screenwriter. However, many comedians from vaudeville and the movies worked this way, even Arthur's father, Groucho.

One criticism that could be valid from Lawrence Quirk states:

> Though neglecting his artistic potential, indeed thwarting it at times in favor of his popular persona, he nonetheless parlayed his chutzpah and strong, driving ego and genuine gifts (however, at times misused and under exploited) into an unstoppable force that made him one of the world's most popular, most instantly recognizable entertainers.[7]

Biographer Quirk has many anecdotal reports about the comedian. He does have a point about Hope's efforts for charity and as a morale booster for our troops in foreign countries. Lawrence Quirk advances the view that Hope's potential was wasted in his enthusiasm to do benefit shows. He questions the reason why he never received an Oscar for his acting. Bob Hope claims he became too busy to pay attention to his career in film. Hope also believes he should have received more recognition for his serious films such as *The Seven Little Foys* and *Beau James.*

Evidence of the youth rebellion against conventional morality may have affected Hope because he wanted to appeal to a wide audience. Also, he always wanted to use up-to-date humor. As already discussed in the previous chapter, his screenwriters in the '60s provided humor that tried to close that gap with a more sympathetic view of the lifestyle of youth. This is especially evident in the 1965 *I'll Take Sweden* and the 1969 *How to Commit Marriage.*

REVISIONIST VIEW

A retrospective examination by critics needs to be considered for all of Hope's films. This need becomes apparent given any close analysis of the previous criticisms. My investigation into all seven Road Pictures shows that, when I made an evaluation based on a few, limited observations, the analysis was faulty. It should be realized that whatever goes out of fashion or taste may later go from rejection to nearly full acceptance. An example of a too-harsh put-down criticism of the Road Pictures follows:

> Very disjointed in structure, these comedies show the influence of the radio variety show. All three principals engage in banter that has a ring of radio, not vaudeville. Each gets a chance at a song or two....In a type of theatricalism that seldom works in the cinema, Bob or Bing directs an aside to the movie audience. Camping in the jungles in *Road to Zanzibar* (1941), Bing tells Dorothy Lamour that movies often have a man singing to a woman, and regardless of where they may be, an orchestra accompanies him. Bing sings "Always You" and, of course, the strains of a full orchestra come from nowhere.[8]

This was a limited view of a structuralist who had some brush with the Road Pictures of Hope and Crosby. There was tighter dramatic structure in many of the '30s comedies, except for the musical and variety shows. I was at fault by looking for a dramatic construction of the past—both in theatre and the cinema. This became a narrow view in my early 1970s work on what I believed to be "the Golden Age of Sound Comedy," the thirties. My sample for evaluation was about three of seven Road Pictures. Now, thirty years later, I realize not only that I did not see the structural patterns of the Road Pictures, but I also judged as a particular genre what I now see as an art form of its own.

After an evaluation of the more direct, conventionally structured *Casanova's Big Night*, a 1954 movie, a more favorable review appeared in my study of the quality of film comedy that evolved in the silent period and came after the thirties.[9] However, my grasp of Hope's acting was viewed as erratic because I continued to be influenced by the critics of the period. Bob Thomas had the same problem—taking the critical comments of the late '70s as valid. One of his most amazing statements, even though he surveys all of Hope's films, is from James Agee's essay on the silent film comedians: "Hope is a good radio comedian with his pleasing presence, but not much more, on the screen."[10]

Naturally, the sixties experienced a look back to the past greatness of the mimes of the '20s, to the kings of comedy—Chaplin, Lloyd, Keaton, and Langdon. This mode, however, is another type of celluloid humor. Agee was championing a particular form and technique of comedy that Thomas seems also to see as lacking in Hope—physical comedy. He even stresses this by comparing Bob Hope with other comedians:

> The Hope talent was not immediately discernable. He was a good dancer, but no Fred Astaire. He had a light, pleasant singing voice. Physically, he lacked the obvious comedic aspects of Groucho Marx or Joe E. Brown. Well, the nose. It did curve like a scimitar, but it wasn't an outrageous prop, like Jimmy Durante's.[11]

I do find Joe E. Brown a superior sight gag comedian, and not just his cavernous mouth when he yells in frustration over some affront. He had the bodily skills of an athlete and could make running, fighting, and dancing extremely funny. He was nearly the equal of the silent screen clowns. Thomas, with his many insightful analyses, errs by comparing Hope to Groucho Marx. Groucho remains a verbal, almost stand-up comedian compared to Hope. Bob did make a transition to the visual medium. Groucho is always Groucho and has limited mimic abilities compared to Hope's many deceptions—especially his Charley's aunt portrayals in such movies as *The Lemon Drop Kid* and *Casanova's Big Night*. Also, Hope creates some of his most risible scenes when he fights a superior swordsman in *Monsieur Beaucaire* and *Casanova's Big Night*.

Bob Thomas makes a solid contribution to the study of Hope's films when he surveys and classifies the comedian's movies. For example, he develops evaluations on"The Comedy Adventures," "The Roads," "The Farces," "The Comedies of Character," and "The Domestic Comedies."[12] In his pioneer effort to classify, this might be considered by some fans as too academic in the same way that some evaluations seem to be neglected or omitted because the works are considered not worth explaining or evaluating. To his credit, he supplements these classifications with plot synopses of all of Hope's features. One classification Thomas might have included is the genre of the revue and musical. Such Hope films as *The Big Broadcast of 1938*, *College Swing*, *Variety Girl*, and *Here Come the Girls* might have received some of his expertise as one who executes a thorough examination of the comedian.

The Road to Hollywood developed as a collaboration between Hope and Thomas. I have stressed the Thomas part of the book because it was one of the better evaluations of the comedian's work to come out in the '70s. Hope handled the reminiscence of his total career, and he gave an opening designation to the first part of the joint effort with the title, "WHERE THERE'S LIFE by Bob Hope." His co-writer scribed the title "HOPE ON FILM: A Survey by Bob Thomas." Hope gets credit for the first half of the book, even though it is generally known that he used ghostwriters for many of his books. This is not to say that many of Bob's own words weren't repeated as the ghost took down his reflections.[13]

Bob Hope may not have wished an analysis of his revue or musical films. He thought his 1939 *Some Like It Hot* (renamed *Rhythm Romance* for television and video tape) was a failure. A revisionist view gives the film more credit than he did. He joked about his effort:

> *Some Like It Hot* was the rock-bottom point in my movie career. After that one, there was no place to go but up. For years afterward, Bing wouldn't let me forget it. Whenever I started to give him the needle about something, he came back with a rejoinder, something like, "By the way, can you come over to the house tonight Bob? We're going to barbecue some steaks and then all sit down and watch *Some Like It Hot*." That shut me up in a hurry.[14]

Ironically, Hope covered all of his films, including his last starring role feature in the 1972 *Cancel My Reservation*, without realizing that the three '60s movies, *Boy, Did I Get a Wrong Number*, *Eight on the Lam*, and *Private Navy of Sgt. O'Farrell* co-starring Phyllis Diller, would be rated his less effective comedies. Contrary to what he expected, *Some Like It Hot* became the subject of a revisionist view. Part of a revised view of the film is Bob's acting, which shows him at his con man best.

Another evaluation of Hope's films includes the retrospective view of the influence of the Road Pictures on other films. There is much evidence that scripter and director Frank Tashlin sprinkled his creation, *The Son of Paleface*, with in-jokes, plus some impossible chase scenes with a 1910 automobile and a wagon. One ludicrous scene has a wheel that comes off the car stabilized by a rope to hold up the back of the automobile. In another, Hope jumps from a balcony to avoid the enemy and crashes through the bed of the wagon. At rapid speed, his legs run to keep up with the dash to elude capture. These fantastic sequences not only have some of the Road Pictures' illogical jokes, but they seem to harken back to the mode of Mack Sennett's silent screen comedy.

The very end of the 1954 *Casanova's Big Night* has a surrealistic ending worthy of the Road Pictures. The leading character pleads with the audience to accept his ending rather than the Paramount studios' plan to have his character's head chopped off. Hope gives his own movie version of how he subdues and kills all against him and escapes. As he inquires who likes his ending, the audience rejects his heroic rewrite of the ending.

It would appear that the 1985 *Spies Like Us* attempted to be a latter-day reincarnation of a Road Picture. A spoof of a lampoon, naturally, doesn't always work. *Saturday Night Live* veterans Chevy Chase and Dan Aykroyd had turned to feature films with some success, but a venture into the province of Bob Hope and Bing Crosby ended up with a two-star rating. From observation it would appear Chase mocked Hope and Aykroyd mimicked Crosby, but the quality of the original comrades on the road didn't work. Chevy occasionally had a quip that had some of the Hope finesse. Dan seems to be on the road to explain things, since he is the intellectual—not the con man Bing portrayed. So the spoof seldom had the nature approaching a parody. Granted, the pair were on a trek as would-be spies, who were only decoys as inferior agents. And they mounted a camel in Pakistan as if they were Bing and Hope in *Road to Morocco*. One brief appearance by the real Bob Hope had some of the wacky nature of the Road Pictures. In a cameo role he knocks a golf ball into a tent where Chevy and Dan are pretending to be medical doctors. Bob asks, "Mind if I play through?" He knocks the golf ball out of the tent. "Doctor, Doctor. I'm glad I'm not sick."

LEGACY

Any assessment of a comedian who has been called one of the most "admired men" and an "icon of comedians" requires an evaluator to examine the possible influence Hope has had on the careers of other comedians. This legacy makes him a significant contributor to his profession as an entertainer.

I have already indicated how Woody Allen admired Hope's delivery of his comic lines and how this contributed to Allen's character as an actor and his overall writing approach in developing films. It is possible to include another Allen—Steve Allen—as a comedian who may have been influenced by Hope. This statement becomes more valid if Steve's personality and his skill as a master of ceremonies come under examination. His sunny, breezy, always curious and friendly demeanor exists in Allen's many television programs. Allen created *The Tonight Show* on September 27, 1954, and developed a formula as a host who introduced and entered into sketches with guests. Allen, as pioneer of this type of show, with *The Tonight Show* staff, laid the foundation that produced the comedian hosts who followed him—Jack Paar, Johnny Carson, and Jay Leno of *Late Night*. They employed the same pattern of entertainment to make this NBC program the longest running in television history. More recently the NBC *Late Night* show with its host has many of the characteristics of Bob Hope's acting style.

In his first feature film, *The Big Broadcast of 1938*, Bob Hope developed the role of a master of ceremonies that employed lame jokes, as he did in the 1960 *The Facts of Life*. What becomes evident on reflection is how all these hosts for *The Tonight Show* possess an amiable, easy-going comic style that relates well to guest entertainers. Hope projected the same persona in his many years as host of the Academy Awards presentations.[15] More than any of these masters of ceremonies, Bob carried this character into his films, as well as into the USO performances for U.S. troops overseas. Obviously, for those who remember his radio and television shows, the same personality became part of the driving force and focus of attention there.

The hosts of *The Tonight Show*, Allen, Paar, Carson, and Leno, never conquered the film medium as Hope did, but another comedian, Steve Martin, who had some experience as a host on

Saturday Night Live, was able to do so. Comedian Martin possesses abilities for film comic characters that have some similarities to those of Bob Hope. Steve, like his predecessor, also acted as a master of ceremonies—on *Saturday Night Live*—however, he never developed similar emcee traits for his film career. In 1979, his success as a comedian in movies began with *The Jerk*. He would be less strident in his acting as he continued with more innovative characters in future films. Some overplaying of the part in *The Jerk*, almost as obnoxious as the moron character Jerry Lewis executed in a number of his movies, might have worked in a television skit, but when extended to a feature did not prove to display the best of Martin's comedic talent.

Steve Martin's career evolved, depicting a variety of amusing personalities that indicated his versatility in character development. As a would-be con artist who stalked beautiful, rich women, he needed a tutor, enacted by a suave Michael Caine in the 1988 *Dirty Rotten Scoundrels*. Steve has some traits of the naïve and even crude character Hope played in the Road Pictures. Bing Crosby had to lead Hope and even trick him in a con game. Martin depicted an unscrupulous Hollywood director who created motion pictures on the cheap by subterfuge in *Bowfinger* (1999). Hope enacted a racetrack tout in the Damon Runyon adaptations, *Sorrowful Jones* (1949) and *The Lemon Drop Kid* (1951). In a more mild type of comedy Martin enacted the lead in the remake of a Spencer Tracy hit with his 1991 version of *Father of the Bride*. Bob handled the father roles in the two '60s films, *I'll Take Sweden* and *Eight on the Lam*. The paternal roles of both Martin and Hope do not lend themselves to the most laughable comedy—at least, in the films given to them. However, both actors show they can act with the restraint necessary for such parts.

Both comedians project a persona that the audience likes and finds pleasurable, even when the character has mental or physical defects—traits that make a personality laughable. In the plot of the movie starring Milton Berle, *Always Leave Them Laughing* (1949), Bert Lahr, playing a vaudeville clown-like policeman, suggests to Berle that a comedian must first be likeable to gain the confidence of the crowd watching him perform. In this film, Milton previously had been playing the brash, loudmouth television comedian—much like his *The Milton Berle Show* that started June 8, 1948, and continued until January 6, 1967. Obviously, this program entertained many people for almost two decades. His verbal and physical overstated style remained something not all critics liked. Berle's acting was often overstatement. Shakespeare's Hamlet advised players not "to tear a passion to tatters." In the movie, Berle supposedly took the vaudevillian's advice. However, the character Milton portrayed couldn't make the transition to more restrained acting. For comic effect Hope lampooned overacting in his portrait of an itinerant actor in the 1944 *The Princess and the Pirate*. Very early in his career, Steve Martin burlesqued a standup comedian striving to get a laugh with crude props such as an arrow that looked as if it pierced his head. His restrained acting, however, grew in such a way that he seemed to be influenced by Bob Hope's comic method.

Francis Davis, an evaluator of Hope's influence on other comic actors, indicated the widespread examples of humorous standup and host entertainers who might have used the comedian as a model:

> Hope's influence has been ubiquitous, both as a stand-up comedian and as a comic actor. Without [Hope] as the prototype, there would be no Johnny Carson, Steve Martin or Bill Murray—to say nothing of Maxwell Smart, Austin Powers ... even M*A*S*H's Capt. Benjamin Franklin "Hawkeye" Pierce.[16]

Davis refers to Alan Alda as Hawkeye in the long-running military sitcom, MASH. The character played by Alda did have some characteristics of the con man Hope and a style of quick repartee and understated punch line. Bill Murray and Don Adams (as Maxwell Smart the bumbling secret agent on television and in a few movies) seem to come closer to the Bob Hope prototype than Mike Myers, who started in television and moved to such movies as *Austin Powers: The Spy Who Shagged Me* (1999). Myers employed caricatures and eccentric humor situations that are unlike Hope vehicles. Bill Murray, however, appeared in a military comedy, *Stripes* (1981), with a character somewhat like Hope in his 1941 *Caught in the Draft*. Both characters in these two movies are misfits in the army who produce humor in their leading roles. Like Hope, Murray had the ability to impersonate a real person in *Where the Buffalo Roam* (1980). In this movie he creates an effective portrait of the eccentric, free-spirited journalist, Hunter S. Thompson. Whereas Bob Hope handled a masterful interpretation of the unconventional vaudeville comedian Eddie Foy in *The Seven Little Foys*, actor Bill Murray developed into a performer of deviant characters as his career progressed. In 1991, Bill's *What About Bob?* presented the movie audience with one of the most likeable oddballs ever witnessed in the medium. His enactment of an intrusive mental patient who invades the life of a psychiatrist's family illustrates how a superior actor can depict a person with severe mental problems as attractive, without offending those who believe such a character is not to be used for comedy.

Both Steve Martin and Bill Murray seem to me to display some of the traits of the Bob Hope style, although whether or not there is a direct influence from their predecessor may be questioned. Hope existed in a milieu of vaudeville and then radio. Most of comedians mentioned have similar styles (delivery and all it entails, both verbal and physical). Besides Woody Allen claiming direct influence, Steve Martin also says he learned from Hope. The generations of Steve Allen, Woody Allen, Don Adams, Alan Alda, Johnny Carson, Steve Martin, and Bill Murray grew up and dwelled in the world of television—with Steve Allen moving from radio to get a firm foothold as a television host. Hope's contemporaries emerged from vaudeville, and all developed radio programs and moved on to television: Jack Benny, George Burns and Gracie Allen, Milton Berle, Ed Wynn, Eddie Cantor, Jimmy Durante, Abbott and Costello, plus many others. As an evaluator of films and comedians for decades, I realize the purveyors of humorous drama influence each other within their own generation. Bob probably received inspiration from Jack Benny from whom, some people believe, Hope received his sliding walk and understated delivery. Bob may have learned from Benny the long pause and a variation of Jack's double take. However, I think the two comedians might have mutually aped each other. During the radio years in the '30s and the transition to both film and television, many comic celebrities engaged in joshing among friends. Benny and Hope exchanged mild insults, as did Hope and Bing Crosby, Benny and Fred Allen, to the point that the banter became a tradition, both on radio and in film.

Almost all major comedians of radio and television served as what is called host or master of ceremonies for their own shows, simply called *The Ed Wynn Show* or *The Jimmy Durante Show*, depending on who served as host. Almost all of these comedians entered the movies. Hope probably became the most successful actor in all the media.

Conan O'Brien's first *Late Night* show was broadcast on September 13, 1993, and benefited from his skill as a writer of articles for *The Harvard Lampoon*. As a writer of sketches, Steve Martin, like O'Brien, moved on to performing. Essayist Francis Davis believes O'Brien uses many of Hope's techniques in his standup routines:

Conan O'Brien, when announcing that his guests that night include a supermodel or leggy movie star, might lick his index fingers and use them to smooth his eyebrows, like Hope primping for what he's only been led to believe will be a romantic rendezvous (it's usually some sort of scheme, with him as the sucker). The host of *Late Night* also occasionally growls when an attractive female guest says something provocative, a variation on Hope's ejaculatory *woof*. And the premise of many of O'Brien's best sketches is either that he's sexually inadequate or that nobody thinks he's funny—two more pages straight out of Hope's book, as O'Brien would be the first to admit.[17]

Bob Hope did exploit the growl—a type of sound similar to a tiger's growl with "g" and a string of "rs," such as g-r-r-r-r—probably more often than he used a "woof." And, after viewing some of Conan's *Late Night* shows, I have seen the eyebrow primping. When he does two jumps and twists around in a dance, he reminds me of another comedian—Danny Kaye. Sometimes he seems to be a cross between Hope and Kaye. He can certainly toss off a line like Hope. At times, he is manic and makes silly gestures and oddball noises, like Kaye about to do a patter song. On his May 18, 2004, show, he mentioned the death of Tony Randall. He indicated that he admired Tony's acting since childhood. Is this another influence on his eclectic style? Like Randall, he is sometimes overly fastidious and, occasionally, fey.

The headline of the July 2003 *Philadelphia Inquirer* might be questioned: "Bob Hope Was One of the Innovators of Screen Comedy."[18] The stress, however, should be placed on "One." Other comedians followed the use of topical gags, plus what evaluator Carrie Rickey in the *Inquirer* calls stepping out of character and talking to the viewer. This was, of course, used extensively in the Road Pictures of Hope and Crosby. It is not exactly one comedian's innovation. Most vaudevillians incorporated this device for a contrived or legitimate ad-lib. For example, Will Rogers took advantage of a mishap as a piece of scenery fell on stage to utter an unscripted joke. He looked at the audience and said simply, "Termites."

It has been reported from many sources, especially in the Arts & Entertainment's *Biography*, that Hope could ad-lib and write his own jokes.[19] From the silent days of such comedians as Charles Chaplin, Harold Lloyd, Buster Keaton, and Harry Langdon plus many others, the stars employed writers to develop gags and a story line for their features. These actors, like Hope and his contemporaries, served as editors of the stories and the gags, thereby they were, if they attained star status, completely in charge of the creative process. A great deal of credit for the quality of Hope's films does depend on the screenwriters. Of course, they had to know his approach to humor:

> "We wrote jokes about his writers," said Larry Gelbart, who went to work for Mr. Hope in 1948 and whose writing credits include the television version of "M*A*S*H" and the movie *Tootsie*. "He knew there was a good joke in having writers. He played off everything. He used every part of his life. His life was his own straight line. Actually he was wittier and smarter off stage. We sort of wrote to a Hope paradigm. ... People loved him because he was so publicly being the fool as we all privately are."[20]

This statement by one of his writers indicates how leading comedians served as editors, and the best of them proved to be excellent judges of the jokes that would suit them and be funny. Naturally, Hope's writers were blessed with many years of experience. Several of the actors mentioned were skilled writers of their own material. Hope probably maintained such a busy schedule that he only had time to collect and alter jokes to fit his own style. Obviously, Woody Allen authored his own lines and screenplays, plus a few stage plays. Steve Martin scripted a modern version of Cyrano de Bergerac with *Roxanne* (1987), as well as *L. A. Story* (1991). Hope has many credits for humorous books, but it is difficult to determine how much he contributed because he had co-authors who probably did the major share of the writing. But Hope, as always, acted as the astute editor of his own writing and that of others who assisted him.

Bob Hope's humor, the range of characters he portrayed, and the value of his motion pictures should be summarized to conclude *The Road to Comedy*. The variety and significance of this comedian's contributions have not always been realized by the public and critics.

Hope continued the tradition of topical comedy linked to political humor. This approach to the world of the risible has been attributed to two of our most famous writers of the past, Will Rogers and Mark Twain. Before his death in the early thirties, Rogers wrote a newspaper column and gave speeches on politics.[21] Often quoted is his statement, "I don't belong to an organized party. I'm a Democrat." Mark Twain approached political humor more allegorically, through his novels such as *A Connecticut Yankee in King Arthur's Court*, where he satirized the attempt to create a Utopia in an imperfect world. The kingdom of Arthur resembled some of the faults of today's government and society. Will Rogers created one-line jokes, thus he is the precursor to Hope. A magazine from the Gold Collectors Series mentions Bob's proclivity toward this type of humor:

> Long before Jay Leno, David Letterman, and Bill Maher made a living lampooning the power elite, Bob Hope was the king of topical humor aimed at kings and presidents alike. Hope opened each radio and television show with a monologue that took its gags straight off the pages of the newspapers. No politician was safe when "Rapid Robert" took the stage. With Hope, there was no sacred cow.[22]

A widely repeated gag by Bob occurred when he played golf many times with President Gerald Ford, whose action of pardoning President Nixon for the Watergate scandal may have cost him his election to a second term. Hope said something close to this one-liner: "If you beat Gerry Ford in golf, he will pardon you." Hope, kidding both Republican and Democratic presidents, took this gentle poke at President John Kennedy and his brother:

> And I think Robert Kennedy has picked some pretty good help. Harvard is emptier than our treasury. It's quite a thing. There are so many professors in the Cabinet, you can't leave the White House without raising your hand.[23]

Bob also carried his topical and political humor into his movies. In the 1940 *The Ghost Breakers*, Hope and Paulette Goddard are menaced by a wandering, stumbling zombie played by Noble Johnson, a bit film actor noted for his ghoul parts. "He's like the Democrats, he doesn't know where he's going," wisecracks Hope. One other facet of the comedian's unusual skill in promoting laughter cannot be determined from his films—his ad-lib abilities. As has been mentioned, the ad-lib could be pre-planned, and the actor gets the credit. Steve Allen, probably one of the best at ad-libbing—even better than Hope—laughed at his own spontaneous humor. Steve explained why he laughed at his jokes. He laughed, he said, because he had never heard the jest before. The only example of this type of humor I could find was tied into the political-topical gag in Bob's humorous book on golf, *Confession of a Hooker*. He delivers an anecdote on Nixon's demeanor during a golf match:

> Nixon acted like he was campaigning, hugging and kissing everyone in sight. I told him, "Mr. President, you're already elected." I thought it was pretty funny, but I didn't notice him laughing.[24]

Examples of Hope's use of monologue humor in films generally are hard to find. Screenwriter Edmund Hartmann explained to me how he wrote detailed monologues for Hope. One of the best occurs in the 1950 *Fancy Pants*, when Hope as a con man butler weaves an elaborate, contrived tale of a British soldier fighting a fierce band of African warriors. Hartmann explained how he wrote this elaborate declamation for Hope. While the comedian executed many monologues in his career in vaudeville, radio, and television, it was a type of humor seldom used in his films.

Actor Hope excelled at a wide range of humor. Some of the types can be classified as spirit of play, understatement, overstatement, invective, running gag, and the revealing gag. Much of Hope's comedy is laced with the spirit of play—a more sunny type of cheerful jostling with jests that may poke fun at authority but are more often understated so that seldom does comedian Bob become sarcastic. His closest colleagues from vaudeville and radio, Jack Benny and George Burns, dealt in wry observations on human foibles. The parsimonious Benny has an often-quoted radio exchange when he is being robbed by a gangster. The petty thug points his gun and says, "Your money or your life." (A big pause, and the robber repeats his threat.) Benny, ever the skinflint, finally replies, "I'm thinking it over." Jack's understated delivery illustrates how the radio comedian learned to underplay. In his movies, Hope utilized the understatement in his asides to the camera in many of the Road Pictures. In the second of the series, the 1941 *The Road to Zanzibar*, Hope engages in the carnival act of sawing a girlfriend in half to gain passage to go back to the United States. Crosby asks him if he knows how to do this magic act. "If I don't," Bob says, "one of us is going back half fare." The punch to this gag comes from the comedian's dry understatement. Benny, Hope, and Burns were experienced and talented comedians who knew how to turn a joke by understatement. Bob did utilize overstatement when he depicted an ineffective character, such as an itinerant actor traveling in the Caribbean. In *The Princess and the Pirate*, Hope practiced his role as an old hag— a cackling witch-like imitation. It is a horribly overacted creation, and the laugh pokes fun at a very poor thespian.

Hope could switch from this type of laughable character to a sophisticated character who uses the put-down. Such invective comedy reveals another classification—a type of insult comedy. This assault on a person goes back to Shakespeare and continues into seventeenth-, eighteenth-, and nineteenth-century dramas. One of the best examples of this type of comedy exists in Hope's last important comedy, *How to Commit Marriage*, in 1969. Hope proves he can match Jackie Gleason, who was the master of the comic insult. The invective usually depends on a situation with rivals, a man versus a man or a woman versus a woman. In some cases, especially the Road Pictures, one person may dominate. Bing Crosby often remains ahead of Bob Hope. In a situation where Bing sells Bob into slavery, strong animosity develops. This rivalry existed most effectively in *Road to Morocco* and may have assisted in the 1942 work receiving such high popular and critical status. The rivalry sometimes switches to an attack on the enemy. In the latter part of many of the Road Pictures, the two become buddies and, in the spirit of play, are like two children delighted to be able to attack and defeat the enemy.

Two other examples of the wide range and variety of humor developed by Hope and his writers were the running gag and the revealing gag. Using the Road Pictures as examples, the running gag involves the incongruous patty-cake performed by Bob and Bing that distracts the enemies so that the pair can knock them unconscious with a surprise blow. Most running gags evolve within one motion picture—a series of repeated jokes that end in a pay-off that is more laughable. This type of gag appears throughout the series, with the funniest as a reversal. The sixth Road Picture, *Road to Bali* released in 1953, shows the duo with a patty-cake routine backfiring. The natives capture them, and this time the deception doesn't work because the islanders duck. Bob and Bing thus knock each other out. The revealing gag doesn't have the prominence of the running gag. It is quite rare. One of the best examples occurs in the '60s film, *Call Me Bwana*, as we observe what looks like a house in Africa. It ends up that Hope's character is obsessed and has collected all the trimmings in his New York apartment, which makes him want to be an explorer like his uncle. The truth of where he lives is revealed as he opens the drapes to show skyscrapers, as the sounds of the traffic below come to the ears of the movie audience.

There always exists the matter of taste that enters the critical or popular evaluation of Hope's films. From an examination of his works, some films rate higher than others. If Bob's movies are classified according to critical and popular acclaim, there will always be a question of personal taste involved. Some treatments and subjects themselves happen to be liked or disliked. Critics hope they are able to be objective; nevertheless, even the average moviegoer may detect subjectivity in films.

The two films that enjoy kudos from evaluators and the public alike certainly seem to be *Road to Morocco* and *The Paleface*. Both pictures were financial successes for Paramount. Also, evaluators and the public praised these works. Anthony Quinn, who played a villainous Sheik, credits *Road to Morocco* with furthering his career. "Quinn swears that the 'Road' pictures made so much money they created opportunities for him he might otherwise not have had."[25] Evaluators generally rate these two films among Hope's best, and they are often mentioned in brief biographic sketches of the comedian's career.

Moving down a notch to second place, *The Princess and the Pirate*, *Monsieur Beaucaire*, *Casanova's Big Night*, and *The Facts of Life* have enough support to be four important motion pictures starring Bob Hope. The three period pictures were a phenomenon to me and to theater and film critic Robert Nott, who writes for the *Santa Fe New Mexican*. We observe how Hope plays with aplomb, and we relish the inadequate con man and impersonator in these three titles. *The Facts of Life* may be controversial, because evaluators dismiss the comedian's '60s pictures as weak works when compared with those from the '40s and '50s. They choose to equate such films as *Call Me Bwana*, *Eight on the Lam*, *Boy, Did I Get the Wrong Number*, and *The Private Navy of Sgt. O'Farrell*. A second showing of some of the films should correct this misconception. Three other movies besides *The Facts of Life* need to be re-examined: *Road to Hong Kong*, *I'll Take Sweden*, and *How to Commit Marriage* attest to the fact that Hope moved to the more permissive comedy of the times and tried to handle material that was more progressive—space travel, liberal sexual mores, and bridging the generation gap.

For the third ranking there is more spread in time, from 1939 to 1957. The 1939 entry, *Never Say Die*, could be classified here because of its satirical thrust. *Fancy Pants* (1950), with co-stars Hope and Lucille Ball, qualifies for its energetic, smooth execution by the stars and director. In 1953, the sixth of the series, *Road to Bali*, makes the list for its innovative ability to keep fresh the formula of the Road Pictures. And the last two of the five in this group, *The Seven Little Foys* (1955) and *Beau James* (1957), demonstrate a change of Hope's skill to that of a serious actor in biographic works. All of the five possess superior screenwriters in this order:

1. *Never Say Die*, writers Don Hartman, Frank Butler, and Preston Sturges

2. *Fancy Pants*, writers Edmund Hartmann and Robert O'Brien
3. *Road to Bali*, writers Frank Butler, Hal Kanter, and William Morrow
4. *The Seven Little Foys*, writers Melville Shavelson and Jack Rose
5. *Beau James*, the instigators of Hope's serious roles, Shavelson and Rose

If the screenwriters for all three categories are examined, it would be revealed that excellent scripters created the vehicles for the comedian to achieve the success he deserved.

I have focused this study on the films of Bob Hope. In vaudeville, radio, and motion pictures he has become an icon for those who followed him as master of ceremonies. He also carried talented reviews of skits, songs, and dances to military personnel from World War II to the Gulf War. Some biographers believe the latter contribution became his most important gift to our society. Raymond Strait, who appeared to be writing a type of exposé book on the comedian by telling about some events that exposed his womanizing, switched to a personal note that revealed he met Bob Hope when he was in the service overseas. Strait wrote:

> He made us feel good. No one ever took his business to the public the way Hope did. He never had to coerce us. We waited in long lines to see him, set our clocks, tape recorders, and VCRs to make sure we didn't miss him in person, on radio, in the movies and on television.[26]

Some time ago I wrote about the comedian that "made us feel good" because he had the foibles we did. Hope is sort of a latter-day Harold Lloyd, from the silent days of cinema. In some ways both of them could have been similar fellow-next-door persons with faults and virtues. You liked such a character because he brought joy even when he was a con man and a person inferior to you. He was likeable. Lloyd and Hope were like the commedia del arte character, Harlequin the Happy. Forever moving, he was cloaked in a gaiety and charm all his own.

And Hope always left us laughing.

Appendix A: Bob Hope Films

TWO REELERS (SHORTS)

Year	Title	Co-stars
1934	*Going Span ish*	Leah Ray.
1934	*Paree, Paree*	Dorothy Stone, Charles Collins.
1935	*The Old Grey Mayor*	Ruth Blasco, Lionel Stander, Sam Wren.
1935	*Watch the Birdie*	Neil O'Day, Arline Dintz.
1935	*Double Exposure*	Johnny Berkes, Loretta Sayers, Jules Epailley.
1936	*Calling All Tars*	Johnny Berkes, Oscar Ragland.
1936	Shop Talk	starring only Bob Hope.

FEATURE MOTION PICTURES

Year	Title	Co-stars
1938	*The Big Broadcast of 1938*	W.C. Fields, Shirley Ross, Martha Raye, Dorothy Lamour, Leif Erikson, Lynn Overland.
1938	*College Swing*	George Burns, Gracie Allen, Edward Everett Horton, Martha Ray.
1938	*Give Me A Sailor*	Betty Grable, Martha Raye Clarence Kolb.
1938	Thanks for the *Memory*	Shirley Ross, Otto Kruger, Laura Hope Crews, Charles Butterworth, Hedda Hopper.
1939	*Never Say Die*	Martha Raye, Paul Harvey, Ernest Cossart.
1939	*Some Like It Hot (Rhythm Romance)*	Shirley Ross, Rufe Davis, Una Merkel.
1939	*The Cat and the Canary*	Paulette Goddard, Douglass Montgomery.

FEATURE MOTION PICTURES (CONTINUED)

Year	Title	Co-stars
1940	*Road to Singapore*	Dorothy Lamour, Bing Crosby, Anthony Quinn.
1940	*The Ghost Breakers*	Paulette Goddard, Willie Best, Anthony Quinn.
1941	*Road to Zanzibar*	Dorothy Lamour, Bing Crosby, Una Merkel.
1941	*Caught in the Draft*	Dorothy Lamour, Eddie Bracken, Lynne Overman.
1941	*Nothing but the Truth*	Paulette Goddard, Leif Erikson, Edward Arnold.
1941	*Louisiana Purchase*	Vera Zorina, Victor Moore, Dona Drake.
1942	*My Favorite Blonde*	Madeleine Carroll, George Zucco, Gale Sondergaard.
1942	*Road to Morocco*	Dorothy Lamour, Bing Crosby, Dona Drake, Anthony Quinn.
1943	*They Got Me Covered*	Dorothy Lamour, Otto Preminger, Lenore Aubert.
1943	*Let's Face It*	Betty Hutton, Phyllis Povah, Zasu Pitts, Eve Arden.
1944	*The Princess and the Pirate*	Virginia Mayo, Walter Slezak, Walter Brennan, Marc Lawrence, Victor McLaglen.
1946	*Road to Utopia*	Dorothy Lamour, Bing Crosby, Douglas Dumbrille.
1946	*Monsieur Beaucaire*	John Caulfield, Majorie Reynolds, Patric Knowles.
1947	*My Favorite Brunette*	Dorothy Lamour, Lon Chaney Jr., Peter Lorre.
1947	*Where There's Life*	Signe Hasso, George Coulouris, William Bendix.
1947	*Road to Rio*	Dorothy Lamour, Bing Crosby, Frank Faylen.
1948	*The Paleface*	Jane Russell, Iris Adrian, Robert Armstrong.
1949	*Sorrowful Jones*	Lucille Ball, William Demarest, Mary Jane Saunders.
1949	*The Great Lover*	Rhonda Fleming, Roland Culver, Roland Young.
1950	*Fancy Pants*	Lucille Ball, Jack Kirkwood, Bruce Cabot.
1951	*The Lemon Drop Kid*	Marilyn Maxwell, Jane Darwell, Lloyd Nolan.
1951	*My Favorite Spy*	Hedy Lamarr, Arnold Moss, Francis L. Sullivan.
1952	*Son of Paleface*	Jane Russell, Bill Williams, Roy Rogers.
1952	*Road to Bali*	Dorothy Lamour, Bing Crosby, Ralph Moody.
1953	*Off Limits*	Marilyn Maxwell, Mickey Rooney, Stanley Clements.
1953	*Here Come the Girls*	Arlene Dahl, Tony Martin, Millard Mitchell.
1954	*Casanova's Big Night*	Audrey Dalton, Joan Fontaine, John Carradine.
1955	*The Seven Little Foys*	George Tobias, Milly Vitale, Billy Gray.
1955	*The Seven Little Foys*	George Tobias, Milly Vitale, Billy Gray.

FEATURE MOTION PICTURES (CONTINUED)

Year	Title	Co-stars
1956	*That Certain Feeling*	George Sanders, Eva Marie Saint, Pearl Bailey.
1956	*The Iron Petticoat*	Katharine Hepburn, James Robertson Justice.
1957	*Beau James*	Alexis Smith, Vera Miles, Darren McGavin.
1958	*Paris Holiday*	Anita Ekberg, Fernandel, Martha Hyer.
1959	*Alias Jesse James*	Rhonda Fleming, Jim Davis, Wendell Corey.
1960	*The Facts of Life*	Lucille Ball, Don Defore, Ruth Hussey.
1961	*Bachelor in Paradise*	Lana Turner, Jim Hutton, Paula Prentiss.
1962	*Road to Hong Kong*	Dorothy Lamour, Bing Crosby, Joan Collins, Cameos: Frank Sinatra, Peter Sellers, David Niven, Dean Martin, Dave King, Zsa Zsa Gabor, Jerry Colonma.
1963	*Critic's Choice*	Lucille Ball, Rip Torn, Jim Backus.
1963	*Call Me Bwana*	Anita Ekberg, Lionel Jeffries, Edie Adams.
1964	*A Global Affair*	Lilo Pulver, Elga Anderson, Michele Mercier.
1965	*I'll Take Sweden*	Dina Merrill, Tuesday Weld, Frankie Avalon.
1966	*Boy, Did I Get a Wrong Number*	Elke Sommer, Phyllis Diller, Cesare Danova.
1967	*Eight on the Lam*	Jonathan Winters, Phyllis Diller, Jill St. John.
1968	*The Private Navy of Sgt. O'Farrell*	Jeffrey Hunter, Phyllis Diller, Gina Lollobrigida, Henry Wilcoxon, William Wellman, Jr.
1969	*How to Commit Marriage*	Jane Wyman, Maureen Arthur, Jackie Gleason, Leslie Nielsen, Paul Stewart.
1972	*Cancel My Reservation*	Eva Marie Saint, Forrest Tucker, Keenan Wynn.

Appendix B: Selected Bob Hope Awards

ACADEMY AWARDS, USA

Year	Award	Category
1941	Honorary Award	In recognition of his unselfish services to the motion picture industry (special silver plaque).
1945	Honorary Award	For his many services to the Academy (Life Membership in the AMPAS).
1953	Honorary Award	For his contribution to the laughter of the world, his service to the motion picture industry, and his devotion to the American premise.
1960	Jean Hersholt	Humanitarian Award.
1966	Honorary Award	For unique and distinguished service to our industry and the Academy (gold medal).

GOLDEN GLOBES, USA

Year	Award	Category
1958	Special Award	For an Ambassador of Good Will.
1963	Cecil B. DeMille Award	

EMMY AWARDS

Year	Award	Category
1966	Emmy	Outstanding Variety Special for: "Bob Hope Presents the Chrysler Theatre" (1963) for the Christmas Special (January 19, 1966).

EMMY AWARDS (CONTINUED)

Year	Award	Category
1984	Governor's Award	

SCREEN ACTORS GUILD AWARDS

Year	Award	Category
1966	Life Achievement Award	

TELEVISION CRITICS ASSOCIATION AWARDS

Year	Award	Category
1993	Career Achievement Award	

AMERICAN COMEDY AWARDS, USA

Year	Award	Category
1995	Lifetime Achievement Award in Comedy	

Appendix C: Selected Bob Hope Honors

1959 Emmy: Trustees' Award "for bringing the great gift of laughter to all peoples of all nations; for selflessly entertaining American troops throughout the world over many years; and for making TV finer by these deeds and by the consistently high quality of his TV programs through the years".

1962 Hollywood Foreign Press Association: Cecil B. DeMille Award.

1985 Kennedy Center Honors Lifetime Achievement Award.

1990 Inducted into the Radio Hall of Fame.

1995 National Medal of Arts: presented by President Bill Clinton.

1997 Congress named Hope an honorary U.S. veteran, citing his decades of entertaining troops around the world. He is the only person to receive that distinction.

1998 Queen Elizabeth conferred Honorary Knighthood on Hope.

Bob Hope has entertained the troops overseas in every war from WWII to the First Gulf War. The U.S. Air Force named a cargo plane "The Spirit of Bob Hope" after the legendary entertainer. The Navy honored him with a ship, the "USNS Bob Hope".

He holds two entries in "The Guinness Book of World Records." One is for having the distinction of being the entertainer with "the longest running contract with a single network, spanning sixty-one years". The second is for being the "most honored entertainer," with over 1,500 awards.

He served as the U.S. Overseas (USO) Entertainment Coordinator from 1941 through 2001 and hosted the Oscars eighteen times. Mr. Hope holds 54 Honorary Degrees and has entertained eleven different Presidents of the United States.

Notes

Chapter 1: Song, Dance, and Gags: From Vaudeville to Radio

1. Bob Hope, *Bob Hope: My Life in Jokes*, 228.
2. Richard Grudens, *The Spirit of Bob Hope*, 8. Les Hope refers to a shortening of his given name, Leslie.
3. William Robert Faith, *Bob Hope: A Life in Comedy*, 16.
4. Bob Hope, *Bob Hope's Own Story: Have Tux, Will Travel*, 55.
5. Lawrence Quirk, *The Road Well-Traveled*, 28.
6. Faith, *A Life in Comedy*, 23.
7. Ironically, Bing Crosby received critical acclaim for one of his superior performances in film when he played a father with a drinking problem in *The Country Girl* (1954).
8. Information gleaned from Lawrence Foy's photo album.
9. Faith, *A Life in Comedy*, 59.
10. Ibid., 71.
11. Jim Harmon, *The Great Radio Comedians*, 99.
12. Ibid., 11.
13. Faith, *A Life in Comedy*, 56.
14. Harmon, *The Great Radio Comedians*, 136.
15. Faith, *A Life in Comedy*, 71.
16. Frank Vreeland, *Foremost Films of 1938*, 335.
17. *Legends of Radio, The Bob Hope Show*, "Guests: Blondie and Dagwood," December 20, 1938 (audio tape).

Chapter 2: Hollywood Embraces a Song and Dance Man

1. An evaluation of musicals in *Time*, June 10, 1929, 19.
2. The production numbers seem to be derived from a feature film or adapted from a stage musical, as indicated in the opening titles. The feature *Fifty Million Frenchmen* has a credit line.

3. This DVD may be obtained through the website of Bob Hope or through Amazon.com.

4. Lawrence Quirk, *The Road Well-Traveled*, 1904.

5. Ibid., 107.

6. David P. Hayes, personal communication on the Internet, Newsgroups/ alt.movies/silent, September 17, 2003.

7. Frank S. Nugent, *New York Times*, March 10, 1938.

8. *American Film Institute Catalog: Feature Films, 1931–1940*, 151.

9. Quirk, *The Road Well-Traveled*, 118.

10. Ironically, Betty Grable would become the pinup photo for the service men during World War II. Shot from the back wearing a bathing suit, the photo accentuates her legs and derriere.

11. This is an opening title shown on the screen. The narration of shots, however, are descriptions of the content by the author of this book.

12. Bob Hope and Bob Thomas, *The Road to Hollywood*, 125.

13. Nugent, *New York Times*, November 23, 1939.

14. A second quote from Kay's All Movie Guide on the Internet.

Chapter 3: Starring Hope During the War Years

1. According to the *American Film Institute Catalog: Feature Films, 1941–1950* (p. 1418), there were three leading actors from the Broadway musical: Victor Moore, Vera Zorina, and Irene Bordoni. This may have provided seasoned acting for the total production of the film version of *Louisiana Purchase.*

2. In a special evaluation section of Hope's *The Road To Hollywood*, Bob Thomas indicates that creator and director Elliott Nugent and screenwriters Walter De Leon and Lynn Starling focused on *The Cat and the Canary* in a way that "played it for laughs." Thomas adds, "The first major film tailored to the talents of Bob Hope, it was critical to his career" (p. 137).

3. An allusion to the 1678 novel *The Pilgrim's Progress* by John Bunyan.

4. *American Film Institute Catalog: Feature Films, 1941–1950*, 1639. The American Film Institute also reports that Hope's screenwriters Melvin Frank and Norman Panama wrote for the comedian's radio show before creating *My Favorite Blonde.*

5. Hope started as host of the Motion Picture Academy Awards in 1960 and continued this role for fifteen years, a record that still stands.

6. *American Film Institute Catalog: Feature Films, 1941–1950*, 1363–1354. Researchers for the American Film Institute indicate that Danny Kaye, who played the role on Broadway, was slated to do the movie instead of Hope but was "left out of negotiations."

Chapter 4: There Was Hope and Hartmann

1. David Fantle and Thomas Johnson, "A Tribute to Bob Hope, Thanks for the Memories," in *Golden Collectors Series*, 27–28.

2. Julian Brown, *Variety: Comedy Movies*, 92.

3. Bosley Crowther, *New York Times*, December 18, 1948, 41.

4. John Harkness, *The Academy Awards Handbook: Revised and Updated 2001 Edition.*

5. From a Walt Disney Company television program, circa 1989.

6. Crowther, *New York Times*, June 6, 1949, 15.

7. *Mary Poppins* is an effective and, to many fans and critics, a superior fantasy-musical overflowing with charm.

Chapter 5: Some Hits and Misses

1. Ed Hartmann had handled the story line of the 1948 *The Paleface*, one of the most acclaimed works of his career. Tishman was a gagman for the movie. He wanted to take over as writer and director for the sequel, and Hartmann was dropped.

2. Hal Erickson, in an evaluation for the All Movie Guide, ranks the sequel as a superior work. It may be a matter of taste.

3. Bendix appeared in *The Life of Riley* television sitcom from 1953 to 1958 (*The Complete Directory to Prime Time Network and Cable TV Shows*, 596).

4. This use of cameos for noted stars began to mushroom with Hope's television specials in the 1970s and 1980s. Well-known actors had a limited use in most of his movies.

5. A. Weiler, *New York Times*, March 30, 1953, 25.

6. Bob Hope with Melville Shavelson, *Don't Shoot, It's Only Me*, 195.

7. *New York Times*, June 27, 1997, 21.

Chapter 6: Neglected and Underrated Movies

1. Goodrich and Hackett were extremely versatile writers, as shown by their handling of Frank Capra's sentimental Christmas favorite, *It's a Wonderful Life* (1946), musicals for Jeanette MacDonald and Nelson Eddy, and an adaptation for stage and screen of *The Diary of Anne Frank*.

2. Hope's wife, unlike the wives of George Burns, Jack Benny, and Fred Allen, did not want to play the comedienne with Bob. Instead, she preferred to remain in a more minor role in vaudeville and radio as an accomplished singer of serious songs.

3. Bosley Crowther, *New York Times*, December 8, 1938, 34.

4. *Webster's New Collegiate Dictionary*, 617.

5. Stanley Green, *Encyclopedia of the Musical Film*, 130–131.

6. Charles Affron, evaluation of *Ninotchka*, *International Dictionary of Films and Filmmakers—#1 Films*, 701.

7. *M-G-M PRESS BOOK*, 1.

8. *M-G-M PRESS BOOK*, 4.

9. Hal Erickson, *Evaluation of "The Iron Petticoat."*

10. Arthur Marx, *The Secret Life of Bob Hope*, 392.

11. Leonard Maltin, *Leonard Maltin's 1999 Movie & Video Guide*, 162, 395.

12. Julian Brown, ed., *Variety: Comedy Movies*, 27.

13. Quirk, *A Road Well-Traveled*, 276.

14. Roger Greenspun, *New York Times*, September 22, 1972, 38.

15. Jay Cocks, *Time*, October 9, 1972, 100.

16. Ibid., 100.

17. Nathan Rabin, "Films That Time Forgot: *Cancel My Reservation*."

Chapter 7: The Rocky Road to Exotic Worlds

1. In *Road to Hollywood*, Bob Thomas recognizes the Road Pictures as a separate genre and gives some interesting evaluations of five of them. He does not discuss *Road to Rio* or *Road to Hong Kong*, suggesting that he does not regard them as important as the other works.

2. In Dorothy Lamour's autobiography, *My Side of the Road* (p. 87), she questions whether Fred MacMurray and Jack Oakie were considered for *Road to Singapore*, calling the report a rumor.

3. Part of the enjoyment for the audiences that followed the Road Picture series is the expected joke to suddenly be switched to surprise variation.

4. There remains a controversy regarding the ad-libs used in the Hope–Crosby pictures. From their radio days, writers could give them lines that would seem to be impromptu. Lamour indicates that she tried to follow the script but was constantly frustrated when they departed from the written dialogue (*My Side of the Road*, 87–88).

5. There are a number of suggestive jokes with sexual connotations, but in the 1940s they were mild because the censors were ever vigilant.

6. The title *Road to Utopia* may be intended as a joke. It might be an inversion joke of what I call the exotic worlds. Not many people think of Alaska as a utopia. More often, we think of utopia as a pleasant place, such as a tropical island located in the Pacific Ocean.

7. Before he became a comedian in film, Benchley was noted for his humorous articles in magazines and as an important dramatic critic. His fruitful career as a writer took place in the 1920s and 1930s.

8. In Maltin's *Movie Comedy Teams* (326–331), this evaluator indicates that the Wiere Brothers had limited success in the movies. They appeared as a team in a secondary part of the plot.

9. Hal Kanter, *So Far, So Funny: My Life in Show Business*, 157.

10. Ibid., 157–158.

11. Such referential inserts may have been some influence by the French New Wave films of the 1950s and 1960s, such as Francois Truffaut's *Shoot the Piano Player*.

12. Evidently, Lamour still was associated with the Road Pictures to the extent that she drew an audience, but the younger woman, Joan Collins, became the lead in *Road to Hong Kong*. Dorothy wanted her part expanded; instead, she took the money.

13. Even in the 1950s, guest appearances were common on the television programs. This may have been an influence on feature motion pictures.

14. *And Now for Something Completely Different* (1971) became the first feature of the Monty Python company. It consisted of a series of sketches similar to those used on British television.

15. Maltin, *Movie Comedy Teams*, 115–116.

Chapter 8: Fade Out on Movies: The Fade In of the Small Screen

1. Bob Thomas in Hope's *The Road to Hollywood* classifies *The Facts of Life* as a domestic comedy. He declares it the best of the genre. It remains one of the most interesting comedies of a couple of adults trying to commit adultery, according to Thomas. He also sees it as an unusually humorous film for Hope.

2. Melvin Frank and Norman Panama were almost the last of an age of effective comedy screenwriters who were influenced by a tradition of excellent authorship in the media of theater, radio, and film. They, like such writers of the '40s and '50s as Hal Kanter and Edmund Hartmann, created sophisticated, humorous dramas similar to *The Facts of Life*.

3. The range of Rip Torn's acting in the media of film and television remains outstanding, from comedy roles in films such as *You're a Big Boy Now* (1966) to serious lead roles such as *Heartland* (1980). Among his many television roles, he appeared on *The Larry Sanders Show* from 1996 to 1998.

4. An excerpt of Hal Erickson, evaluation on the Internet of *The Bachelor in Paradise*, from All Movie Guide.

5. Kanter, *So Far, So Funny*, 247. Kanter expresses what many screenwriters found humiliating about writing for Hope: he would bring in his radio or television writers for more gags Writers often thought their contribution to the story was sufficient.

6. The curtain line for the 1946 *Road to Utopia* has the son of Hope and Lamour walking into the room as a young Bing Crosby. Hope has a very similar line to the audience: "We adopted him," to assure the viewer that Crosby had nothing to do with the procreation of their son.

7. *New York Times*, August 12, 1965. Reviewer Howard Thompson may have been a prude because the innuendoes are relatively mild. The teenage parties with music (Frankie Avalon's department) were a mere cliché of the beach pictures of the decade. This could have soured his evaluation.

8. What I call the Silent Kings of Comedy—Chaplin, Lloyd, Keaton, and Langdon—avoided fantastic gags and only used them for dream sequences.

9. William Robert Faith, *Bob Hope, A Life in Comedy*, 324–325.

10. Other comedians entered with television programs before Hope took the plunge, and he wisely decided to use the periodic special broadcast.

11. Hope and his daughter Linda Hope created a book called *Bob Hope: My Life in Jokes*, a collection of one-liners with some brief monologues. This one was given in an early TV program that is not clearly documented here (p. 81).

12. From a 2002 DVD released by Hope Enterprises, Inc., *America's Favorite Funnyman: Highlights From the Best of Bob Hope*, the comedian narrates this retrospective of television excerpts. Hope states: "Here's where it all began—Easter Sunday, April 9, 1950. . ."

13. Hope is reported to have entered many skits and gave his guests short appearances (*Variety*, April 11, 1951).

14. From a review in *Broadcasting*, March 30, 1953.

15. A look at the sixth edition of *The Complete Directory to Prime Time Network and Cable TV Shows* (1995) shows the variety and range of presentations from 1946 to recent years.

16. There are a number of sketches from the decades of Hope's television career released on VHS and DVD, but to date no complete programs. Bob Hope Enterprises, Inc., has retained the rights. If there are releases of total programs, it is possible some gems may be found among them.

Chapter 9: Through the Decades with Hope's Films: 1934 to 1972

1. Hope and Thomas, *The Road to Hollywood*, 125.

2. John Baxter, *Hollywood in the Thirties*, 86.

3. Hope and Thomas, 127.

4. Ibid., 154–155.

5. See Chapter 8 for a description of why *The Facts of Life* is an excellent movie.

Chapter 10: Assesment: Bob Hope's Legacy

1. The ineffective pretender might be considered one of Hope's best character types. He is often forced to take on a role that he cannot fully master. However, the impersonation remains credible because the audience sees through the deception and finds it laughable.

2. This newspaper article appeared in the early part of World War II, and the source is from personal memory only. No doubt it remained in my memory because it was so shocking in an age that had strict censorship. Hope had to clean up the language that sometimes slipped through the many live radio broadcasts in the early 1940s.

3. Since Bob Hope's daughter, Linda Hope, had the position of producer of his television specials and collector of his jokes in *My Life in Jokes*, there are few off-color anecdotes and quips in this book.

4. Hope, *My Life in Jokes*, 103.

5. Hope and Thomas, *The Road to Hollywood*, 157.

6. Marx, *The Secret Life*, 99.

7. Quirk, *The Road Well-Traveled*, 314.

8. Donald W. McCaffrey, *The Golden Age of Sound Comedy: Comic Films and Comedians of the Thirties*, 183–184.

9. Ibid., 184.

10. Thomas, *The Road to Hollywood*, 119–120. This quote comes from James Agee's "Comedy's Greatest Era," *Life*, September 5, 1949, 70–88.

11. Ibid., 121.

12. Ibid., 127–157.

13. The full title of the book and the authors shows the comedian taking the credit. It reads like this with larger print given to the star: *THE ROAD TO HOLLYWOOD: My 40-year Love Affair with the Movies*, by *BOB HOPE* and *Bob Thomas*.

14. Hope and Thomas, *The Road to Hollywood*, 28.

15. Hope handled the master of ceremonies role for the Academy Awards more than any other emcee. He hosted the Oscars eighteen times.

16. Francis Davis, "Bob Hope, Prisoner of War," *The Nation*, June 30, 2003, 35–37.

17. Ibid., 36–37.

18. Carrie Rickey, *Philadelphia Inquirer*, July 28, 2003 (from Internet reproduction, Star-Telegram.com).

19. Arts and Entertainment Channel, *Biography*, "Bob Hope: America's Entertainer," released on DVD through Hope Enterprises, Inc., 2003.

20. Todd S. Purdum, "Bob Hope, Before He Became the Comedy Establishment," *New York Times*, April 20, 2003, 7.

21. An important headliner in vaudeville, Will Rogers became an effective Hollywood actor and starred in many films, such as the 1933 *David Harum* as a small town banker who reflected the practical politics of rural America.

22. Fantle and Johnson, "Thanks for the Memories," 66.

23. Ibid., 67.

24. Bob Hope as told to Dwayne Netland, *Bob Hope's Confessions of a Hooker: My Lifelong Love Affair with Golf*, 71.

25. Raymond Strait, *Bob Hope: A Tribute*, 163.

26. Ibid., 450.

Selected Bibliography

Baxter, John. *Hollywood in the Thirties.* New York: A. S. Barnes, 1968.

Brooks, Tim, and Earle Marsh. *The Complete Directory to Prime Time Network and Cable TV Shows: 1946–Present,* 6th ed. New York: Ballantine Books, 1995.

Brown, Julian, ed. *Variety: Comedy Movies.* New York: BDD Promotional Books Company, Inc., 1992.

Davis, Frances. "Bob Hope, Prisoner of War." *The Nation* (June 30, 2003): 35–37.

Erickson, Hal. *Evaluation of "The Bachelor in Paradise."* All Movie Guide. http://www.moviegallery.com/product.cgi?product_id=027616154934.

———. *Evaluation of "The Iron Petticoat."* All Movie Guide. http://www. moviegallery.com/amg_info.cgi?v_id=v++++96755.

Faith, William Robert. *Bob Hope: A Life in Comedy.* New York: De Capo Press, 1982, 2003.

Fantle, David, and Thomas Johnson. "Bob Hope, Thanks for the Memories," *A Tribute to Bob Hope, Golden Collectors Series,* Vol. 3, No. 1. London: London Publishing Co., 2003.

Fein, Irving. *Jack Benny: An Intimate Biography.* New York: G. P. Putnam's Sons, 1976.

Green, Stanley. *Encyclopedia of the Musical Film.* New York. Oxford University Press, 1981.

Grudens, Richard. *The Spirit of Bob Hope.* Stony Brook, NY: Celebrity Profiles Publishing, 2002.

Hanson, Patricia King, and Amy Dunkleberger, Eds. *The American Film Institute Catalog of Motion Pictures Produced in the United States. Feature Films, 1931–1940.* Berkeley, CA: University of California Press, 1993.

———. *The American Film Institute Catalog of Motion Pictures Produced in the United States. Feature Films, 1941–1950.* Berkeley, CA: University of California Press, 1999.

Harkness, John. *The Academy Awards Handbook: Revised and Updated 2001 Edition.* New York: Pinnacle Books, 2001.

Harmon, Jim. *The Great Radio Comedians*. Garden City, NY: Doubleday & Company, Inc., 1970.

Hope, Bob. *I Never Left Home*. New York: Simon & Schuster, 1944.

Hope, Bob, as told to Pete Martin. *Bob Hope's Own Story: Have Tux, Will Travel*. New York: Simon & Schuster, 2003.

Hope, Bob, as told to Dwayne Netland. *Bob Hope's Confession as a Hooker: My Lifelong Love Affair with Golf*. New York: Doubleday, 1988.

Hope, Bob, and Linda Hope. *Bob Hope: My Life in Jokes*. New York: Hyperion Books, 2003.

Hope, Bob, and Melville Shavelson. *Don't Shoot, It's Only Me*. New York: G. P. Putnam's Sons, 1990.

Hope, Bob, and Bob Thomas. *The Road to Hollywood*. New York: Doubleday, 1977.

Kanter, Hal. *So Far, So Funny: My Life in Show Business*. Jefferson, NC: McFarland & Company, Inc., 1999.

Kroll, Jack. "Springing Eternal." *Newsweek*. 11 August 2003: 62–63.

Lamour, Dorothy, as told to Dick McInnes. *My Side of the Road*. Upper Saddle River, NJ: Prentice-Hall, 1980.

Maltin, Leonard. *Leonard Maltin's 1999 Movie & Video Guide*. New York: Signet Book, 1998.

———. *Movie Comedy Teams*. New York: Signet Book, 1970.

Marx, Arthur. *The Secret Life of Bob Hope: An Unauthorized Biography*. Fort Lee, NJ: Barricade Books, Inc., 1993.

McCaffrey, Donald W. *The Golden Age of Sound Comedy: Comic Films and Comedians of the Thirties*. New York: A. S. Barnes, 1973.

Rabin, Nathan. "Films That Time Forgot: *Cancel My Reservation*." *The Onion A. V. Club*, 37, no. 20 (2001). http: www.theavclub.com/fttf/index.php? issue=3721.

Strait, Raymond. *Bob Hope: A Tribute*. New York: Pinnacle Books, 2003.

Tucker, Ken. "Bob Hope." *Entertainment Weekly*. 8 August 2003: 30, 32, 35.

Vreeland, Frank. *Foremost Films of 1938: A Yearbook of the American Screen*. New York: Pitman Publishing Corporation, 1939.

Index

About the Author

DONALD W. MCCAFFREY is Professor Emeritus in the Department of English at the University of North Dakota, where he taught cinema, theater, and literature for nearly 30 years. He is the author of several books, including *The Golden Age of Sound Comedy, Assault on Society: Satirical Literature to Film*, and *Guide to the Silent Years of American Cinema* (Greenwood, 1999).